Abstract of Account Information of
FREEDMAN'S SAVINGS AND TRUST
New Orleans, Louisiana

1866–1869

Compiled and Indexed
by

Linell L. Hardy

HERITAGE BOOKS
2009

HERITAGE BOOKS
AN IMPRINT OF HERITAGE BOOKS, INC.

Books, CDs, and more—Worldwide

For our listing of thousands of titles see our website
at
www.HeritageBooks.com

Published 2009 by
HERITAGE BOOKS, INC.
Publishing Division
100 Railroad Ave. #104
Westminster, Maryland 21157

Copyright © 1999 Linell L. Hardy

All rights reserved. No part of this book may be reproduced or transmitted in any form or by any means, electronic or mechanical, including photocopying, recording or by any information storage and retrieval system without written permission from the author, except for the inclusion of brief quotations in a review.

International Standard Book Numbers
Paperbound: 978-0-7884-1137-3
Clothbound: 978-0-7884-8244-1

Dedication

This volume is dedicated to my family, John Colbert,
Naima Colbert, Naomi Hardy,
and Henry Colbert
and to those
who have come before
and those who will follow.
May a greater understanding of who we
are help mold future generations.
A special thanks to
Mrs. Thelma Frazier
whose dedication to her students gives
me hope for the generations to come.

Introduction

For about 15 years I have been researching my family's history and have found working with the records available for the African - American families the most challenging. The source material is hard to come by and few indexes are found. Over the years, in search of clues to ancestors long passed, I have acquired a small collection of microfilm from the National Archives. Late in the fall of 1996 I started thinking about putting some of that microfilm into a form that could benefit more researchers. As not everyone has access to microfilm readers and the information is not indexed so it takes many hours to find that one elusive name in the midst of thousands. This genealogical abstract is the result.

The information is abstracted from the accounts of the Freedman's Savings and Trust Branch in New Orleans, Louisiana. The microfilm number from the National Archives is 816 roll 12 account numbers 5 - 1018 dating from June 20, 1866 to Mar. 11, 1869. Many of the depositors are former slaves and information pertaining to plantations and former owners may be found in some records. Many of the accounts contain names of family members, occupation, age, place of birth, residence and a regiment if the person served in the military. I have kept it in the format that was in the original records and have done my best to keep it as accurate to the original document as possible. There were no page references in the original only account #'s.

The name index includes only full names and I have done my best to guess the last name when one is not included for the individual. I apologize ahead of time for any inaccuracies involved in the process of indexing the names.

Copies of the original documents are available from the National Archives or they can be ordered from me at a cost of $4.00 for the first entry and $1.00 for each additional entry ordered at the same time. Just send the account numbers you'd like copies of along with a mailing address and a check or money order made payable to Linell Hardy, 8171 Arthur St. Cotati, CA 94931. Allow 4-6 weeks for delivery.

Good luck in your research!!!

National Archives
Microfilm #816 Roll #12

Freedman's Savings and Trust
New Orleans
Accounts #5-1018
June 20, 1866- Mar. 11, 1869

Account Number - 5
Name - John Washington
Date of Application - June 18, 1866
Father or Mother? Married?- Margaretta E. A. Washington
Place of Birth- New Orleans, La
Residence - White Terpsichore & Melpomene 418
Occupation - Tin smith

Account Number- 7
Name- William Cooper
Date of Application - June 20, 1866
Name of Master - Nelson Maritche
Father or Mother? Married?- Amelie Dunford
Name Of Children- Sister: Mary Dunlap
Place of Birth- New Orleans La
Residence- Barracks Street No.93
Occupation- Clerk
Remarks 1.) later crossed out - in case of death, all sums to his credit in the Bank go to his sister Mary Dunlap. 2.) not crossed out -Wife can draw and E. Leviste can draw

Account Number- 10
Name- Amelie Durnford
Date of Application- June 23, 1866
Name of Master- Durnford Andrew
Plantation- "The Rosalie" Durnford lower Coast
Father or Mother? Married? Benit Durnford husband
Place of Birth- Louisiana
Residence- St. Louis St. No.19
Occupation- Cook
Remarks- Wm Cooper #7 can draw, E. Leviste can draw

Account Number- 11
Name- William Hall
Date of Application- June 25, 1866
Name of Master- Jean Pralon
Plantation - "city"
Father or Mother? Married?- Eliza Hall
Name of Children- none
Place of Birth- Richmond, Virginia
Residence- Corner Appollo & Clio 301
Occupation- "Baker" at U.S. Bakery Julia St.
Remarks- No money to be paid to any one but Wm Hall

Account Number- 12
Name- Dudley Robertson
Date of Application June 30, 1866
Father or Mother? Married?- Sarah Robertson
Name of Children- William, Henry, Aga Smooth
Place of Birth- Hanover, King William Co. Virginia
Residence- 93 Liberty Street
Occupation- Sawyer

Account Number - 14
Name- Mrs. Ellen Baptiste Lubin
Date of Application- July 2, 1866
Name of Master- Free
Father or Mother? Married? Yes
Name of Children- Marguerite & Mary Lubin
Place of Birth- New Orleans La
Residence- Burgundy between Ursulines & Hospital Sts.
Occupation- Laundress

Account Number- 15
Name- John Edmond
Date of Application- July 2, 1866
Father or Mother? Married?- Charlotte Morris
Name of Children- Julia & Mary Lorenza Edmond
Place of Birth- New Orleans La
Residence- Barrack Street No. 93
Occupation- Carpenter

Account Number- 20
Name- Hiram Carter
Date of Application- July 10, 1866
Name of Master- A. Flash

1

Father or Mother? Married?- Father Hiram Carter
Place of Birth- Augusta Georgia
Residence- St. Ann between Prieur & Roman
Occupation- Steward
Remarks- Louisa Saxton 133 Walker St. Augusta, Ga I am be his wife.

Account Number - 24
Name- Edward Williams
Date of Application- July 12, 1866
Name of Master- N.R. Jennings
Plantation- city
Father or Mother? Married?- Martha Williams
Place of Birth- Parish of St. Tammany
Residence- 203 Triton Walk
Occupation- Carpenter
Signature- Yes

Account Number- 25
Name- Celestin Royal
Date of Application- July 12, 1866
Name of Master- Ramar Arnaud
Plantation- city
Name of Children- Celestine & Sophia Royal
Place of Birth- Baton Rouge La
Residence- Poydras No. 389
Occupation- Laborer

Account Number- 26
Name- Warren Drake
Date of Application- July 14, 1866
Name of Master- A.C. Lecount
Plantation- Magnolia- Nachitoches
Name of Children- Warren Drake Jr. at Fairdwill, North Carolina
Place of Birth- Fairdwill, North Carolina
Residence- Baronne 185
Occupation- Carpenter

Account Number- 28
Name- Rebecca Johnson
Date of Application July 16, 1866
Name of Master- J. C. Alvord
Father or Mother? Married?- to Wm C. Johnson
Name of Children- none
Place of Birth- Richmond, Virginia
Residence- Corner Camp & 4th St.
Occupation- Laundress

Account Number- 34
Name- John Henry Dorsey
Date of Application- July 20, 1866
Name of Master- Thomas Maddox
Plantation- "Lakeland" Rapides Parish
Father or Mother? Married? John Dorsey not married
Place of Birth- Charles Co. Maryland
Residence- 463 Victory Street
Occupation- Carpenter
Remarks- Fathers name John Dorsey lives on Rapides Bayou Red River- His mother Ann Dorsey is also living at Rapides Bayou.
Signature- yes

Account Number- 36
Name- William Simpson
Date of Application- July 23, 1866
Name of Master- Hypolite Chretien
Plantation- Grand Coteau Opelousas
Father or Mother? Married?- Annie Simpson
Name of Children- Francois & Nelly & Mary Simpson
Place of Birth- Surrey Co. Virginia
Residence- History Street No. 12
Occupation- Shoemaker
Remarks- The three children were from a former wife, Annie Simpson being his second. He declares all funds deposited in this Bank must go to his children.
Signature- yes

Account Number- 37
Name- Marie Therese Anderson
Date of Application- July 26, 1866
Father or Mother? Married?- William Anderson
Name of Children- Joseph Emile Anderson
Place of Birth- New Orleans La
Residence- Chartres St. No. 112
Occupation- Furnished Rooms Keeper
Remarks- Mr. Emile Leviste is authorized to draw.

Account Number- 38

Name- Bristor Foreman
Date of Application- July 28, 1866
Name of Master- Dennis Simmons & Co.
Father or Mother? Married?- single
Regiment and Company- Co. A 36th regt. U.S.CT. discharged
Residence- Norfolk, Va Union St. No. 36
Signature- On Signature Book

Account Number- 41
Name- John Sanders
Date of Application- Aug. 6, 1866
Name of Master- C.C. Lathrop
Plantation- Life Ins. Co.
Father or Mother? Married?- Celie Sanders
Name of Children- Ive, Jve(?), Emilia Sanders
Place of Birth- near Annapolis Md
Residence- Magazine, Julia & St. Joseph
Occupation- Peddler
Signature- yes

Account Number- 43
Name- Melie Mather
Date of Application- Aug. 9, 1866
Father or Mother? Married?- widow
Name of Children- Adolphe Tureand, Samuel Lougus
Place of Birth- Louisiana
Residence- 193 St. Joseph St.
Occupation- Midwife

Account Number- 45
Name- Mrs. Elizabeth Dore
Date of Application- Aug. 13, 1866
Father or Mother? Married?- to Chs. Dore
Name of Children- none
Place of Birth- New Orleans La
Residence- Richard Street No.15
Occupation- Washer woman

Account Number- 46
Name- Woodson Jones
Date of Application- Aug. 13, 1866
Father or Mother? Married?- Rachel Jones
Name of Children- Frederic, Easter, Sophia Jones and Woodson Jones 2 yrs. old
Place of Birth- Campbell Co. Virginia, 10 miles from Hamilton Courthouse
Residence- corner Common and Bolivar
Occupation- employed on Jackson R.R
Remarks- Fathers name Frederick- heard he died in Va- Mothers name Dalphe- dead when I was 10 or 12 yrs. old. Brothers Frd Pleasant, Joe, Manson, Stevens & Spotman- don't know where they are.

Account Number- 49
Name- John Carter
Date of Application- Aug. 23, 1866
Name of Master- Francis Cook
Plantation- John Mc Macartney
Father or Mother? Married?- none
Name of Children- Simon Carter born in October 1847
Place of Birth- New Orleans La
Residence- corner Melpomene & Bacchus
Occupation- "Waiting on Gentlemen"
Remarks- Married Jan. 25, 1847 to Mary Jane Prerie. Jan. 17, 1870- Residence corner Terpsichore & Rampart works at Loan Pledgrass
Signature- yes

Account Number- 50
Name- Mrs. Celine John Jackson
Date of Application- Aug. 28, 1866
Name of Master- Mr. Robin
Plantation- city
Height and Complexion- black
Father or Mother? Married?- yes
Name of Children- none
Place of Birth- West Baton Rouge
Residence- Good children & corner Annette
Occupation- Washer and Ironer
Remarks- Father's name Harry Carter- died in Ancimate(?) when I was a small girl- Mother's name Darkey Riley- died in West Baton Rouge when I was a little girl- Andre Kelper her brother died since the war.
Signature- X

Account Number- 51
Name- Pleasant Gill
Date of Application- Aug. 29, 1866
Name of Master- Wm. Hays
Plantation- Brashear City
Father or Mother? Married?- Elizabeth Scott
Names of Children- Agnes, Hannah & Michael Gill
Place of Birth- Sussex Co. Virginia
Residence- Gravier Street 247
Occupation- Driver (team)

Account Number- 52
Name- Jerome Woods
Date of Application- Sept. 11, 1866
Name of Master- came from Texas- Dec. 8, 1833 sent away from mother when 9 yrs. old
Height and Complexion- 51 Mar. 22, 1869 Brown
Father or Mother? Married?- don't know father, mother Mary- Mary Elizabeth Woods dead
Name of Children- Jerome & William Woods & Samuel Woods (Sam dead)
Place of Birth- Dixon Springs, Smith Co. Tennessee
Residence- 1) Roman 44 1/2 Palmyra & Common 2) 448 So. Fayette St.
Occupation- 1) Journeyman 2) Lamp lighter
Remarks- wife died 4 Sept. 1868 - Mother in Tenn. - has no recollection of any brother or sister.
Signature- X

Account Number- 54
Name- Felix C. Antoine
Date of Application- Sept. 13, 1866
Father or Mother? Married?- Elizabeth "Hutchinson" Antoine
Name of Children- Lewis C. Antoine
Place of Birth- New Orleans La
Residence- Prieur St. No. 3 or Bertrand St.
Occupation- Brick Layer
Remarks- he is to come and give his signature.

Account Number- 55
Name- C.C. Antoine
Date of Application- Sept. 13, 1866
Father or Mother? Married?- Maria Ross
Name of Children- Joseph Antoine
Place of Birth- New Orleans La
Residence- Prieur St. No. 3 or Bertrand St.
Occupation- Barber
Signature- yes

Account Number- 56
Name- Betsy Johnson
Date of Application- Sept. 17, 1866
Name of Mistress- Mrs. Marie Louise Etienne
Name of Children- Joe Salomon Johnson
Place of Birth- Rock bridge Co. Virginia
Residence- Kerlerec Street No.12
Occupation- Washer woman
Remarks- In case of death all money deposited to go to her son Joe S. Johnson

Account Number- 57
Name- A.J. Davis
Date of Application- Sept. 19, 1866
Name of Children- A.J. Davis Jr.
Place of Birth- New Orleans La
Residence- 65 Gasquet St.
Occupation- Porter
Signature- yes

Account Number- 59
Name- Albert Parker
Date of Application- Sept. 24, 1866
Place of Birth- New Orleans La
Residence- Calliope between Pryamid & Nayades
Occupation- Wagon Driver

Account Number- 60
Name- Harriet Cobb
Date of Application- Sept. 24, 1866
Name of Master- Philip Chandler
Plantation- Whitehall Pointe Coupee La
Father or Mother? Married?- Robert Cobb
Place of Birth- Montross, Westmoreland Co. Va
Residence- corner Derbigny & Columbus
Occupation- Servant

Remarks- In case of death wants the money to go to Cyrus Ellis for the benefit of her two younger sisters Emily Anna & Charlotte Watson.

Account Number- 61
Name- Rosetta Robinson
Date of Application- Sept. 25, 1866
Name of Children- Dr. A.W. Lewis
Place of Birth- Caroline Co. Va
Residence- Richmond Va
Remarks- This deposit was made by Dr. A.W. Lewis to have a transfer on Richmond VA- Edwin Walker Lewis son of Dr. A.W. Lewis.

Account Number- 62
Name- Andrew J. Baptiste
Date of Application- Sept. 25, 1866
Name of Master- Abe Cogfield
Plantation- Red River Nachitoches La
Regiment and Company- 9th U.S. Cavalry
Place of Birth- Nachitoches La
Occupation- Soldier

Account Number- 64
Name- Widenay Woodney
Date of Application- Sept. 29, 1866
Name of Master- Otto Basil
Plantation- Otto Brasil Red River
Father or Mother? Married?- father's name Willis Thomas
Regiment and Company- was formerly of 4th U.S.C Cavalry Co. G
Place of Birth- below Vicksburg Miss.
Residence- at Baptiste opposite St. Bernard's Parish right bank
Occupation- Journeyman

Account Number- 66
Name- Graham Bell
Date of Application- 1) Oct. 2, 1866 2) changes Mar. 31, 1869
Name of Master- Came to Louisiana in 1852
Height and Complexion- Born in 1845 Brown
Father or Mother? Married?- father Sam, mother Nancy "Bright" Turner, stepfather Wm Turner, wife Mary E. Bell

Name of Children- Lewis Bell 5 (1869) & Ida Victoria 8 mos. (1869)
Place of Birth- Miss.
Residence- 1) St. Andrew No. 304 2) Dryades St. between 1st and 2nd
Occupation- 1) Carriage Driver 2) Dining Room Servant
Remarks- 1) age 21years 4 mos. 3 weeks 2) Nathan died in Miss- since Graham was 3 years old Mother lives in same town with Graham- children dead Spenser Jackson & John - brother Sam. in N. O. , Allen (dead), Bui (dead), sister Maria wife of Henry Stewart In Natchez, some sisters dead- Mother had 8 children.
Signature- yes

Account Number- 67
Name- Anthony Gray and his wife Ellen Gray
Date of Application- Oct. 3, 1866
Height and Complexion- age about 50
Father or Mother? Married?- fathers name- don't remember mothers name Dicy- I left her in Va- I was a very small child, yes- Ellen Gray
Place of Birth- near Fluvana Courthouse Virginia
Residence- 3rd Street- now on Washington St. between Clara & Magnolia
Occupation- Drayman
Remarks- has no relatives at all- that he knows of- for descriptive of Ellen Gray see record after 1018.
Signature- X

Account Number- 68
Name- Reverend Anthony Ross
Date of Application- Oct. 4, 1866
Father or Mother? Married?- Emeline Ross
Place of Birth- Anna Rolla Co. Maryland- 40 miles from Baltimore on the western shore
Residence- Bolivar St. between Poydras & Perdido No, 145
Occupation- Minister of Wesley's Chapel

Account Number- 69

Name- Henry Lang Parker
Date of Application- Oct. 4, 1866
Father or Mother? Married?- aged 16 years
Regiment and Company- during the war ward room boy on the Iron clad No. 27
Place of Birth- New Orleans La
Residence- Calliope between Prytania & St. Charles
Occupation- Porter in offices

Account Number- 70
Name- Stephen Priestley
Date of Application- Oct. 4, 1866
Plantation- Priestley's Plantation
Father or Mother? Married?- Charlotte Priestley
Place of Birth- Priestley's Plantation St. James La
Residence- Terpsichore St. 418
Occupation- Laborer

Account Number- 72
Name- Addison Jenkins
Date of Application- Oct. 4, 1866
Father or Mother? Married?- Susan Jenkins
Place of Birth- Orange Co. Va
Residence- 105 Liberty Street
Occupation- Runner in the U.S. Engineer Dept.
Remarks- His deposit made this day is $6.00 in silver to be paid on call in like currency.

Account Number- 74
Name- Mars Murrell
Date of Application- Oct. 6, 1866
Father or Mother? Married?- Diana Murrell
Name of Children- Martha Ann Murrell
Place of Birth- St. Augustine Florida
Residence- First St. No. 320 near Dryades (?)
Occupation- Porter at Poursine & Co.

Account Number- 75
Name- Alexander Dumas
Date of Application- Oct. 6, 1866
Father or Mother? Married?- Maria Simms Dumas
Name of Children- Alexander, Charlotte & Harriet Dumas
Place of Birth- New Orleans La
Residence- Perdido St. No. 159
Occupation- Porter in a Commission house
Signature- yes

Account Number- 78
Name- William Johnson
Date of Application- Oct. 8, 1866
Name of Master- Lawyer Pierce
Father or Mother? Married?- Mary Johnson
Name of Children- Johnny Johnson
Place of Birth- Washington City
Residence- corner St. Peter & Gravier
Occupation- Drayman

Account Number- 79
Name- Joseph Stevenson
Date of Application- Oct. 8, 1866
Father or Mother? Married?- Daphne Stevenson
Name of Children- none
Place of Birth- Davidson Co. Tennessee
Residence- 218 Felicity Road
Occupation- Drayman

Account Number- 80
Name- Alexander Armstrong
Date of Application- Oct. 8, 1866
Regiment and Company- formerly of 6th Col. Regt. Co. F
Place of Birth- New Orleans
Residence- Craps between Mandeville & Marigny
Occupation- Cigar Maker
Signature- yes

Account Number- 81
Name- James Bumbray
Date of Application- Oct. 8, 1866
Name of Master- Henry Doyle
Father or Mother? Married?- Mary Bumbray
Name of Children- James Bumbray Jr.
Place of Birth- Fauquier Co. Virginia
Residence- Howard between Poydras & Perdido 136
Occupation- Warehouse man at John

Marks & Co. Fatzo Marks & Co.
Remarks- Father's name Enoch Bumbray.
Signature- yes

Account Number- 82
Name- April Neck
Date of Application- Oct. 8, 1866
Name of Master- Doet Thomas
Place of Birth- Charleston S.Ca
Residence- Philippa, corner Girod
Occupation- Hod Carrier for Bricklayer
Remarks- Mother's name Lucy- sisters names Mary, Hester all in Charleston. Brother's name Isaac Nair & Scipio Jenkins in Charleston.

Account Number- 83
Name- Ancel Bunton
Date of Application- Oct. 8, 1866
Name of Master- Sumpter Turner
Father or Mother? Married?- Martha Bunton
Name of Children- Frederic, Catharine, Ancel Bunton
Place of Birth- Sumner Co. Tennessee
Residence- Dryades between St. Andrew and Josephine
Occupation- Cooper
Remarks- Father William Bunton- Mother Annie Bunton.

Account Number- 84
Name- Richard B. White
Date of Application- Oct. 8, 1866
Father or Mother? Married?- Delila White
Place of Birth- New Orleans La
Residence- Gravier St. 417
Occupation- Barber
Remarks- Brothers Harry, Samuel P. & Joseph White.

Account Number- 85
Name- Joseph Alexander Thompson
Date of Application- Oct. 8, 1866
Father or Mother? Married?- Sarah Ann Washington
Name of Children- James Henry Thompson
Place of Birth- Decatur, Georgia
Residence- 248 Baronne Street

Occupation- Office Cleaner
Remarks- Mother's name Judith Hillborn in Lamar Co. Texas.

Account Number- 86
Name- John Lewis
Date of Application- Oct. 8, 1866
Name of Master- Levee Steam Cotton Press Co.
Height and Complexion- Black 54 yrs. old
Father or Mother? Married?- Sarah Lewis
Name of Children- Julia, Edward Lewis (dead)
Place of Birth- Eastern Shore Maryland
Residence- Miro between Mauir & St. Ann
Occupation- works at Cotton Presser
Remarks- Mother and father dead. Edward his son got drowned on the 4th March 1869 about 100 miles above Vicksburg Miss.

Account Number- 87
Name- Esau Taylor
Date of Application- Oct. 8, 1866
Name of Master- Widow M.A. Amson
Father or Mother? Married?- Lucinda Taylor
Name of Children- Step child Rosella Rice
Place of Birth- Louisville, Kentucky
Residence- Circus St. near Poydras Market
Occupation- working in Rope & Bagging Store

Account Number- 88
Name- Levi Johnson
Date of Application- Oct. 9, 1866
Name of Master- William Diamond & before was owned by R. J. Latting
Height and Complexion- Black aged about 48
Father or Mother? Married?- not
Place of Birth- Greensville near Augusta Georgia
Residence- Thalia No. 144
Occupation- Drayman
Remarks- no father nor mother, no

relations whatever

Account Number- 89
Name- Oliver Moore
Date of Application- Oct. 9, 1866
Father or Mother? Married?- Anna Moore
Name of Children- Maria Moore
Place of Birth- Edgeville District S. Ca
Residence- Thalia 244 between Bacchus & Apollo
Occupation- Drayman
Remarks- His father and mother dead. His brothers names are Cesar & James Moore living in South Ca sisters names are Cynthia & Susan Moore in South Ca Maria Moore inscribed Dec. 6th.

Account Number- 90
Name- Wm R. Harris
Date of Application- Oct. 9, 1866
Height and Complexion- Black 54 years old
Father or Mother? Married?- Maria Harris
Regiment and Company- formerly with 155th NY vols.
Place of Birth- Prince George Co. Maryland
Residence- Perdido between Prieur & Johnson
Occupation- works at Cotton Presser
Remarks- No relations but his wife.

Account Number- 91
Name- Margaret Jane Brown
Date of Application- Oct. 9, 1866
Height and Complexion- Light Complexion
Name of Children- Nancy Brown
Place of Birth- The Sales- near Bowling Green Ky
Residence- 186 Dryades Street
Occupation- Washer & Ironer
Remarks- The son's name is William Henry Maxey and resides in Vicksburg Miss.

Account Number- 92
Name- Jeremiah Johnson
Date of Application- Oct. 12, 1866
Father or Mother? Married?- Mary Johnson
Name of Children- William Lewis, Robert Thomas, & Laura Johnson
Regiment and Company- formerly of 80th U.S.C.T. Co. B
Place of Birth- Huntsville Alabama
Residence- Liberty St. No. 102
Occupation- House Servant

Account Number- 94
Name- Charles Braxton
Date of Application- Oct. 12, 1866
Height and Complexion- Black
Regiment and Company- 116th U.S.C.T. Co. K
Place of Birth-Lexington Ky
Residence- with Regiment
Occupation- Soldier
Remarks- Mother's name Keser Braxton, father's name Frederick Braxton.

Account Number- 95
Name- Samuel Trotter
Date of Application- Oct. 14, 1866
Father or Mother? Married?- Mary Trotter
Place of Birth- Rohan Co. North Ca
Residence- Galvez Street No. 31
Occupation- Drayman
Remarks- Eliza, Joe, Sam, Sarah, Mary, & Letitia Trotter all his children, left them 38 years ago in Rohan Co. near Sauesbury N. Ca.

Account Number- 96
Name- Benjamin Miller
Date of Application- Oct. 15, 1866
Father or Mother? Married?- Henrietta Miller
Name of Children- Ben and Love Miller
Place of Birth- Wilson Co. above Nashville Tenn.
Residence- Franklin between Perdido and Poydras
Occupation- Drayman
Remarks- Name of children- Ben and Love Miller- when last heard from were in Texas- In case of death wants money to go to wife Henrietta.

Account Number- 97
Name- Harry Warren
Date of Application- Oct. 15, 1866
Father or Mother? Married?- Nancy Warren
Place of Birth- Bullskin, Shelby Co. Kentucky
Residence- Lafayette St. 239
Occupation- Drayman
Remarks- Sister Margaret Warren- brothers Amos & Silas Warren all in Shelbyville Shelby Co. Ky

Account Number- 98
Name- Frank Green
Date of Application- Oct. 16, 1866
Height and Complexion- Bright- 14 years old
Place of Birth- New Orleans
Residence- 185 Barrack St.
Occupation- Working in Office
Remarks- Name of father Isaac Gregory- name of mother Ann Gregory

Account Number- 99
Name- Ebenezer Barry
Date of Application- Oct. 16, 1866
Regiment and Company- formerly of 77th U.S.C.T. Co´J or I & consolidated into 10th U.S.Heavy Art'y. Co. M
Place of Birth- Tuscaloosa Alabama
Residence- Boarding on Lafayette St.
Occupation- Laborer
Remarks- Sisters name Eliza, Hannah oldest brother name Randolph used to belong to a man by the name of Sears.

Account Number- 100
Name- Lewis Gilbert
Date of Application- Oct. 17, 1866
Height and Complexion- 10 years old
Remarks- Deposit made by Sarah Gilbert for Lewis Gilbert her son.

Account Number- 101
Name- James C. Williamson
Date of Application- Oct. 17, 1866
Father or Mother? Married?- Mary Adele Williamson
Name of Children- Anna, James C., & Harriet Williamson
Place of Birth- Charleston S.Ca.
Residence- 74 Basin St.
Occupation- House Carpenter
Remarks- His wife and children live in Charleston S. Ca.

Account Number- 102
Name- James Henry
Date of Application- Oct. 17, 1866
Father or Mother? Married?- Nancy Henry
Place of Birth- Matthews Co. Virginia
Residence- 271 Felicity St.
Occupation- Porter in Store
Remarks- No father no mother or relatives.
Signature- yes

Account Number- 103
Name- Mrs. Widow Harriet Atkins
Date of Application- Oct. 18, 1866
Place of Birth- Wake Co. Virginia
Residence- corner Gravier & St. Paul
Occupation- Cook Shop
Remarks- Widow Atkins husbands name was Thomas Atkins. The money was drawn by Joseph Green No. 121 Franklin St. and Mrs. Joseph Raymond- Mrs. Atkins God child.

Account Number- 104
Name- Nicey Henrietta Morse
Date of Application- Oct. 18, 1866
Name of Children- Isabella, Henrietta, Georgiana, George, & Alexander Morse
Place of Birth- Eastern Shore Maryland city of Burlon
Residence- Perdido between Howard & St. Paul
Occupation- Cook
Remarks- Name of husband Henry Morse.

Account Number- 106
Name- William H. Day
Date of Application- Oct. 19, 1866
Father or Mother? Married?- Mary H. Day
Regiment and Company- formerly from 4th U.S.C.T. Co. D
Place of Birth- Elmira New York

Residence- Baronne St. No. 90
Occupation- Carpenter

Account Number- 107
Name- Marinda Sanders
Date of Application- Oct. 20, 1866
Name of Master- Mother's name was Georgiana- I left her in Nashville Tenn. when I was 4 years old- mother used to belong to W. Pettis
Height and Complexion- Light
Father or Mother? Married?- Daniel Sanders
Name of Children- none
Place of Birth- Nashville
Residence- 170 Basin St.
Occupation- Seamstress
Remarks- No relations whatever- Oct. 7, 1869- I now live at No. 10 Treme (?) St.
Signature- yes

Account Number- 108
Name- William Andres
Date of Application- Oct. 22, 1866
Father or Mother? Married?- Lizzie Stewart Andres
Name of Children-Margaret Steward
Regiment and Company- formerly of 6th Regt. 60 day vols. Co. G
Place of Birth- New Orleans La
Residence- 189 Royal St.
Occupation- Carpenter
Signature- yes

Account Number- 109
Name- Humphrey Cooper
Date of Application- Oct. 22, 1866
Name of Master- W. Gossum (?) at Ocognan Va
Father or Mother? Married?- Maria Cooper
Place of Birth- Fairfax Co. Va
Residence- corner 1st & Coliseum
Occupation- Cook

Account Number- 110
Name- Samuel Tillman
Date of Application- Oct. 22, 1866
Father or Mother? Married?- Jane Tillman
Name of Children- stepson's name Alfred

Lacoste
Regiment and Company- formerly of 7th La vols. 60 days Co. A
Place of Birth- New Orleans La
Residence- Bertram between Gravier & Perdido
Occupation- N.O. Gas works
Remarks- Mother's name Emilia Davis.
Signature- yes

Account Number- 112
Name- Nathaniel Watkins
Date of Application- Oct. 24, 1866
Regiment and Company- 36th Regt. Co. F
Remarks- This day discharged from service and going to Norfolk, Va given him a transfer card.

Account Number- 113
Name- James Linton
Date of Application- Oct. 24, 1866
Regiment and Company- C 36th Regt. U.S.C.T.
Remarks- This day discharged going to Norfolk, Va gave him a transfer card.

Account Number- 114
Name- Alfred Fletcher
Date of Application- Oct. 24, 1866
Regiment and Company- 36th U.S.C.T. Co. D
Remarks- This day discharged going to Norfolk, Va gave him a transfer card.

Account Number- 115
Name- Major Meekins
Regiment and Company- Co. K 36th Regt.
Remarks- This day discharged going to Norfolk, Va gave him a transfer card.

Account Number- 116
Name- Edward Fields
Date of Application- Oct. 27, 1866
Name of Master- Left Tenn. in 1863 came to N.O.
Height and Complexion- 28 Dark Brown
Father or Mother? Married?- Fanny Fields
Place of Birth- Jackson, Madison Co.

Tenn.
Residence- Bolivar St. 156 removed to 237 Baronne St.
Occupation- Drayman
Remarks- Mother's Name Aime Fields in Memphis Tenn. Feb. 1869 in N.O. Mother died in Jackson Tenn over 20 years ago- brothers William in Memphis & Guy in N.O. & Manuel in Philadelphia & John in N.O. & Sam and Goliath in St. Lewis & Robert in Memphis & Archy dead- sisters Elizabeth wife of Ben Caruthers- Slatia Ann dead.
Signature- yes

Account Number- 118
Name- Peter Joseph
Date of Application- Oct. 29, 1866
Father or Mother? Married?- Cora Joseph
Regiment and Company- formerly of Co. A 92nd U.S.C.T.
Place of Birth- New Orleans La
Residence- Melpomene between Willow & Claiborne
Occupation- Bricklayer
Remarks- Mother's name Margaret Frost
Signature- yes

Account Number- 119
Name- William Morgan
Date of Application- Oct. 29, 1866
Place of Birth- Nashville Tenn.
Residence- Johnson St. near Canal
Occupation- Barber
Remarks- Sister's name Louisa Morgan, when last heard from about 7 years ago was in this city- no other relatives.

Account Number- 120
Name- George Green
Date of Application- Oct. 29, 1866
Father or Mother? Married?- Margaret Green
Place of Birth- New Orleans La
Residence- St. Charles between St. Joseph & Delord (?)
Occupation- Drayman
Remarks- Mother's name Dinah Brackstone

Account Number- 121
Name- Isiah Norwood
Date of Application- Oct. 29, 1866
Father or Mother? Married?- Mary Norwood
Place of Birth- Clinton La
Residence- Palmyra St. No. 117
Occupation- Carpenter
Remarks- Mother's name Eliza
Signature- yes

Account Number- 122
Name- David Teelers
Date of Application- Nov. 1, 1866
Name of Master- Elijah Parker
Plantation- Parkers Plantation
Place of Birth- Parkers Plantation, on Bayou Boeuf close to Cherryville
Residence- Burgundy St. 135
Occupation- working in a wood yard
Remarks- Mother's name, Annie, last heard from was on Ouchita River close to Monroe. Sister's names Melly, Nancy, brothers Simon Teelers- fathers (?) name Simon Teeler.

Account Number- 123
Name- Peyton Randall
Date of Application- Nov. 1, 1866
Name of Children- Emilia & Walker Randall
Place of Birth- Common Co. Va
Residence- at N.O. Gas Works
Occupation- Laborer in Gas Works Co.
Remarks- Brother's name is Aaron Bradley leaving at Pass Manchac- formerly belonged to Mrs. Wood of Cotton Press.
Signature- yes

Account Number- voided entry
Name- Charles Waldon
Date of Application- Nov. 1, 1866
Regiment and Company- Co. H of Col. Plumley's Regt. of Colored Troops/ formerly of New Orleans La
Residence- Gasquet St.
Occupation- Blacksmith
Remarks- no relatives whatsoever.

Account Number- 124
Name- E.P. Royal
Date of Application- Nov. 2, 1866
Height and Complexion- 40 Black
Father or Mother? Married?- Victorine Royal - father Philip and mother Syllis
Place of Birth- Iberville Parish
Residence- Poydras between Clara and Claiborne 389 later entry 369 Esplanade St.
Occupation- Laborer
Remarks- Pastor of M.E. Church on LaHarpe St. 3rd District. Father died in N.O. about 25 years ago- Mother died about 30 in N.O. Brothers Celestine in N.O., Martin down on the coast- Sister Louisa in St. Charles Parish- brother James dead & sisters Polly & Sarah dead.
Signature- yes

Account Number- voided entry
Name- Isaac Whalan
Date of Application- Nov. 3, 1866
Father or Mother? Married?- Martha Whalan
Name of Children- Harriet Whalan now Mrs. Cavanaugh
Place of Birth- Montgomery Maryland
Residence- Josephine between Coliseum & Prytania
Occupation- Ginner
Remarks- Harriet Whalan resides in Galveston Texas

Account Number- 126
Name- Alexander Bailey
Date of Application- Nov. 5, 1866
Father or Mother? Married?- Adeline Bailey
Place of Birth- Clarksville Tenn.
Residence- 147 Clio St.
Occupation- Carpenter
Signature- yes

Account Number- 127
Name- Phebe Wallace
Date of Application- Nov. 6, 1866
Name of Master- Chanorde de Graffenreid in Chester Co. S. Ca
Name of Children- Anna & George Lee
Place of Birth- Newbern NC
Residence- Dryades St. 260
Occupation- General house Servant
Remarks- Both children reside in Chester Co. South Carolina

Account Number- 128
Name- Benjamin Harrison
Date of Application- Nov. 6, 1866
Father or Mother? Married?- Fanny Sels Harrison
Name of Children- David & Sarah Harrison
Place of Birth- Dinwiddie Co. Va- 10 miles from Dinwiddie Courthouse
Residence- corner Coliseum and Jackson
Occupation- Upholster & Mattrass Maker
Remarks- Martha Harrison his daughter is now Martha Fields- Rudolph Harrison his son lives with him.

Account Number- 129
Name- Maria Gadson
Date of Application- Nov. 7, 1866
Name of Master- William Tennant in Charleston
Place of Birth- Charleston S. Ca
Residence- Custom House corner Rampart at W. Letchford
Occupation- Cook
Remarks- Her sister's name is Binah Williamson residing in Charleston S. Ca

Account Number- 131
Name- George Allen
Date of Application- Nov. 12, 1866
Name of Master- Father's name Charles Allen died in city on St. Charles St. next to Mr. Slocomb when he was a child.
Regiment and Company- 73rd U.S.C.T. Co. K
Place of Birth- New Orleans La
Residence- Perdido & St. Paul near Corner
Occupation- Slater
Remarks- Name of mother is Rebecca Glasco- sisters Caroline & Rosa Glasco- brother Joe killed in Texas during the war- Had a child Monerva- died when he

was in the Army. Niece can draw see her record # 2234.
Signature- x

Account Number- 132
Name- Roxana Robertson
Date of Application- Nov. 12, 1866
Height and Complexion- Black
Father or Mother? Married?- Husband Alfred Robertson
Name of Children- Ben Jackson Baker & Mary Susan Baker
Place of Birth- King Wm Co. Va
Residence- Claiborne between Poydras & Perdido
Occupation- Peddling
Remarks- Mother's name Celina Jackson resides in King Wm Co. Va.

Account Number- 133
Name- Albert Parker & wife
Date of Application- Nov. 12, 1866
Father or Mother? Married?- Julia Parker
Name of Children- see below
Place of Birth- Caroline Co. Va
Residence- 145 Calliope
Occupation- Warehouse man
Remarks- children's name Richard & James Parker

Account Number- 134
Name- Jacob Cheek
Date of Application- Nov. 12, 1866
Regiment and Company- 4th La vols. 60 days Co. I
Place of Birth- Mecklemburg Co. N. Ca
Residence- Franklin No. 42
Occupation- Blacksmith
Remarks- Sisters name Susan Cheek when last heard from was in Mecklemburg Co. N. Ca- uncle's name James Cheek in same Co. N. Ca (later entry) This deposit may be paid to Louisa Smith who lives on Custom House St. corner Pryor- (signed Jacob Cheek) Louisa Smith is
yellow complexion medium height, dark hair & eyes, about 30- her mother is named Rachel- sister Clara- Father Noah.

Account Number- 136
Name- Denson Flory
Date of Application- Nov. 15, 1866
Name of Master- Andrew Flory
Regiment and Company- Co. K-36th U.S.C.T.
Residence- Norfolk Va
Occupation- farmer
Remarks- name of mother Mary Ann Flory- given him a transfer on Norfolk Va

Account Number- 137
Name- John Turner
Date of Application- Nov. 16, 1866
Father or Mother? Married?- Mary E. Turner
Name of Children- Susan V. Robertson
Place of Birth- Frederick Co. Maryland
Residence- corner Miro & Bienville
Occupation- Clergyman

Account Number- 198
Name- Milton Harris
Date of Application- Nov. 20, 1866
Name of Master- John Davidson
Name of Children- son's name Walter Harris
Regiment and Company- 76th U.S.C.T. Co. K private
Place of Birth- Nashville Tenn.
Residence- corner Franklin & Poydras
Occupation- Slater
Remarks- his mother Fanny Johnson alias Fanny Blue- last heard from in Texas. Brother Madison Harris is a slater also.

Account Number- 199
Name- George Moore
Date of Application- Nov. 21, 1866
Name of Master- Graham Moore
Plantation- Currico Co. N. Ca
Regiment and Company- Corpl. Co. B 36th U.S.C.T.
Place of Birth- Currico Co. N. Ca
Residence- Magazine St. near the Market
Occupation- Laborer
Remarks- Alick, Melden, Elie Moore his brothers are in Newbern N.C.

Account Number- 200
Name- Sarah Washington
Date of Application- Nov. 21, 1866
Name of Master- Isaac Patton in Richmond Va now living in this city- came to Miss. (Vicksburg) one or two years before the war.
Height and Complexion- Dark Griff age 29
Father or Mother? Married?- Ludrick & Silvy Single-had husband Thomas Fisher she is not living with
Place of Birth- Brunswick Co. Va
Residence- 334 Canal St.
Occupation- Washer & Ironer
Remarks- Description given and money deposited by Dr. A.W. Lewis. (later entry) Father died in Va-when she was about 10- left mother in Va- brother Coleman Washington killed in army- She came to N.O. before surrender- Sister Ermine (wife of Henry Ivius) dead. Robert Merritt her nephew, a lad about 16 years is the only relative she has. He also belonged to Isaac Patton.
Signature- Dr. A.W. Lewis

Account Number- 203
Name- Franklin Frizzell
Date of Application- Nov. 23, 1866
Name of Master- Johnson Frizzell
Father or Mother? Married?- Louisa Frizzell
Name of Children- David, Harriet & Johnson Frizzell
Regiment and Company- 36th U.S.C.T. Co. D
Place of Birth- Pitt Co. North Ca
Residence- St. Thomas- Max alley
Occupation- Laborer
Remarks- This deposit is made out from a certificate of Deposit of W. Sperry of $75. & for which transfer was asked from Newbern.

Account Number- 204
Name- William Ballard
Date of Application- Nov. 23, 1866
Name of Master- Stephen Walker
Father or Mother? Married?- Margaret Ballard
Regiment and Company- Sergt. Co. E 116th U.S.C.T.
Place of Birth- Jessamine Co. Nicholasville KY
Residence- Camp Greenville La
Occupation- Soldier- before war a farmer

Account Number- 205
Name- Edward Major
Date of Application- Nov. 26, 1866
Name of Master- James Shortridge
Height and Complexion- Black 48 yrs. old
Father or Mother? Married?- Maria Major
Place of Birth- James Island Charleston South Ca
Residence- Prieur between Perdido and Poydras
Occupation- Laborer in Cotton Presses
Remarks- No other relatives

Account Number- 207
Name- Louisa Jerridan
Date of Application- Nov. 30, 1866
Place of Birth- King Wm Co Va
Residence- Lafayette between Franklin & Liberty
Occupation- Sicknurse
Remarks- no relatives whatever- In case of sickness and want of money she would send Aline Narcisse (Aline signed) with her book (later entry) Laura Morse can draw

Account Number- 208
Name- Charlotte Hayden
Date of Application- Nov. 30, 1866
Name of Master- Deshields
Name of Children- Josephine, Catherine, John, & Frederick Hayden
Place of Birth- Eastern Shore Md
Residence- 494 Magazine St.
Occupation- Cook, Washer & Ironer
Remarks- Deposit made by Dr. A.W. Lewis

Account Number- 212
Name- Jacob Parris
Date of Application- Dec. 8, 1866
Regiment and Company- 36th U.S.C.T Co. C discharged

Place of Birth- Spartanburg S.Ca
Residence- St. Thomas St.
Occupation- Soldier
Remarks- Mother Milberry Parris- Thompson's Creek, Spartanburg Dist. S.Ca

Account Number- 215
Name- Adeline Biggs
Date of Application- Dec. 15, 1866
Father or Mother? Married?- Louis Biggs
Name of Children- Louis Biggs
Place of Birth- Donaldsonville La
Residence- corner Common & Rampart
Occupation- Furnished Rooms Keeper
Remarks- Her brother's name is Joseph Fuller (Oct. 20, 1867) Resides now on Lafayette St. No. 124
Signature- yes

Account Number- 216
Name- Celestine Clayton
Date of Application- Dec. 17, 1866
Name of Children- Marie Martinez
Place of Birth- New Orleans La
Residence- Custom House No. 144
Occupation- Furnished Rooms Keeper
Remarks- Deposit this day made to her name by her brother John G. Seldon.

Account Number- 217
Name- Joseph Hawkins
Date of Application- Dec. 18, 1866
Height and Complexion- Black
Regiment and Company- Co. C 116th U.S.C.T.
Residence- Camp in N.O.
Occupation- Soldier
Remarks- Book given for Hawkins to Thomas Robbins Co. C 116th.

Account Number- 218
Name- Josephine Chamburger
Date of Application- Dec. 22, 1866
Father or Mother? Married?- John Chamburger
Place of Birth- Louisville Kentucky
Residence- corner St. Louis and Treme
Occupation- Furnished Rooms
Remarks- Ennis Ray mother lives in Lockland Ohio near Cincinnati

Account Number- 221
Name- William Beard
Date of Application- Dec. 24, 1866
Father or Mother? Married?- single
Place of Birth- Stanton, Augusta Co. Va
Residence- Common St. 127
Occupation- Barber
Remarks- His mother Mrs. Jane Beard resides in Rockbridge, Rockbridge Co. Va.

Account Number- 223
Name- Thomas Johnson
Date of Application- Dec. 28, 1866
Father or Mother? Married?- Judith Johnson
Place of Birth- Longgreen Co. Md
Residence- Terpsichore St. No. 418
Occupation- Laborer
Remarks- no other relatives

Account Number- 224
Name- Henry King
Date of Application- Dec. 29, 1866
Name of Master- Been here since 1834
Height and Complexion- 57 Black
Father or Mother? Married?- Elisha & Bridget Sally King
Name of Children-Abraham 28 & Esther 26 (wife of Bill) King
Place of Birth- Eastern Shore Somerset Co, Md
Residence- Baronne between Julia & Girod 208 (later entry) 218 St. Charles
Occupation- House Servant generally
Remarks- Father died in Maryland- Mother died there after Father- children Elisha & Elizabeth dead- children both in the city- brothers Homer in Md- Sharper & James & Leven all dead- sister Margaret wife of ___ Harris & Leah sold away from Md- Hester (dead) & Milly in Md.
Signature- yes

Account Number- 225
Name- Gustavus A. Thomas
Date of Application- Dec. 29, 1866
Name of Master- Geo W. Green
Plantation- Fairview Settlement Concordia La
Father or Mother? Married?- widower

Name of Children- Mary Jane & Prince Albert Thomas
Regiment and Company- served as teamster U.S.A.
Place of Birth- Fauquier Co. Va
Residence- Vanwinkle Plantation Pointe Coupee
Occupation- Farmer

Account Number- 227
Name- Madison Harrison
Date of Application- Jan. 2, 1867
Name of Master- James Davidson- city
Father or Mother? Married?- Malvina Harrison
Name of Children- none
Regiment and Company- formerly of Co. G 97th U.S.C.Inf.
Place of Birth- Brownsville Tenn
Residence- corner Annunciation & Pleasant 700
Occupation- Slater
Remarks- Name of brothers Wilson Harrison- city Edmond Harrison leaves in Tenn.

Account Number- 228
Name- Robert Hodge
Date of Application- Jan. 2, 1867
Name of Master- left Va when small boy
Height and Complexion- 6 feet Black
Father or Mother? Married?- parents Billy & Sally wife Mary
Place of Birth- Alexandria Va
Residence- 141 Perdido between Howard & Liberty
Occupation- Minister of the Gospel at Canton La
Remarks- No relatives whatever, Mr. Robert Hodge is 66 years old. (later entry) left parents in Va. Wife died in N.O. about 12 yrs. ago- in 1853. Brothers Bill and Jam both in Va & George sold away before Robert was- Sister Caroline in Alexandria- Preaches in Carrollton in M.E. Church. Mrs. Jane Hodge his wife may draw deposit money.
Signature- yes

Account Number- 229
Name- Alexander Singleton

Date of Application- Jan. 3, 1867
Name of Master- Marcelin Breaux
Plantation- 5 miles above Thibodeauxville La
Father or Mother? Married?- not married
Name of Children- none
Place of Birth- Southampton Va
Residence- Calliope St. 151
Occupation- Wood sawyer
Remarks- Knows nothing about any of his relatives.

Account Number- 230
Name- Mrs. Eliza Parker (& Mr.)
Date of Application- Jan. 3, 1867
Father or Mother? Married?- to Charles Parker
Name of Children- Annie Brown
Place of Birth- Fredericksburg Va
Residence- 204 St. Joseph St.
Occupation- Hairdresser
Remarks- Her mother's name is Ann Brown.

Account Number- 231(?)
Name- Caroline Boyer (widow)
Date of Application- Jan. 3, 1867
Name of Master- Capt. T.L. Macon
Father or Mother? Married?- Widow
Name of Children- none
Place of Birth- Athens Clark Co. Ga
Residence- Carondelet St. between Lafayette & Girod
Occupation- Nurse
Remarks- Father's name Claiborne Edwards in Athens Ga.

Account Number- 233
Name- Wm Davenport
Date of Application- Jan. 5, 1867
Father or Mother? Married?- Maria Davenport
Name of Children- none
Place of Birth- Cumberland Co. Va
Residence- 148 Canal St.
Occupation- House servant
Remarks- Wm Davenport died April 24, 1871- Alphus W. Cray identified widow & certified death of Mr. D.

Account Number- 234

Name- Betsy Malbourn
Date of Application- Jan. 5, 1867
Name of Master- Henry Cairnes, city
Father or Mother? Married?- widow
Place of Birth- Gloucester Co. Va
Residence- 182 Annunciation St.
Occupation- Cook
Remarks- Brother's name William White, his children Francis, Chloe, Carter & Robert White. In case of sickness Mary Armstrong is authorized on presentation of book to draw her money.
Signature-x

Account Number- 236
Name- Martha Ann Fields
Date of Application- Jan. 7, 1867
Name of Master- J.P. Shortridge
Father or Mother? Married?- Howard Fields
Place of Birth- Liberty, Clay Co. Missouri
Residence- Bienville St. 268
Occupation- Washing & Ironing
Remarks- Knows nothing about her relatives.

Account Number- 237
Name- Jane Riche
Date of Application- Jan. 7, 1867
Father or Mother? Married?- Lewis Riche
Name of Children- Louis, Charley, Mary, Sally, Margaret Jane, William Riche
Place of Birth- Charleston S. Ca
Residence- Perdido St. 255
Occupation- seamstress
Remarks- In case of sickness would send her book for draft by either Louis or Mary Riche her children. To none others money should be paid.

Account Number- 238
Name- Joseph Collins
Date of Application- Jan. 8, 1867
Name of Master- John Robertson, city
Place of Birth- Nashville Tenn.
Residence- Cypress between Bolivar and Claiborne
Occupation- Steam boating
Remarks- Has a mother- does not know where she is - name Candess Cyrus.

Signature- yes

Account Number- 241
Name- Peter Mathews
Date of Application- Jan. 14, 1867
Name of Master- Dr. George Tucker
Plantation- Homeward, Lafourche La
Height and Complexion- Black
Father or Mother? Married?-Jane Ann Mathews
Name of Children- Peter, William Henry Mathews
Place of Birth- Wilmington Hanover Co. N.Ca
Residence- Harvey's Canal Parish Jefferson La
Occupation- Farmer

Account Number- 247
Name- Rachel Richardson
Date of Application- Jan. 19, 1867
Name of Master- Dr. Daret
Plantation- city
Father or Mother? Married?- not married
Name of Children- none
Place of Birth- Charleston S. Ca
Residence- at Mr. Tilton's corner Dryades & Canal
Occupation- Servant
Remarks- Her sister's name is Amanda Berdon in Charleston S. Ca.

Account Number- 251
Name- Susan Thompson
Date of Application- Jan. 21, 1867
Name of Master- Henry Ficius
Plantation- city
Father or Mother? Married?- widow of Cornelius Thompson
Name of Children- none
Place of Birth- near Richmond Va
Residence- Josephine between Liberty and Benton
Occupation- Cook, Washer & Ironer
Remarks- no relatives- In case of sickness she authorizes John A. Murrey to draft with her book whatever money she would need or the whole
Signature- John A. Murrey

Account Number- 254(?)

Name- John Harris
Date of Application Jan. 24, 1867
Name of Master- Millis Fuller
Plantation- Chuot (?) Pass Attakapas
Height and Complexion- Black
Father or Mother? Married?- not
Name of Children- John Henry, Henry James, Geo. W. Harris
Place of Birth- Richmond Va
Residence- No. 8 Toulouse St.
Occupation- Peddler
Signature- yes

Account Number- 255
Name- Mrs. Eliza Hunter
Date of Application- Jan. 28, 1867
Name of Master- In case of sickness or when she could not come, she authorizes Mr. John Duncan to draw part or the whole of her money deposited in this bank.
Father or Mother? Married?- James Hunter
Name of Children- none
Place of Birth- Winchester Co. Va
Residence- Lafayette between Basin and Ramparts 259
Occupation- Washing & Ironing
Remarks-Father's name Jerry Allen, sister Jane Allen, brother Alfred Allen all in Winchester Va.
Signature- x

Account Number- 257
Name- Henry Williams
Date of Application- Jan 29, 1867
Father or Mother? Married?- Mathilda Williams
Place of Birth- Midway Woodfort Co. Ky
Residence- 63 Claiborne St.
Occupation- Waiter at Crown Verandah Hotel (later entry) drives a cart
Signature- yes

Account Number- 258
Name- Mrs. Lizzie Hampton
Date of Application- Jan. 30, 1867
Father or Mother? Married?- to Wade Hampton
Place of Birth- Petersburg Va
Residence- 129 St. John Poydras & Perdido
Occupation- Seamstress & Chambermaid
Remarks- Either husband or wife can draft for deposits

Account Number- 259
Name- Eli Jones
Date of Application- Jan. 30, 1867
Name of Master- Mrs. Clark Adams
Plantation- Parish of Iberville
Father or Mother? Married?- not
Regiment and Company- formerly in U.S. Navy Recgship (?) Vermont discharged in NY
Place of Birth- Parish of Iberville La
Residence- corner Melpomene & Magnolia
Occupation- Drayman at Shakespeare's Foundry
Remarks- Mother's name Caroline Washington, in city- sister's name Susan Jones, Mathilda Washington.
Signature- yes

Account Number- 260
Name- Lucy Jackson widow
Date of Application- Jan. 31, 1867
Name of Master- Lestor Prudhomme
Plantation- Nachitoches Red River La
Father or Mother? Married?- widow of Thomas Jackson
Name of Children- Julia Ann, Catherine, Prescilla Jackson
Place of Birth- Wilmington N. Ca
Residence- Main St. between Treme & Marais
Occupation- Washer & Ironer
Remarks- Any of the three daughters can draw money with book.

Account Number- 262(?)
Name- Mathilda Rivers
Date of Application- Feb. 2, 1867
Name of Mistress- Mrs. Eliza Farrar
Plantation- city
Height and Complexion- Black 25yrs. old
Place of Birth- Jackson Miss.
Residence- 16 Basin St.
Occupation- Dining Room Servant

Remarks- No mother- fathers name Charles Weston -is living but knows not where he is- Brother's names Albert and Richard Weston- somewhere in Miss.

Account Number- 263
Name- Edward Burke & Wife
Date of Application- Feb. 5, 1867
Father or Mother? Married?- Emma Burke his wife
Place of Birth- Jefferson Co. Missouri
Residence- Urania St. between Coliseum & Prytania
Occupation- Plasterer & Whitewasher
Remarks- The deposit made this day is made for a/c of both Edward Burke & wife all the other deposit that may be made will be the same way.

Account Number- 266
Name- Adeline Tillman
Date of Application- Feb. 5, 1867
Father or Mother? Married?- Henry Tillman her husband
Place of Birth- Havoe (?) Co. Va
Residence- 156 Franklin St.
Occupation- Sick Nurse
Remarks- Has brother by the name of Henry Green, living in this city.

Account Number- 268
Name- Robert Smith
Date of Application- Feb. 7, 1867
Name of Master- Geo. Arnold Holt
Plantation- city
Height and Complexion- Black
Father or Mother? Married?- not
Regiment and Company- formerly Captain's Steward on board of gunboat Fearnot U.S.N.
Place of Birth- Black River Neck near Baltimore Md
Residence- Bienville, Marais, Villere
Occupation- Cook
Remarks- no relatives at all

Account Number- 269
Name- Esther King
Date of Application- Feb. 13, 1867
Father or Mother? Married?- not- 25 yrs. old
Place of Birth- New Orleans La
Residence- Baronne, Julia & Girard 208
Occupation- House Servant
Remarks- Her father's name Henry King- mother's name Sally King.

Account Number- 270
Name- William Carter
Date of Application- Feb. 14, 1867
Father or Mother? Married?- Mathilda Carter
Place of Birth- Chesterfield Co. Va
Residence- 307 Common St.
Occupation- Laborer
Remarks- Brother's name Joseph Carter- wife's sister's name Susan Macknami(?)

Account Number- 271
Name- Ambrose Parrent
Date of Application- Feb. 15, 1867
Name of Master- Charles Cox
Plantation- Bayou Lafourche 5 miles from Donaldson
Height and Complexion- Black
Father or Mother? Married?- Mary Ann Parrent
Name of Children- Ann, Adeline Parrent
Place of Birth- Maryland State knows not where
Residence- Carondelet, Girod & Lafayette 145
Occupation- Laborer
Remarks- Wife cannot draw even with an order.

Account Number- 272
Name- Julia Christian
Date of Application- Feb. 18, 1867
Name of Master- James Davis
Plantation- city
Height and Complexion- Black
Father or Mother? Married?- to Armstead Christian
Name of Children- Henry Christian
Place of Birth- Stanford Ky
Residence- Washington, Prytania & St. Charles No. 220
Occupation- Washer & Ironer

Account Number- 273

Name- Emma Augustus
Date of Application- Feb. 18, 1867
Name of Master- M.B. Brady
Plantation- city
Father or Mother? Married?- widow
Name of Children- none
Place of Birth- Mount Pleasant Va
Residence- corner Thalia & White
Occupation- Hairdresser
Remarks- Stepson's name is Nathan Augustus- no other relatives living- husband's name William Augustus (dead)

Account Number- 274
Name- William Crump
Date of Application- Feb. 19, 1867
Height and Complexion- Light black 21 yrs. old
Father or Mother? Married?- not
Name of Children- none
Regiment and Company- 4th Cav. Co. A discharged
Place of Birth- New Orleans La
Residence- corner Main & Rampart (later entry) Barrack between Roman & Derbigny(?)
Occupation- Laborer
Remarks- Father's name Jack Crump- mother Mary Crump both in city- bothers John & Edward in city- sister Fanny in city & Ellen at Lake Providence & Mary in city.
Signature- yes

Account Number- 275
Name- Elizabeth Burl
Date of Application- Feb. 20, 1867
Height and Complexion- yellow
Father or Mother? Married?- not
Name of Children- none
Place of Birth- Leesburg Laudun Co. Va
Residence- Second, Appollo & Bacchus
Occupation- Nursing at Mr. Davis
Remarks- Mothers name Mrs. Emily Robinson somewhere in Va. (later entry) corner St. Charles & Triton Walk "James House"
Signature- yes

Account Number- 277

Name- Andrew Talbot
Date of Application- Feb. 20, 1867
Height and Complexion- Black
Father or Mother? Married?- not
Name of Children- none
Regiment and Company- Co. H 116th U.S.C.T. discharged
Place of Birth- Danville Boyle Co. Ky
Residence- Carrollton La
Occupation- Gardner
Remarks- Deposited card no. 1280 from Louisville(?) of $150. - on which $50. were paid.

Account Number- 278
Name- John Armor
Date of Application- Feb. 21, 1867
Name of Master- Free
Height and Complexion- Light- 16 years old
Father or Mother? Married?- not
Name of Children- none
Place of Birth- New Orleans
Residence- 133 Bienville St.
Occupation- Barber
Remarks- no father nor mother- sister's name Estelle Armor in N.Orleans
Signature- yes

Account Number- 281
Name- Ed Hopkins
Date of Application- Feb. 23, 1867
Height and Complexion- Light 19 years
Father or Mother? Married?- not
Name of Children- none
Place of Birth- New Orleans La
Residence- Perdido between St. John & Franklin
Occupation- Steam boating
Remarks- Mother's name Edith Williams city- no other relatives.

Account Number- 282
Name- James Jenkins
Date of Application- Feb. 23, 1867
Name of Master- Meyer McGee
Plantation- Washington Parish
Height and Complexion- 21 yrs old Black
Regiment and Company- 10th U.S.C.A. Heavy Co. C discharged
Place of Birth- Charleston S. Ca

Residence- Marine Hospital City
Occupation- Assistant Teacher
Remarks- Medard Jenkins father's name in Savannah Georgia- Gilbert Jenkins brother's name- Jane, Mary Jenkins his sisters all in Georgia.
Signature- yes

Account Number- 283
Name- Pierre Raymond
Date of Application- Feb. 25, 1867
Father or Mother? Married?- Clothilde Raymond his wife
Name of Children- Arthur Raymond from 1st wife- Frederick Robert from last wife
Place of Birth- New Orleans La
Residence- 251 St. Louis St.
Occupation- Carpenter
Signature- yes

Account Number- 284
Name- William Morris
Date of Application- Feb. 25, 1867
Name of Master- Left Maryland year before Santa Anna & Genl. Taylor commenced fighting- lived 41 miles below N.O. for 6 years
Height and Complexion- Black 49 (Mar. 1868 entry)
Father or Mother? Married?- Littleton & Elsie wife Lydia Morris dead
Name of Children- none (Mar. 1868) Maria's Children Alexine 28 wife of Simon Smith & Augusta Morris 27
Place of Birth- Eastern Shore, Caroline Co. Md
Residence- Felicity Road, Perssania & Coliseum
Occupation- Engineer
Remarks- Alexine Morris is in Jefferson (Mar. 1868 entry) Former wife Maria dead. Augusta in N.O. Maria's children Justina 29, Sam 28 and one other all in Maryland. No children by Lydia. Father died in Va in 1863- mother died when he was a baby- don't remember her. Maria's children (?)lier & William Henry both dead- Brothers David Lockman & Daniel Gross in Md- Sisters Alerenia(?) & Annette & Louisa & Surenna all in Md.
Signature- x

Account Number- 285
Name- William Smith
Date of Application- Mar 2, 1867
Place of Birth- Petersburg Va
Residence- Hercules St.
Occupation- Gardner
Signature- Does not write

Account Number- 287
Name- Samuel Murphy
Date of Application- Mar. 5, 1867
Father or Mother? Married?- Emilia Place
Name of Children- none
Regiment and Company- 20th NY Co I(?) J(?)
Place of Birth- Middleburg, Schoharie Co. NY
Occupation- 2nd Engineer on Steamer Legram
Signature- yes

Account Number- 288
Name- Mary Diana Braxton
Date of Application- Mar. 5, 1867
Father or Mother? Married?- Widow
Name of Children- George Green & Louisa Blye
Place of Birth- Norfolk Va
Residence- St. Charles, Delord & St. Joseph
Occupation- Washing & Ironing
Remarks- Her son George Green is empowered to draw money for her, on presenting the bank book.
Signature- Does not write

Account Number- 289
Name- Save Williams
Date of Application- Mar. 6, 1867
Name of Master- John Johnson
Plantation- Plaquemines "Concession Pon(?)
Height and Complexion- Black
Father or Mother? Married?- Martine Williams
Name of Children- Joseph, Pauline & Alfred
Regiment and Company- Co. E 74th U.S.C.T.
Place of Birth- Fauquier Va

Residence- Galvez St. Ann & Marie
Occupation- Blacksmith
Remarks- Winston Williams his father- died when Save was a boy in Va- Hannah was left in Va Fauquier Co., when Save started to come here in 1852- brother Wellington Williams came here with him, but he never saw him since. June 10, 1869 Williams now resides on Villere St. between Bienville & Conti.
Signature- x

Account Number- 292
Name- Joseph Bailey
Date of Application- Mar. 8, 1867
Name of Master- Joe Rawley
Plantation- Clinton La
Height and Complexion- Black
Father or Mother? Married?- Not
Name of Children- none
Regiment and Company- Co. A 80th U.S.C.I.
Place of Birth- 5 miles from Amite River La
Residence- Carrollton, Douglas Grocery
Occupation- Farmer

Account Number- 294
Name- Joseph E. Hollond
Date of Application- Mar. 11, 1867
Father or Mother? Married?- Sarah Ann Holland
Name of Children- none
Regiment and Company- Co. I 74th U.S.C.T.
Place of Birth- Monticello Co. Va
Residence- Clara, Perdido & Gravier
Occupation- Cooper
Remarks- Bank book lost see No. 490.
Signature- yes

Account Number- 295(?)
Name- Turner W. Johnson
Date of Application- Mar. 11, 1867
Father or Mother? Married?- Emily Letche Hays
Place of Birth- Columbia S.Ca
Residence- 180 Terpsichore St. Appollo & Bacchus
Occupation- Cooper
Remarks- Father's name Abraham Johnson- mother Mason Johnson both dead.
Signature- yes

Account Number- 297
Name- Ann Eliza Brown
Date of Application- Mar 12, 1867
Father or Mother? Married?- widow
Name of Children- none

Account Number- 298(?)
Name- Spencer Stanford
Date of Application- Mar. 12, 1867
Height and Complexion- Light
Father or Mother? Married?- not
Regiment and Company- 137 Alabama U.S.T.
Place of Birth- Biloxi, Miss
Residence- New Orleans La
Occupation- Steam boating
Remarks- Mother's name Delia Stanford in city.
Signature- Does not write

Account Number- 300
Name- Henry Williams deposited by Alexander Burridge
Date of Application- Mar. 16, 1867
Height and Complexion- Colored about 30 years
Father or Mother? Married?- not
Name of Children- none
Place of Birth- Lexington Ky
Residence- Corner Felicity & Rampart
Occupation- Steam boating on Steamer Lee
Remarks- Henry Williams is deaf & dumb- Mother's name Delia Burridge. Money to be drawn by Williams or by Alexander Burridge.

Account Number- 302
Name- Margaret Johnson
Date of Application- Mar. 18 , 1867
Name of Children- Abraham Johnson
Place of Birth- Baltimore Md
Residence- 116 Camp St.
Occupation- House Servant
Remarks- In case of sickness authorizes her son Abraham Johnson to draw her money.

Account Number- 304
Name- Andrew Hunter
Date of Application- Mar. 19, 1867
Name of Master- Formerly lived at Memphis Tenn. Has been here since the war.
Height and Complexion- about 47 Black
Father or Mother? Married?- Dr. Rice & Lily wife Margaret Shield
Name of Children- Ellen about 14 & Alfred 24 yrs.
Regiment and Company- 7th U.S.C.T. Co. E
Place of Birth- Sumner Co. above Nashville Tenn.
Residence- No. 243 (forgot name of street)
Occupation- Steward private house
Remarks- Andrew has other children by Louisa Sanders- John 24, William 22, Patsy 23, Will dead- They all were sold away from Memphis to Ala.- William was here about 6 mos. ago. His father was in Houston Texas 20 yrs. ago when he was there- his mother died there 21 yrs. ago last Aug. Brother John in N.O. & William (don't know where he is) & Frederick (don't know where he is)- sister Mary & Martha wife of Robinson Burrill- Has a brother Phillip (don't know where he is).
Signature- x

Account Number- 305
Name- Fanny Cazenau
Date of Application- Mar. 20, 1867
Height and Complexion- Light
Father or Mother? Married?- single
Name of Children- William Harrison 4 mos. old
Place of Birth- Bay St. Louis Miss.
Residence- corner Carondelet Walk & Johnson
Occupation- House Keeper
Remarks- Deposited by her agent Mr. J.W. Harrison- who can draw on

Account Number- 306
Name- Moses Townsend
Date of Application- Mar. 21, 1867
Name of Master- Latapie
Plantation- city

Father or Mother? Married?- Roxeann Townsend
Name of Children- none
Place of Birth- North Carolina raised in Logan Co. Ky
Residence- Claiborne near corner Conti
Occupation- Office Servant

Account Number- 307
Name- John Piermont
Date of Application- Mar. 22, 1867
Name of Master- Peter Hitman
Plantation- Uhope Plantation, Rapides La
Height and Complexion- Black 32 yrs. old
Father or Mother? Married?- Mary Jane Piermont
Place of Birth- Rapides Parish La
Residence- St. Paul St. No. 129
Occupation- Laborer
Remarks- Father's name William Piermont in Rapides Parish La- 3 sisters Margaret, Rebecca, Julia Ann Piermont

Account Number- 308
Name- Henry Worthen
Date of Application- Mar. 22, 1867
Name of Master- Dr. W. Dean in charge of 39th U.S.C.T.
Height and Complexion- Black
Father or Mother? Married?- single
Regiment and Company- 39th U.S.C.T. 1st Detachment
Place of Birth- Charleston S. Ca
Residence- Camp at Greenville Post La
Occupation- acting Hospital Steward 39th U.S.C.T.
Remarks- Deposited by Surgeon Beal

Account Number- 309
Name- James Dutton
Date of Application- Mar. 22, 1867
Height and Complexion- Black
Father or Mother? Married?- Single
Regiment and Company- 4th detachment 39th U.S.C.I.
Place of Birth- Ky
Residence- Post Greenville La
Occupation- Cook In Hospital of 39th U.S.C.T.

Remarks- Deposited by Surgeon Beal

Account Number- 310
Name- William Alexander
Date of Application- Mar. 22, 1867
Height and Complexion- Black
Father or Mother? Married?- single
Regiment and Company- 39th U.S.C.I.
Residence- Camp at Greenville La
Occupation- Soldier

Account Number- 310
Name- Elizabeth Davis
Date of Application- Mar. 23, 1867
Height and Complexion- Black
Father or Mother? Married?- John Davis
Name of Children- John Albert Burney
Place of Birth- Green Co. Ky
Residence- Kerlerec St. 214
Occupation- Washer woman
Remarks- J.A. Burney her son is in Galveston Texas.

Account Number- 313
Name- Felix Lindor
Date of Application- Mar. 27, 1867
Height and Complexion- 5 feet Black
Father or Mother? Married?- Eliza Maurice Lindor
Name of Children- Marie Adele Lindor 4 mos. old
Regiment and Company- Co. H 74th U.S.C.T.
Place of Birth- Bayou Lafourche Ascension Parish La
Residence- St. Bernard Ave. Prieur & Johnson
Occupation- Pupil of Missionary Theological School
Remarks- Coralie Michel his mother in city- Lorenza, Irma, Modeste Philips his sisters- all in city.
Signature- yes

Account Number- 314(?)
Name- Rosetta Taylor
Date of Application- Mar. 28, 1867
Name of Master- William Brothers
Plantation- city
Height and Complexion- Black about 50 yrs. old

Father or Mother? Married?- Widow of Frank Taylor (later entry) Philip Packer
Name of Children- Georgiana Wilson & William & Aleck Allen
Place of Birth- Norfolk Va
Residence- Baronne St. near Triton Walk
Occupation- Cook
Remarks- When she was sold away from Norfolk in 1847, she left her children there- heard from them since the blockade of the city- In case of death and the children could not be found she wants her money to go to Emma Johnson. (later entry) Husband can draw Philip Packer.

Account Number- 316
Name- Margaret Augustus
Date of Application- Apr. 1, 1867
Height and Complexion- Black about 45 yrs.
Father or Mother? Married?- Perry Augustus
Name of Children- none had 4 children all dead
Place of Birth- Bourbon Co. Ky
Residence- Basin St. Poydras & Perdido
Occupation- Washer and Ironer
Remarks- Rose Coundry her mother in Sterling, Bourbon Co. Ky - ___ Coundry her father dead- came here about 16 yrs. ago from Ky

Account Number- 317
Name- Robert Washington Bowie
Date of Application- Apr. 3, 1867
Father or Mother? Married?- Nancy Bowie
Name of Children- none
Place of Birth- Baltimore Md
Residence- 140 Franklin St.
Occupation- Teacher
Signature- yes

Account Number- 318
Name- Paul Bonseigneur
Date of Application- Apr. 4, 1867
Father or Mother? Married?- not
Name of Children- none
Place of Birth- New Orleans La
Residence- 333 Liberty St.

24

Occupation- Stevedore
Signature- yes

Account Number- 319
Name- Jordan B. Noble
Date of Application- Apr. 5, 1867
Father or Mother? Married?- not
Name of Children- Mrs. Pascal & J. Massana (?)
Place of Birth- Augusta Georgia
Residence- Clio St. No. 218
Occupation- Musician
Signature- yes

Account Number- 320
Name- Stevens Strange
Date of Application- Apr. 5, 1867
Height and Complexion- Light 55 years old
Father or Mother? Married?- Cornelia Strange
Name of Children- John Strange 20 yrs. old
Place of Birth- Winchester Va
Residence- Thalia, Camp & Prytania
Occupation- Barber
Remarks- Mrs. Strange is a hairdresser. In case of his death Mr. Strange wants that his wife Cornelia Strange should inherit whatever amount of funds he might have deposited in this branch.
Signature- x witnessed by Noble Gannon

Account Number-323
Name- Anderson Randall
Date of Application- Apr. 8, 1867
Father or Mother? Married?- Rosine Randall
Name of Children- none
Regiment and Company- cook in 4th Ky Cavalry 1864
Place of Birth- Lagrange Georgia
Residence- 327 White St.
Occupation- Steam boating
Remarks- Mowning Colquitt his mother and Washington Colquitt his father- both of them were living in Harris Co. Georgia about 10 years ago.
Signature- cannot write

Account Number- 324
Name- Simon Augustin
Date of Application- Apr. 8, 1867
Plantation- Telesford Roman- St. James La
Height and Complexion- Black 35 years old
Father or Mother? Married?- Charlotte Augustin
Name of Children- none " wife pregnant"
Place of Birth- St. James Parish La on Telesford Roman Plantation
Residence- Monroe St. Carrollton La
Occupation- Laborer
Remarks- Sisters name Theresa married to Nelson Collins, resides with him. No other relatives.
Signature- does not write

Account Number- 325
Name- Alfred Hale
Date of Application- Apr. 8, 1867
Father or Mother? Married?- Viney Hale
Name of Children- none
Place of Birth- Jonesboro, Washington Co. Tenn.
Residence- Shreveport La
Occupation- Farming
Remarks- Albert & Maria & Violet Hale- his brother and sisters, were at Jonesboro when Alfred left 30 years ago- never heard of them since. Brought in by Mr. Saville.
Signature- does not write

Account Number- 326
Name- Rev. J.P. Newman
Date of Application- Apr. 8, 1867
Residence- 158 Julia St.
Occupation- Minister
Signature- yes

Account Number- 327
Name- Mrs. Truelive Malone
Date of Application- Apr. 8, 1867
Name of Mistress- in Va Mrs. Nancy Bakum in Orange Co. Va where she left two of her children- the other one was with John Porter.
Father or Mother? Married?- Montelius Malone

Name of Children- John, Louisa & Susan Wright
Place of Birth- Orange Co. Va
Residence- Perdido St. Howard & Liberty
Occupation- Washer & Ironer
Remarks- When she left Orange Co. 23 years ago, she left her children there, they were very young- has heard of them last about 20 years ago. Wears specs, 2 front teeth upper jaw.

Account Number- 328
Name- Salomon Robert Malone
Date of Application- Apr. 11, 1867
Height and Complexion- Black 44 yrs.
Father or Mother? Married?- Charlotte Ann Moses
Name of Children- Levi Moses 15 yrs. old
Regiment and Company- 76th U.S.C.T. Co. D
Place of Birth- Boone Co. Ky
Residence- No. 15 Bertrand Common & Gravier
Occupation- Teacher
Remarks- Jane Herrim his sister in city.
Signature- yes

Account Number- 329
Name- Newman Taylor
Date of Application- Apr. 11, 1867
Height and Complexion- Black 22 yrs. old
Place of Birth- Bowling Green Ky
Residence- Roman St. corner Canal
Occupation- Dining Room Servant
Remarks- Father's name Vincent Taylor in city- Henrietta, Esther, Cornelia & Lucy Ann Taylor his sisters all in city has brothers- Jordan, Ed & Henry Taylor.
Signature- does not write

Account Number- 330
Name- John Duncan Smith
Date of Application- Apr. 12, 1867
Height and Complexion- Black 43 years old
Father or Mother? Married?- Sarah Lewis
Place of Birth- Nashville Tenn.

Residence- 239 Lafayette, Basin & Circus
Occupation- Office Cleaner
Remarks- Mother's name Rachel Smith in city- sister's name Maria Williams.
Signature- yes

Account Number- 331
Name- Edward Anderson
Date of Application- Apr. 16, 1867
Height and Complexion- Black 19 years old
Father or Mother? Married?- not
Name of Children- none
Place of Birth- New Orleans La
Residence- Rampart, Josephine & St. Andrews
Occupation- Steam boating
Remarks- Mother's name Harriet May- stepfather's name William May- has no brothers or sisters- but a little girl 6 yrs. old raised by his mother is called Frances May.
Signature- yes

Account Number- 332
Name- Charles Reed
Date of Application- Apr. 16, 1867
Name of Master- John N. Mott in Mobile
Height and Complexion- Black 72 years old
Father or Mother? Married?- Delia Reed
Name of Children- Thomas & Laura Reed
Place of Birth- Williamsburg Va
Residence- Mobile Ala
Occupation- Drayman
Remarks- Charles Reed was a depositor in our Mobile Branch.
Signature- does not sign

Account Number- 333
Name- Elizabeth Washington
Date of Application- Apr. 17, 1867
Father or Mother? Married?- Aaron Washington
Name of Children- none
Place of Birth- Baltimore
Residence- Perdido St. No. 218
Occupation- Washer & Ironer
Remarks- John Carpenter her father & Isabella Carpenter her mother are in

Millersville near Baltimore- Mrs. E. Washington has no children- has a stepchild called Twissie Washington.
Signature- does not write

Account Number- 334
Name- Mrs. Hannah Jefferson
Date of Application- Apr. 18, 1867
Height and Complexion- Black
Father or Mother? Married?- Thomas Jefferson
Name of Children- none
Place of Birth- Eastern Shore Maryland
Residence- 31 Claiborne St.
Occupation- Washer & Ironer
Remarks- Mrs. Jefferson has no relatives whatever.
Signature- does not sign

Account Number- 335
Name- Alonzo Lewis
Date of Application- Apr. 22, 1867
Height and Complexion- Black 27 yrs. old
Father or Mother? Married?- Henrietta Lewis
Regiment and Company- 86th U.S.C.T. Co. D
Place of Birth- New Orleans La
Residence- 268 Lafayette St.
Occupation- Gasfitter & Brass finisher
Remarks- Alexander Lewis & Esther Lewis his father & mother's names- brother Adam Lewis.
Signature- yes

Account Number- 336
Name- Ann Robertson
Date of Application- April 22, 1867
Height and Complexion- Black
Father or Mother? Married?- Jack Robertson
Name of Children- Elijah & Jack Robertson
Place of Birth- Alexandria La
Residence- Carrollton Market St. La
Occupation- Washer & Ironer
Remarks- Rose Thompson her mother at Alexandria Va.

Account Number- 337
Name- Edward Bailey
Date of Application- Apr. 22, 1867
Height and Complexion- Black 22 years
Father or Mother? Married?- not
Name of Children- none
Regiment and Company- D. 10th Heavy Arty. Cold.
Place of Birth- Halifax Co. North Ca
Residence- Carrollton, Bouligny St.
Occupation- Laborer
Remarks- Mother's name Jane is living on Bayou Grosse Tete La, sisters name Sylvester- his brothers name Albert.
Signature- does not write

Account Number- 338
Name- Robert F. Walk
Date of Application- Apr. 23, 1867
Father or Mother? Married?- Kitty Walk
Name of Children- none
Place of Birth- Norfolk Va
Residence- 19 Gasquet, Liberty & Franklin
Occupation- Carpenter
Remarks- Ann Eliza Walk his sister resides in Norfolk, Va- has no other relatives.
Signature- yes

Account Number- 339
Name- Ann Murrell
Date of Application- Apr. 23, 1867
Father or Mother? Married?- John Murrell
Name of Children- Mary Jane Murrell 25 yrs. old
Place of Birth- Alexandria Va
Residence- 173 St. Charles St.
Occupation- Washer & Ironer
Remarks- Son's name Joseph Murrell- Mary Morris her sister lives in Alexandria Va- Mrs. Murrell came here about 22 or 23 years ago. Husband can draw.

Account Number- 340
Name- O.J. Flagg
Date of Application- Apr. 26, 1867
Height and Complexion- White
Father or Mother? Married?- Mary Flagg
Name of Children- none
Place of Birth- Whitesborough NY

Residence- Parish St. Charles La
Occupation- Employed by U.S.
Signature- yes

Account Number- 341
Name- David Page
Date of Application- Apr. 26 1867
Height and Complexion- Black
Father or Mother? Married?- Diana Page
Name of Children- James, Emily Page 7 & 16 yrs. old
Regiment and Company- Co. E 86th U.S.C.T.
Place of Birth- Botetourt Co. Va
Residence Douglas St. 474
Occupation- Laborer
Remarks- Fanny Young his sister lives in this city. James & Emily Page are his children by two different women. He has not as yet any children from Diana Page his present wife.
Signature- yes

Account Number- 342
Name- John Griggs
Date of Application- Apr. 27, 1867
Height and Complexion- Black 36 years old
Father or Mother? Married?- Ann Griggs
Name of Children- Mary & Alice Griggs
Regiment and Company- 86th U.S.C.T. Co. F
Place of Birth- Currituk Co. North Ca
Residence- Cypress near Derbigny No. 54
Occupation- Laborer
Remarks- He came in the city in 1861- Mary and Alice Griggs his two daughters are 15 & 12 yrs. old respectively- They are in Moyak Currituk Co. North Ca. of Ann Griggs his actual wife - he has no children.

Account Number- 343
Name- John Lee
Date of Application- Apr. 29, 1867
Name of Master- "Father's name George Richardson died in N. Ca don't know when mother's name Margaret Lee In Virginia.
Height and Complexion- 21 years old Black
Father or Mother? Married?- single
Regiment and Company- 36th U.S.C.I. Co. E
Place of Birth- Cumberland Co. N. Ca
Residence- in Garrison Duty at Ship Island Miss.
Occupation- Laborer before Enlisting
Remarks- Sisters Sarah & Maria in Va- brothers Joseph Lee & Major Lee in Virginia. This deposit is made by Mr. St. Calair Mandeville U.S. Claim agent- subject to his order (John Lee's) John Lee belongs to 39th U.S.C.I. Co. B in garrison on Ship Island Miss. by consolidation Lee belongs now May 1869 to Co. G 25th U.S.I. at Jackson Barracks.
Signature- yes

Account Number- 344
Name- Byron Gownes
Date of Application- April 29, 1867
Regiment and Company- 36th U.S.C.I. Co. C
Place of Birth- Pitt Co. N. Ca
Residence- on Garrison duty at Fort Pike
Occupation- Soldier
Remarks- This deposit is made by Mr. St. Calair Mandeville U.S. Claim agent- subject to B. Gownes order
Signature- does not write

Account Number- 345
Name- John Burke
Date of Application- Apr. 30, 1867
Height and Complexion- Black about 42 yrs.
Father or Mother? Married?- Emily Robertson Burke
Name of Children- none
Regiment and Company- 4th Calv. Colored Co. A
Place of Birth- Charleston S. Ca
Residence- 309 Terpsichore near Dryades
Occupation- White washer & Laborer
Remarks- Came here in 1853- when he left Charleston his sisters Daphne, Phelis & Rebecca were living in Charleston. Daphne was at Mr. John C.

Potter's place.
Signature- yes

Account Number- 346
Name- John Olmstead
Date of Application- Apr. 30, 1867
Father or Mother? Married?- Hurlde Olmstead
Name of Children- Caroline 2 yrs. old
Place of Birth- Pittsylvania Co. Va
Residence- 205 Howard St.
Occupation- Blacksmith
Remarks- No relatives whatever- Overdrawn $10.
Signature- yes

Account Number- 347
Name- Daniel McKensy
Date of Application- May 1, 1867
Height and Complexion- yellow 55yrs. old
Father or Mother? Married?- Maria McKensy
Name of Children- Martin McKensie 22 yrs.
Place of Birth- Beaufort S. Ca
Residence- Lafayette St. between Roman & Prieur
Occupation- Cook
Remarks- The money in case of sickness of either Mr. McKensie & his wife Maria- may be paid to their son on presentation of book. P.S. Aug. 19, 1870 Mr. Ford our depositor gives notice that both Daniel & Maria McKensy died across the lake- This account closed Jan. 25, 1871 by receipt of Martin Ford which see- S Perry
Signature- Does not write

Account Number- 348
Name- Mrs. Ann Dossy Johnson
Date of Application- May 1, 1867
Father or Mother? Married?- widow
Name of Children- Lazarus & Moses Thompson
Place of Birth- Marcibian Town Md
Residence- Custom house between Burgundy & Ramparts
Occupation- Seamstress
Remarks- Mrs. Johnson has a daughter in this city Mrs. Alice Bright married to Mr. Cornelius Bright.
Signature- x

Account Number- 349
Name- Henry Taylor
Date of Application- May 2, 1867
Father or Mother? Married?- Maria Taylor
Name of Children- Reuben & Kitty Taylor 10 & 8 Yrs. old
Regiment and Company- 92nd U.S.C.T. Co. G
Place of Birth- Washington City
Residence- Girod, Baronne & Philippa
Occupation- Hosteler on Gravier St.
Remarks- No relatives living
Signature- does not write

Account Number- 350
Name- Samuel Luke
Date of Application- May 2, 1867
Height and Complexion- 37 years old
Father or Mother? Married?- Corinne Luke
Name of Children- Lewis & Johnson Luke 18 & 4 yrs old (later entry Lewis now dead)
Regiment and Company- 86th U.S.C.T. Co. G
Place of Birth- Parish St. James La
Residence- Triton Walk Carondelet & St. Charles
Occupation- Carpenter
Remarks- Lewis & Johnson are his children by two different women- He has no children from Corinne Luke his wife. (later entry) Wife Corrine Luke can draw. Corinne born New Orleans age 42 years has scar on left side of lower lip. Don't look so old- Father Francois- mother Rasberry - brothers none- sisters none.
Signature- x

Account Number- 351
Name- Peter Ricks
Date of Application- May 2, 1867
Height and Complexion- Black 48 years old
Father or Mother? Married?- Isabella Ricks

Name of Children- Theodore, Hermogene & Elizabeth Ricks
Place of Birth- Montgomery Co. Md
Residence- 135 Perdido St.
Occupation- Office Cleaner
Remarks- Peter Ricks came here from Washington City in 1848- has always lived here since.
Signature- does not write

Account Number- 352
Name- Edwin Roberts
Date of Application- May 3, 1867
Height and Complexion- Black 45 years old
Father or Mother? Married?- Julia Roberts
Name of Children- Mary Jane Roberts 9 mos. old
Regiment and Company- 75th U.S.C.T. Co. I
Place of Birth- Charleston S.Ca
Residence- Magazine St. 299
Occupation- Painter
Remarks- Mothers' name Agar Owen- sisters name Susan Owen- brothers name William Owen. When Mr. Roberts left Charleston about 10 yrs. ago , his mother, sister & brother were in Charleston.
Signature- yes

Account Number- 353
Name- Mrs. Mary Beard
Date of Application- May 3, 1867
Father or Mother? Married?- John Beard
Name of Children- Andrew Henderson 15 yrs. old
Place of Birth- Culpepper Va
Residence- Dryades St. near Poydras
Occupation- Washer & Ironer
Remarks- She was sold from Culpepper Va in 1853- she there left Abraham, Jacob, Isaac & Margaret her children in Culpepper. They were owned by Capt. Daniel Brown in Culpepper- her name in Culpepper was Mary Brown. In case of death, she wants her husband John Brige to get the money for her children. (later entry) Pay only to both together.

Account Number- 354
Name- Reuben Braxton
Date of Application- May 4, 1867
Height and Complexion- Black 49 yrs. old
Father or Mother? Married?- Claremtime Braxton
Name of Children- none
Place of Birth- Hanover Co. Va
Residence- corner Canal & Dorgenois
Occupation- Gardener
Remarks- When he left Va 24 yrs. ago his mother Lucy Braxton & his father Reuben Braxton- his brother Tom Braxton, were living in Hanover Co. - his brother belonged to Mrs. Widow Foster in Richmond Va.
Signature- does not write

Account Number- 355
Name- Bennett Young
Date of Application- May 4, 1867
Height and Complexion- Black 50 yrs. old
Father or Mother? Married?- Fanny Young
Place of Birth- King & Queen Co. Va
Residence- 182 Liberty St.
Occupation- Drayman
Remarks- Mr. B. Young has no children, but has an adopted child of the name of Robert Daunoy about 15 yrs. old- wife can draw.
Signature- yes

Account Number- 356
Name- John Griffin
Date of Application- May 8, 1867 (updated Mar. 13, 1869)
Name of Master- Been here since first year after war broke out.
Height and Complexion- Black pox marked 24 yrs. (age 29 July/69)
Father or Mother? Married?- (Maria Adams- mother) Nancy Gale Griffin
Name of Children- none (Allen 6 mos.)
Place of Birth- Vicksburg Miss
Residence- Bacchus, Palmyra & Euteie {?} (First corner Liberty)
Occupation- Dray driver (Steam boating)
Remarks- Fathers name Allen Griffin

living in Vicksburg at Mr. Butler's Hotel Keeper (child Emma dead- mother died 23 yrs. ago in Vicksburg- brothers Monroe Hammus in Vicksburg & Washington in Vicksburg- sisters Rosy wife of Wm Lovely in N.O. & Charlotte widow of Tom Smith in Vicksburg & Mary Ann wife of Henry Wilson in Vicksburg.)

Account Number- 357
Name- Aga Harris
Date of Application- May 9, 1867
Height and Complexion- Black about 45 yrs. old
Father or Mother? Married?- Joe Harris
Name of Children- none
Place of Birth- Gujla 30 miles from Richmond Va
Residence- Felicity Road 219
Occupation- Washer & Ironer
Remarks- Left Va 26 years ago- her brothers John, David & Anderson Braxton & sisters Annikus, Harriet & Rose Braxton were living with their master Edward Turpin in Gujilano Co. Peter Cosey can draw his record Natchez Miss. -{?} Prytania- Laborer 42 yrs. see black nails of left hand.

Account Number- 358
Name- Arthelia Morris
Date of Application- May 10, 1867
Height and Complexion- Light Black
Father or Mother? Married?- not Married
Name of Children- Henry- Harriet & Susan
Place of Birth- Norfolk Va
Residence- Philip St. St. Denis & Dryades
Occupation- Cook
Remarks- When she left Norfolk Va about 20 years ago her son Henry was 6 yrs' old, Harriet 4 yrs. & Susan 2 yrs. old they were slaves of Jacob Miller- Her mother's name is Jane Walker she was the wife of Salomon Morris.

Account Number- 359
Name- Emma Bailey
Date of Application- May 13, 1867
Height and Complexion- Black 50 yrs. old
Father or Mother? Married?- not Married
Place of Birth- Livingston Co. Ky
Residence- Joseph St. Bouligny
Occupation- Midwife
Remarks- Came from Livingston Co. Ky 33 yrs. ago - brother Elijah Wheeler, Lavissa Wheeler her sister are living in Livingston Co. Ky. Angeline Knole can draw in case of sickness born- Nelson Co. Ky age- about 38- Occupation- Washer woman- 15 Camp- Mother Annie Mae Father George. Tall & Fat - light complexion.
Signature-

Account Number- 361
Name- Joseph Leduc
Date of Application- May 14, 1867
Height and Complexion- White
Regiment and Company- Co. B 1st Inf. U.S.A.
Place of Birth- White Hall, Washington Co. NY
Residence- Sailors Home
Occupation- Soldier
Remarks- Father's name Joseph Leduc mother's Sarah Mellon Leduc both dead.
Signature- does not write

Account Number- 360
Name- Gustavus A. Andrews
Date of Application- May 14, 1867
Height and Complexion- White
Regiment and Company- 1st Inf. Co. B
Place of Birth- LaPorte Co. Ind.
Residence- USA
Occupation- Soldier
Remarks- Sister's name Ellen L. Andrews Ridgeville, Manatowok Co. Wisconsin.
Signature- yes

Account Number- 362
Name- Andrew White
Date of Application- May 16, 1867
Height and Complexion- Black 43years old
Father or Mother? Married?- Eliza White
Name of Children- Fanny, Cherry, Andrew White

Regiment and Company- 86th U.S.C.T. Co. H
Place of Birth- Augusta Georgia
Residence- Poydras St. No. 428
Occupation- Laborer
Remarks- Three years ago he left Marianna, Jackson Co. Florida- His mother Hanna belonging to the Tanner family was residing there.

Account Number- 364
Name- Thomas Fax
Date of Application- May 22, 1867
Father or Mother? Married?- Mary Fax
Name of Children- Sarah Fax
Regiment and Company- 7th Reg. La vol. 60 days Co. C
Place of Birth- Petersburg Va
Residence- 277 St. Louis Robertson & Claiborne
Occupation- Porter
Remarks- No other living relatives.
Signature- yes

Account Number- 365
Name- The Union Benevolent Association of the City of New Orleans
Date of Application- May 23, 1867
Signature- Graham Bell, Treasurer

Account Number- 366
Name- Isaac Washington Brown
Date of Application- May 31, 1867
Height and Complexion- Black 36 years old
Father or Mother? Married?- Mary Brown
Name of Children- none
Regiment and Company- 76 U.S.C.T. Co. K
Place of Birth- Pleasant Valley, Washington Co. Md
Residence- St. Philip between Claiborne & Derbigny
Occupation- Laborer
Remarks- Arrived here in 1853 from Baltimore- his father Steven Brown was then living in Pleasant Valley Md- Dorthea Thomas is authorized to draw his money- about 22 years old Black complexion.

Account Number- 367
Name- Bienville Duplantier
Date of Application- May 31, 1867
Father or Mother? Married?- Louisa Duplantier
Name of Children- none
Place of Birth- West Baton Rouge La
Residence- Tchoupitoulas between St. James & Market
Occupation- Laborer
Remarks- Father's name Alfred Duplantier.
Signature- yes

Account Number- 368
Name- Elijah Berry
Date of Application- June 1, 1867
Height and Complexion- Black 40 yrs. old
Father or Mother? Married?- widower
Name of Children- none
Place of Birth- Fredericksburg Va
Residence- Canal 243 Franklin & Treme
Occupation- Tin Smith
Remarks- Polly Berry his mother is now living in Woodville Miss.- also his sister Ellen Collins in Woodville Miss.
Signature- yes

Account Number- 369
Name- Richard Robertson
Date of Application- June 3, 1867
Height and Complexion- Light & Freckled 45 yrs. old
Father or Mother? Married?- Johanna Robertson
Name of Children- none
Regiment and Company- 86th U.S.C.I. Co. B
Place of Birth- New Orleans La
Residence- 107 Carondelet corner Girod
Occupation- Cook
Remarks- No relatives whatever.
Signature- does not write

Account Number- 370
Name- Friday Porter Jr.
Date of Application- June 3, 1867
Height and Complexion- Black 20 yrs. old
Father or Mother? Married?- none

Place of Birth- west Pearl River La
Residence- Indian Village West Pearl River
Occupation- Laborer
Remarks- Father's name Friday Porter- sisters names Lucinda, Savilla & Adeline Porter all in Indian Village.
Signature- yes

Account Number- 371
Name- Violet
Remarks- Mother's name Ann Wood- sister's names Mary Mitchell & Lucy Baldwin- all three can draw.
Signature- does not write

Account Number- 372
Name- Joseph A. Gulick
Date of Application- June 7, 1867
Height and Complexion- White 18 yrs. old
Place of Birth- Cincinnati Ohio
Residence- 689 Magazine
Occupation- Clerk
Remarks- Father's name John W. Gulick resides Mammoth Illinois
Signature- yes

Account Number- 373
Name- Beneficial Benevolent Society
Date of Application- June 8, 1867 - organized Nov. 13, 1852 & incorporated May 9, 1867- {officers changed July 15, 1872}
Remarks- The first deposit of $510. was made for the society by Dennis Thompson and Henry Davis No. 115 Ursulines St. and 193 Rampart St.- Ceclis {?} Polk, president- C.W. Johnson, secty. All checks to be signed by these two officers & bear the seal of Society.

Account Number- 374
Name- Miller C. Strong
Date of Application- June 8, 1867
Name of Master- transfer from Mobile
Height and Complexion- Brown
Name of Children- Comelia Clinton
Place of Birth- Middleton Conn.
Residence- Franklin, Hunt & Lipscomb Mobile
Occupation- Clergyman
Remarks- Transfer card forwarded by him through letter to Rev. Joseph Dutch of Zion Church and to him paid this day on Identification.

Account Number- 375
Name- George Spruel
Date of Application- June 10, 1867
Height and Complexion- Black 49 yrs. old
Father or Mother? Married?- Eliza Spruel
Name of Children- Charles Spruel
Place of Birth- Washington Co. N. Ca
Residence- St. Anthony between Claiborne & Prosper No. 157
Occupation- Cooper & House Carpenter
Signature- does not write

Account Number- 376
Name- Henry Mitchell
Date of Application- June 14, 1867
Height and Complexion- Black 57 years old
Father or Mother? Married?- Rosanna Mitchell
Name of Children- Emma, Plummus, Leontine & Mary Mitchell
Place of Birth- Raleigh N. Ca
Residence- Freret Perdido & Gravier 103
Occupation- Laborer
Signature- does not write

Account Number- 377
Name- John Purcell Jr.
Date of Application- June 20, 1867
Height and Complexion- Very light
Regiment and Company- 123rd New Hampshire Co B
Place of Birth- New Orleans La
Residence- Rampart St. St. Louis & Toulouse 144
Occupation- Steam boating
Signature- yes

Account Number- 378
Name- Denis Green
Date of Application- June 20, 1867
Height and Complexion- Black 37 yrs. old

Regiment and Company- 86th U.S.C.I. Co. F
Place of Birth- St. Marys Co. Md
Residence- Marine Hospital
Occupation- Night Watchman Marine Hospital
Remarks- Came here during Mexican WAR from Maryland.
Signature- does not sign

Account Number- 379
Name- Henderson Carter
Date of Application- June 25, 1867
Height and Complexion- Black 53 yrs. old
Father or Mother? Married?- Mary Jane Carter
Place of Birth- Washington D.C.
Residence- Gravier Bolivar & St. Jane
Occupation- Blacksmith
Remarks- Has been in this city 39 years.
Signature- does not write

Account Number- 380
Name- Robert Brown
Date of Application- June 28, 1867
Name of Master- (later entry) Wife can draw- Ann Brown born Va raised Gloucester Co. Va- age 45 Griff- father Norbin Butchern mother Mary.
Father or Mother? Married?- Ann Brown
Name of Children- William, Mary Ann & Emma Brown
Place of Birth- Davidson Co. Tenn.
Residence- 284 1/2 Perdido St.
Occupation- Cotton Sampler
Remarks- Mrs. Ann Brown, his wife has full authority to draw the whole or any part of all the monies deposited by Mr. Robert Brown. Nov. 22, 1873 son W.A.B. can draw any amount. signed W.A. Brown
Signature- does not write- witnessed Adolph Bencar

Account Number- 381
Name- John F. Winston
Date of Application- June 28, 1867
Father or Mother? Married?- Caroline Winston
Regiment and Company- 7th U.S.C.T. La Co.
Place of Birth- Green Co. Ky
Residence- 295 Poydras St.
Occupation- Restaurant in Custom House
Remarks- Is a licensed minister of Free Mission Baptist Church
Signature- yes

Account Number- 382
Name- Daniel Jones
Date of Application- July 1, 1867
Height and Complexion- Black 37 yrs. old
Father or Mother? Married?- not
Place of Birth- Logan Co. Ky near Middletown
Residence- Hercules near Calliope at Mr. Cray Caldwell
Occupation- Porter at J. W. Shearer & D.A. Givens
Remarks- Mother's name Mathilda Rutherford in Logan Co. Ky.
Signature- does not sign

Account Number- 383
Name- Mahala Chapman
Date of Application- July 3, 1867
Height and Complexion- Black 30 yrs. old
Father or Mother? Married?- Chadwick Chapman
Name of Children- Nelly, Alfred, Julia Chapman
Place of Birth- Frogtown, Boone Co. Ky
Residence- Terpsichore, Bacchus & Dryades
Occupation- Washer & Ironer
Remarks- Left Boone Co. 25 yrs. ago.
Signature- does not write

Account Number- 384
Name- Floyd Wyche
Date of Application- July 3, 1867
Place of Birth- Meridian, Madison Co. Ala
Residence- 41 Union St.
Occupation- Office Attender
Remarks- Martha Campbell his sister resides in Bossier Parish near Collensburgh La.
Signature- yes

Account Number- 385
Name- Emile Donato
Date of Application- July 3, 1867
Height and Complexion- Light Brown
Father or Mother? Married?- Helen Roberts Donato
Name of Children- Joseph Donato
Place of Birth- Opelousas St. Landry, La
Residence- Aux Cayes Haiti
Occupation- Brick Layer & Slater
Remarks- $140- depositor and for which a draft on Branch NY was given- No. 4 July 3, 1867- Amt. deposited by Hermogene Rafael

Account Number- 386
Name- Edom Burnett
Date of Application- July 5, 1867
Father or Mother? Married?- Charlotte Burnett
Place of Birth- Rutherford Co. Tenn.
Residence- 408 Franklin Melpomene & Terpsichore
Occupation- Laborer, dealer in wood & coal
Remarks- Mrs. Burnett has a child by the name of Marsha Becson.
Signature- yes

Account Number- 387
Name- William Harris Pres. of Christian Band Benevolent Society
Date of Application- July 6, 1867
Name of Master- Born in Washington D.C.- came to Louisiana in 1829- Fathers name Richard Harris was then living in Washington. Mother's name Daphne- he left in Washington.
Father or Mother? Married?- Maria Harris
Place of Birth- Society meets at St. Paul's Church of Reverend W. Ant'y Ross.
Occupation- Bricklayer
Remarks- No Drafts can be made except by Mr. Harris' orders. Deposit made by Mr. Chas. McRae treasr. Brothers name Richard & Peter Harris- when he left Washington.
Signature- yes

Account Number- 388
Name- Patrick Winston
Date of Application- July 8, 1867
Name of Master- Father's name Tom died a long time ago in Columbus- Clara died in Columbus- brother Elias Winston lives in Columbus Miss.
Height and Complexion- Black 45 yrs.
Father or Mother? Married?- Mary Winston
Regiment and Company- Co E 78th U.S.C.T.
Place of Birth- Columbus Miss
Residence- Poydras St. 311
Occupation- Laborer at Pooley & Harkell lumber yard
Remarks- Resides in this city since his muster out of service two years ago- July 2, 1869 resides now on Willow St. between Cypress & Lafayette.
Signature- does not write

Account Number- 389
Name- Andrew Jackson
Date of Application- July 12, 1867
Father or Mother? Married?- Frances Jackson
Name of Children- Andrew & Elmira Jackson
Place of Birth- Greenville Co. Va
Residence- Bank St. Miro & Tonti
Occupation- Cotton Sampler
Signature- yes

Account Number- 390
Name- John H. Stewart
Date of Application- July 13, 1867
Name of Master- (later entry) Left Augusta when quite small & came to Montgomery Ala- been here since surrender
Height and Complexion- (later entry) 39 Black
Father or Mother? Married?- not (later entry) Emanuel & Nancy parents
Name of Children- none
Place of Birth- Augusta Ga
Residence- Lake end Pontchartrain (later entry) 153 St. Louis St.
Occupation- Pastry Cook on Steamer Laura

Remarks- Left Augusta in 1837- knows that he has a sister whom he thinks goes by the name of Sallie Monroe at or near Charleston S. Ca. (later entry) Wife Nelly left him- brother Page in Selma Ala. Father died in Athens Ga some 10 yrs ago- mother died in Mobile in 1860.
Signature- yes

Account Number- 391
Name- Giles Bush
Date of Application- July 15, 1867
Name of Master- (later entry) Left Natchez till 1863
Height and Complexion- Black 27 years
Father or Mother? Married?- Mary Bush (later entry) Sandy & Jenny parents
Regiment and Company- Co. B 86th U.S.C.I.
Place of Birth- Natchez Miss.
Residence- 432 Lafayette St.
Occupation- Hostler
Remarks- His brothers Dick, William & George Bush & sister Rose Bush are residents of Natchez Miss. (later entry) children Sam & others dead- sister Mary, Rose & Alice all dead- brothers all in Cairo- Father died in Army at Vicksburg, mother lived in Cairo Ill- with his brother Noah- sister Dinah in N.O.
Signature- yes

Account Number- 392
Name- Anna Pierre
Date of Application- July 15, 1867
Height and Complexion-Light
Father or Mother? Married?- Mr. Pierre
Place of Birth- Virginia- knows not where
Residence- corner Ursulines & Tonti
Occupation- Washer & Ironer
Remarks- Deposited by Mr. A.L. Young. Mrs. Pierre is legitimately married, but has not lived with her husband for the last 9 years though not divorced- she has no relatives whatever- she wants that in case of death what money she may have in the bank be paid to Mr. Young- Mr. Young is empowered to draw money out.

Account Number- 393
Name- William Sylvester
Date of Application- July 16, 1867
Height and Complexion- Black 19 years old
Regiment and Company- 39th U.S.C.T. Co. C
Place of Birth- Washington Co. N.Ca
Residence- Camp at Greenville La
Occupation- Soldier
Remarks- His father's name is Jessie Whitley & his sisters Mahala, Margaret & Fanny are living in Washington Co. N.Ca

Account Number- 394
Name- Walton Green
Date of Application- July 22, 1867
Height and Complexion- Black
Father or Mother? Married?- Elizabeth Green
Name of Children- Mary Jane Green
Regiment and Company- Co. H 86th U.S.C.T.
Place of Birth- Richmond Va.
Residence- Pass Christian Harrison Co. Miss.
Occupation- Farmer
Remarks- His wife and daughter reside with him at Pass Christian Miss.

Account Number- 395
Name- Harriet Maybray
Date of Application- July 26, 1867
Name of Master- Fathers name Major Wilkinson- died in Tennessee a long time ago- brothers names Peter, Samuel & Major were all living when I came here.
Father or Mother? Married?- Green Maybray
Place of Birth- Knox Co. 12 miles from Knoxville Tenn.
Residence- Calliope St. No.212
Occupation- Washer & Ironer
Remarks- When she came here her mother Kesar Wilkinson was in Kansas that was 18 years ago- Aug. 7, 1869 lives now on Fourth St. between Dryades & St. Denis

Account Number- 396
Name- William Aber
Date of Application- July 29, 1867

Height and Complexion- Light
Father or Mother? Married?- Sophie Aber
Name of Children- William Aber 5 mos. old
Regiment and Company- 82nd Co. B U.S.C.I.
Place of Birth- Baton Rouge La
Residence- corner Market & Paccanier St.
Occupation- School teacher
Remarks- The sum of five dollars per month may be paid to Mrs. Sophie Aber on presentation of book.
Signature- yes

Account Number- 397
Name- Jonas Turner
Date of Application- July 29, 1867
Regiment and Company- 82nd Co. B U.S.C.T.
Place of Birth- Jefferson Co. Ala
Residence- Baton Rouge Broadstreet La
Occupation- Farmer
Remarks- Phil, Thomas, Melinda -14-12-10 years old were ran off by the rebels from Bayou Sara & he does not know as yet where they are- their mother's name is Barbara Julian.

Account Number- 398
Name- James J. McMyler
Date of Application- July 30,1867
Height and Complexion- White
Place of Birth- Great Britain
Residence- Carondelet 86
Occupation- Store Keeper
Remarks- No person to draw any part of the moneys deposited but Mr. J.J. McMyler himself.
Signature- yes

Account Number- 399
Name- Harriet Humphrey
Date of Application- July 30, 1867
Father or Mother? Married?- widow
Name of Children- Mary Louise Bruno
Place of Birth- New Orleans La
Residence- LaHarpe between Prieur & Roman
Occupation- Washer & Ironer

Remarks- The deposit was made for her by W.E.P. Royal.

Account Number- 400
Name- Jordan Madoss
Date of Application- July 31, 1867
Height and Complexion- Black
Father or Mother? Married?- Lucy Madoss
Regiment and Company- Co. D 82nd U.S.C.T.
Place of Birth- Lewisville, Miss.
Residence- Liberty between Common & Gravier No. 70
Occupation- Laborer
Remarks- Darly Turner his mother resides In Lewisville Miss.
Signature- does not write

Account Number- 401
Name- Tony Hall
Date of Application- July 31, 1867
Name of Children- Sarah, Jennie, & Narcissa Hall
Regiment and Company- 78th U.S.C.T. Co. D 1st Sergt.
Place of Birth- Fairfield Dist. S. Ca
Residence- Presently at Marine Hospital
Occupation- Cook
Remarks- His three daughters 9 months ago were residing in Columbia S. Ca their mother's name is Caroline Francis.
Signature- yes

Account Number- 402
Name- Hubbard Moore
Date of Application- July 31, 1867
Height and Complexion- Black
Name of Children- Mathilda Moore
Regiment and Company- Co. D 84th U.S.C.T.
Place of Birth- Lynchburg Va
Residence- Philip St.
Occupation- Sailor on Lake Schooner Palmedo
Remarks- His daughter Mathilda Moore is residing in Baton Rouge with her grandmother Sarah- her mothers name is Angeline Taylor.
Signature- does not sign

Account Number- 403
Name- Charles Williams
Date of Application- Aug. 1, 1867
Father or Mother? Married?- Mary Williams
Name of Children- James Williams 18 yrs. old
Regiment and Company- 78th U.S.C.T. Co. B
Place of Birth- Saulsbury Dist. S. Ca
Residence- Philip St. near Bacchus
Occupation- Plasterer
Remarks- About 38 years ago when he came to this city, his mother Maria Diggs was sent to Texas- doesn't know if she is living or dead.

Account Number- 404
Name- Ida Beaumont
Date of Application- Aug. 1, 1867
Father or Mother? Married?- widow
Name of Children- Peter & Maria Louisa Beaumont
Place of Birth- New Orleans, La
Residence- St. Joseph St. No. 208
Occupation- Washer & Ironer
Remarks- The husband Peter Beaumont died two years ago- was orderly Surgl. Co I 84th U.S.C.I.- her son Peter is 18 & Maria Louisa 14 yrs. old.
Signature- does not write

Account Number- 405
Name- Cyrus McWarren alias McMurren
Date of Application- Aug. 1, 1867
Name of Master- Father's name John McMurren is living in N. Ca
Height and Complexion- Black
Father or Mother? Married?- _____ Cheney
Regiment and Company- 78th Co. B U.S.C.T.
Place of Birth- Elizabeth City N. Ca
Residence- Basin, Julia & Girod
Occupation- House Servant
Remarks- Has a sister in Vicksburg by the name of Ellen Brady- wife died Mar. 12, 1869.
Signature- yes

Account Number- 406
Name- Aaron Jackson
Date of Application- Aug. 1, 1867
Father or Mother? Married?- not
Name of Children- Sarah Jackson 16 yrs. old
Regiment and Company- Cdry(?) Sergt. Co A 78th U.S.C.T.
Place of Birth- Prince William Co. Va
Residence- Delord St. corner Magnolia
Occupation- Stevedore
Remarks- Sarah Jackson's mother's name is Ida- she formerly belonged to Mr. Charles Derbigny.

Account Number- 407
Name- Oliver Russell
Date of Application- Aug. 3, 1867
Father or Mother? Married?- Louisa Russell
Regiment and Company- 7th regt. Co. A La vols. 60 days
Place of Birth- Norfolk Va
Residence- Julia Magazine & Tchoupitoulas
Occupation- Painter
Remarks- no relatives at all

Account Number- 408
Name- Anatole L. Boree
Date of Application- Aug. 5, 1867
Father or Mother? Married?- Josephine Boree
Name of Children- Marie Louise, Auguste Louis & Aurore Adelaide Boree
Place of Birth- New Orleans La
Residence- Derbigny St. No. 34
Occupation- Commission Merchant
Signature- yes

Account Number- 409
Name- Silas Ryan
Date of Application- Aug. 5, 1867
Height and Complexion- Black
Name of Children- Frank & Melinda Ryan
Regiment and Company- Co. G Corpl. 87th U.S.C.T.
Place of Birth- Brutee Co. N. Ca
Residence- St. Mary St. Carrollton
Occupation- Laborer
Remarks- Silas Ryan left his two children in 1863 at Plaquemines La- does not

know if they are there yet- mother's name of Frank was Ann- and Melinda's mother was named Julia- both mothers dead.
Signature- does not write

Account Number- 410
Name- William Smith
Date of Application- Aug. 6, 1867
Height and Complexion- Black 5ft. 9 in.
Name of Children- Henrietta & Laura Smith
Regiment and Company- Private Co. C 78th U.S.C.T.
Place of Birth- Petersburg Va
Residence- corner Felicity & Circus
Occupation- Laborer
Remarks- The mother of Henrietta & Laura is Sarah.
Signature- does not write

Account Number- 411
Name- Henry Horton
Date of Application- Aug. 6, 1867
Height and Complexion- Black
Father or Mother? Married?- Lucy Horton
Name of Children- Leonore Horton
Regiment and Company- Sergt. Co. D 78th U.S.C.T.
Residence- Jefferson St. Corner Homer
Occupation- Mechanic- in Algiers House Carpenter
Remarks- Lucy's mother's name is Sarah- Both of them were left at Newtown Co. Ga thirteen years ago.
Signature- does not write

Account Number- 412
Name- Nat Porter
Date of Application- Aug. 7, 1867
Height and Complexion- Black 31 yrs. old
Father or Mother? Married?- not
Name of Children- none
Regiment and Company- Private Co. G 86th U.S.C.T.
Place of Birth- Attakapas Franklin Co. La
Residence- Claiborne, Dumaine & St. Ann

Occupation- Laborer
Remarks- His sister Cecile Porter living with him is the only relative he has.
Signature- does not write

Account Number- 413
Name- George Smith
Date of Application- Aug. 7, 1867
Height and Complexion- Black 37 years old
Father or Mother? Married?- Harriet Smith
Name of Children- none
Regiment and Company- Private Co. D 84th U.S.C.T.
Place of Birth- Fauquier Co. Mary Hill Plantation Va
Residence- Carrollton Corner Eagle & Tampa
Occupation- Laborer
Remarks- 17 yrs. ago when he left Fauquier his mother Nellie, father Paul Smith, his sisters, Mary, Esther & Elizabeth Smith were living at Mary Hill Plantation owned by Gus Jennings.
Signature- yes

Account Number- 414
Name- Jules Nalciers
Date of Application- Aug. 8, 1867
Regiment and Company- Musician F. Co. 84th U.S.C.T.
Place of Birth- New Orleans La
Residence- Prosper St. near St. Bernard St.
Occupation- Laborer
Remarks- 3 years ago he left his place 10 miles from Morganza near Texas Landing- his sister Marie & his brother Auguste Nalciers were living there.

Account Number- 415
Name- William Hyland
Date of Application- Aug. 10, 1867
Height and Complexion- White
Father or Mother? Married?- not
Regiment and Company- 17th U.S.I. unassigned to Co.
Place of Birth- Co. Wicklow Ireland
Residence- Sedgwick Hospital
Occupation- Soldier

Remarks- Left Ireland in 1858 at that time his mother Mrs. Julia Hyland, and Ann Hyland his sister were living in Co. Tyrone Ireland.
Signature- yes

Account Number- 416
Name- Daniel Shaw
Date of Application- Aug. 12, 1867
Height and Complexion- Black 35 yrs. old
Father or Mother? Married?- Christiana Shaw
Name of Children- Mary Ann Shaw
Regiment and Company- Priv. Co. K 84th U.S.C.T.
Place of Birth- Pike Co. 9 miles from the line of Pike & Lincoln Co. Missouri
Residence- 143 Religious St.
Occupation- Sawyer
Remarks- Mary Ann Shaw his daughter is living in Clarksville Miss.- her mother's name was Harriet Shaw.
Signature- does not write

Account Number- 417
Name- Edward Blan
Date of Application- Aug. 12, 1867
Height and Complexion- Black 21 years
Regiment and Company- Corporal Co. I 84th U.S.C.T.
Place of Birth- Tanner's Plantation Terrebonne La
Residence- Dryades, Washington & Sixth
Occupation- Carpenter
Remarks- Maria Blan his mother is dead Schack Blan his father and his sisters Emily, Susan & Elizabeth are living at Tanner's Plantation Terrebonne La.
Signature- yes

Account Number- 418
Name- John Bender
Date of Application- Aug. 12, 1867
Height and Complexion- Light Black 32 yrs.
Father or Mother? Married?- Harriet Bender
Regiment and Company- Co. B. 84th U.S.C.T.
Place of Birth- Washington D.C.
Residence- Circus St. No. 100
Occupation- Baker
Remarks- His father Chs. Bender 9 years ago was in Washington D.C. his sister Oathanna Bender was also there.
Signature- does not write

Account Number- 419
Name- William Berkins
Date of Application- Aug. 14, 1867
Height and Complexion- Black 21 yrs. old
Father or Mother? Married?- Christiana Berkins
Regiment and Company- Priv. Co. B. 84th U.S.C.I.
Place of Birth- Bayou Plaquemines Iberville La
Residence- Rousseau near corner Jackson
Occupation- Laborer
Remarks- His mother Lid Green and his sister Betty Smith are living at Bayou Plaquemines Iberville Parish La.
Signature- yes

Account Number- 420
Name- Henderson L. Smoot
Date of Application- Aug. 14, 1867
Regiment and Company- 87th U.S.C.T. Co C
Place of Birth- Avoyelles La
Residence- corner Dryades & Philippe
Occupation- House Servant
Remarks- Father's name Eliah Smoot, mother's name Nancy Smoot both of them living at Bayou Glaize Avoyelles Parish.
Signature- yes

Account Number- 421
Name- William Perniell
Date of Application- Aug. 15, 1867
Height and Complexion- Black
Father or Mother? Married?- Dicia Perniell
Regiment and Company- Co. F 84th U.S.C.I.
Place of Birth- Bayou Sara West Feliciana La

Residence- corner Great men & Union
Occupation- Laborer
Remarks- Charles Perniell - Jane Perniell his father & mother are living in West Baton Rouge.
Signature- does not write

Account Number- 422
Name- Henry Bell
Date of Application- Aug. 16, 1867
Height and Complexion- about 22 yrs. old
Regiment and Company- Iron Clad Mount City Land man U.S.N.
Place of Birth- Columbus Miss.
Residence- 206 St. Charles St.
Occupation- Servant
Remarks- Jane Bell his mother resides No. 14 Treme St. in this city.
Signature- does not write

Account Number- 423
Name- Stephen Council
Date of Application- Aug. 17, 1867
Height and Complexion- Black 39 yrs. old
Father or Mother? Married?- Julia Ann Council
Name of Children- Adam Council 4 years old (later entry) Mary Council
Place of Birth- Attleys 30 miles from Richmond Va
Residence- St. Andrew Locust & Magnolia
Occupation- Laborer
Remarks- About nine years ago when he left Attley Va his mother Lucy Council was there also his sisters Amanda, Kitty & a brother by the name of Edmond.
Signature- does not write

Account Number- 424
Name- Peter Ambry
Date of Application- Aug. 17, 1867
Height and Complexion- Black 21 yrs. old
Regiment and Company- Co. H 84th U.S.C.T.
Place of Birth- Iberville Parish La
Residence- St. Philip between Treme & Marais

Occupation- Laborer
Remarks- Mathilda White his mother resides in Opelousas at Mr. Eugene Daville's Plantation
Signature- does not write

Account Number- 425
Name- Rev. Henry Green
Date of Application- Aug. 19, 1867
Height and Complexion- about 65 yrs. old Black
Father or Mother? Married?- Elizabeth Louisa Green
Place of Birth- Montgomery Co. near Rockville District of Columbia
Residence- 3rd St. between Dryades & St. Denis
Occupation- Minister
Remarks- Has an adopted child by the name of Hannah 9 years & 6 mos. old. Has several brothers but has no idea of their whereabouts.
Signature- yes

Account Number- 426
Name- Rev. R.K. Diossy
Date of Application- Aug. 21, 1867
Place of Birth- New York
Residence- Franklin St. Mary Parish
Occupation- Minister
Remarks- This deposit ($328.30) was made by Mr. A.C.McDonald for his a/c.

Account Number- 427
Name- Parish Green
Date of Application- Aug. 21, 1867
Height and Complexion- Black 22 years old
Regiment and Company- G 82nd. Reg. U.S.C.T.
Place of Birth- North Bend Bayou Boeuf La
Residence- Freret, Cypress & Julia
Occupation- Laborer
Remarks- His sister Mrs. Ann Washington lives on Philippa St. between Lafayette & Girod- fifteen years he left his mother Mellie Green at Bayou Boeuf La on Mr. John Pierce's plantation but she belonged to Mr. Bill Proctor. (later entry) Father was in Bayou Rouge when

parish (?) left him- he is now Bayou DeGlaze- mother in Jefferson Texas. Has not seen mother since 7 yrs. before the war- sister Elizabeth dead & Dinah up Red River at Stafford plantation- brother David in Texas with mother & Anderson, Wesley & Lewis all in Texas.

Account Number- 428
Name- Jacques Joseph Daniels
Date of Application- Aug. 21, 1867
Height and Complexion- 42 years
Father or Mother? Married?- Lucile Daniels
Name of Children- Antoinette, Emile & Victoria Daniels
Regiment and Company- 73rd Regt. Co. C U.S.C.I.
Place of Birth- New Orleans La
Residence- St. Ann, Villere & Robertson
Occupation- Bricklayer
Remarks- Has a sister by the name of Rosalie Alexis, residing with him.
Signature- yes

Account Number- 429
Name- Joseph Tatum
Date of Application- Aug. 21, 1867
Residence- Plantation near Vidalia- Arnoldlia plantation
Occupation- Laborer
Remarks- Jos Tatum is a cripple- one leg turning inside- He leaves near Vidalia La Concordia Parish- is working now for Major Kaulle(?) close to Vidilia- this money id deposited for his a/c by Mr. Dunford Bureau agent for that Parish.

Account Number- 430
Name- Edward Thompson
Date of Application- Aug. 23, 1867
Height and Complexion- Yellow 25 years
Father or Mother? Married?- Ann Thompson
Regiment and Company- Co. A 82nd U.S.C.T.
Place of Birth- Hinds Co. Miss
Residence- corner Customhouse & Derbigny No. 336
Occupation- Drayman
Remarks- His wife Ann Thompson has a son by a former marriage by the name of John Wesley Cooke.

Account Number- 431
Name- Samuel Smith
Date of Application- Aug. 24, 1867
Height and Complexion- Light Brown 35 years old
Place of Birth- Eastern Shore Maryland
Residence- Circus St. 240 Julia & Girod
Occupation- Steam boating 2nd Pantry man on Lake Steamer Laura
Remarks- Has no other relatives living- thinks he has a sister living whom he was separated from 15 years ago- at Mobile Ala. both of them belonged to Capt. John James Crawford- her name is Sarah.

Account Number- 432
Name- Mary Ann Campbell
Date of Application- Aug. 24, 1867
Height and Complexion- Light
Father or Mother? Married?- Jacob Campbell
Name of Children- none
Place of Birth- Baltimore Md
Residence- Rampart, Customhouse & Bienville Sept. 25, 1869 she now lives at No. 140 Rampart St. Between Toulouse & St. Peter
Occupation- Chambermaid
Remarks- Philip Coca, a Methodist minister in Baltimore is her uncle. Either George Williams or Jacob Cheeks can draw her deposits by presenting her book.
Signature- does not write

Account Number- 433
Name- Robert Marshall Jr.
Date of Application- Aug. 24, 1867
Height and Complexion- White
Regiment and Company- 78th U.S.C.I. Co. A 1st Lt.
Place of Birth- Scotland Glasgow
Residence- New Orleans La
Occupation- Civil Engineer
Remarks- Presently Register of Voters in Parish of Concordia- His father and mother are in New York State.
Signature- yes

Account Number- 434
Name- Beverly White
Date of Application- Aug. 26, 1867
Height and Complexion- Mulatto 32 years old
Father or Mother? Married?- Sophia Leymour White
Name of Children- Samuel White 3 months old
Regiment and Company- Co. I 84th U.S.C.I.
Place of Birth- Harper's Ferry Va
Residence- Philip St. 367 between Bacchus & Dryades
Occupation- Bricklayer
Remarks- Only his grandmother living, Fanny Johnson in Thibodeauxville La.
Signature- does not write

Account Number- 435
Name- Ralph Burrow
Date of Application- Aug. 27, 1867
Height and Complexion- Black
Father or Mother? Married?- single
Regiment and Company- 97th U.S.C.T.
Place of Birth- St. James Parish La
Residence- New Orleans La
Occupation- Laborer
Remarks- Transfer No. 36 from Mobile Ala.

Account Number- 436
Name- Henry Hodge
Date of Application- Aug. 29, 1867
Height and Complexion- Mulatto 43 years old
Father or Mother? Married?- Elisa Hodge
Name of Children- John Henry Hodge 3 weeks old
Regiment and Company- Lands man on board of US Steamer Kensington
Place of Birth- Boston Mass
Residence- Thalia No. 173 Camp & Prytania
Occupation- Laborer
Remarks- Was taken prisoner by the Rebels in 1863 in Sabine Pass and kept a prisoner until June 7, 1865.
Signature- does not write

Account Number- 437
Name- Ella Robertson
Date of Application- Aug. 29, 1867
Height and Complexion- Light Black
Father or Mother? Married?- single
Place of Birth- Richmond Va
Residence- St. Andrew in front of St. Denis St.
Occupation- Housework
Remarks- Mahala Robertson her mother was sold from Va by Thomas J. Glenn of Richmond Va about 12 years ago. Apr. 3, 1873 says she was married about 9 mos. ago to Thomas Hutchinson.
Signature- does not write

Account Number- 438
Name- Jacob Johnson
Date of Application- Aug. 31, 1867
Height and Complexion- Black 32 years old
Father or Mother? Married?- Constance Johnson
Name of Children- Jacob & Josephine
Place of Birth- Rockingham Co. Harrisonburg Va
Residence- Roman, Common & Palmyra
Occupation- Laborer
Remarks- No other relatives living.
Signature- does not write

Account Number- 439
Name- Auguste Baptiste
Date of Application- Sept. 2, 1867
Father or Mother? Married?- Prescilla Davis
Regiment and Company- La 60 day vols. Co. F
Place of Birth- New Orleans La
Residence- Hospital Bourbon & Dauphin No. 100
Occupation- Laborer
Remarks- Mother's name Victorine Baptiste residing on Main St. between Johnson & Galvez
Signature- does not write

Account Number- 440
Name- Jessy Henry
Date of Application- Sept. 2, 1867
Height and Complexion- Black 42 years

old
Father or Mother? Married?- Sally Henry
Regiment and Company- 96th Co. K
U.S.C.T.
Place of Birth- Washington City
Residence- Broadway St. Greenville La
Occupation- Gardener
Remarks- Sally his wife has six children
from a previous husband.
Signature- does not write

Account Number- 441
Name- James Wilson
Date of Application- Sept. 3, 1867
Height and Complexion- Black 22 years
old
Regiment and Company- Co. I 84th
U.S.C.I.
Place of Birth- New Orleans La
Residence- Peace St. No. 7 Caracaloo &
Moreau
Occupation- Laborer
Remarks- Mother's name Margaret
Wilson- brothers names William &
Joseph Wilson all living together on
Peace St., Mrs. Harriet Wilson, Joe's
wife also lives with them.
Signature- yes

Account Number- 442
Name- Hamilton Weeks
Date of Application- Sept. 4, 1867
Height and Complexion- Black 26 years
old
Father or Mother? Married?- Annie Eliza
Weeks
Name of Children- Rebecca Weeks 2
years old
Regiment and Company- Co. E 78th
U.S.C.T.
Place of Birth- Newtown, St. Mary Parish
La
Residence- Religious between Race &
Robin
Occupation- Cooper
Remarks- Henry Weeks alias
Blacksmith his father- Katy Weeks his
mother- Both residing in Newtown, St.
Mary Parish La.
Signature- does not write

Account Number- 443
Name- Alfred Johnson
Date of Application- Sept. 4, 1867
Height and Complexion- 33 years old
Black
Father or Mother? Married?- Rachel Ann
Johnson
Name of Children- Silas Johnson 12
years old
Regiment and Company- Co. F 84th
U.S.C.T.
Place of Birth- Cheneyville La
Residence- Boutte Station La
Occupation- Laborer
Remarks- His boy Silas Johnson is from
a former wife Jeanette- He does not
know whether she is alive or dead- His
boy when he last heard of was in
Lafourche, on Mr. Johnson's Plantation.
Signature- does not write

Account Number- 444
Name- Mark Harris
Date of Application- Sept. 4, 1867
Height and Complexion- Black 38 years
old
Father or Mother? Married?- Eliza Harris
Regiment and Company- Co. G 84th
U.S.C.T.
Place of Birth- North Ca near Saulsbury
Residence- Boutte Station St. Charles
La
Occupation- Laborer
Remarks- Washington, Allison, & Julia,
Lizzie Harris his brothers and sisters are
living in Rapides Parish close to
Cheneyville.

Account Number- 446
Name- John McNease
Date of Application- Sept. 7, 1867
Regiment and Company- Co. I 117th
Reg.U.S.C.T.
Remarks- Transfer from Louisville Ky
with no other remarks.

Account Number- 445
Name- Barry Scott
Date of Application- Sept. 7, 1867
Regiment and Company- Co. I 117th
Reg.U.S.C.T.

Remarks- Transfer from Louisville Ky with no other remarks on descriptive list.

Account Number- 447
Name- David Ray
Date of Application- Sept. 7, 1867.
Regiment and Company- Co. I 117th Reg.U.S.C.T.
Remarks- Transfer from Louisville Ky with no other remarks.

Account Number- 448
Name- William Moman
Date of Application- Sept. 7, 1867
Height and Complexion- Light Black 22 years old
Regiment and Company- Co. I 117th Reg.U.S.C.T.
Place of Birth- Campbell C. Va
Residence- Greenville La
Occupation- Laborer
Remarks- Transfer from Louisville Ky without any other remarks. Subsequent descriptions given by Moman.
Signature- does not write

Account Number- 449
Name- William Givins
Date of Application- Sept. 7, 1867.
Regiment and Company- Co. A 117th Reg.U.S.C.T.
Remarks- Transfer from Louisville Ky with no other remarks.

Account Number- 450
Name- William Chace
Date of Application- Sept. 7, 1867.
Regiment and Company- Co. D 117th Reg.U.S.C.T.
Remarks- Transfer from Louisville Ky with no other remarks.

Account Number- 451
Name- Thomas Hill
Date of Application- Sept. 9, 1867
Height and Complexion- Black 60 years old
Father or Mother? Married?- Mary Hill
Name of Children- Joseph Hill 14 years old
Regiment and Company- Co. I 96th U.S.C.T.
Place of Birth- Grass Creek Plantation King & Queen Co. Va
Residence- Liberty between 2nd & 3rd
Occupation- Tanner & Leather finisher
Remarks- No other relatives here. Mrs. Mary Hill is authorized to draw any amount to Mr. T. Hill's cr. on presentation of book.
Signature- Mary Hill Mr. Hill does not write.

Account Number- 452
Name- John McNease
Date of Application- Sept. 9, 1867
Height and Complexion- Black 21 years old
Regiment and Company- Co. I 117th U.S.C.T.
Place of Birth- Santa Anna Harrison Co. Ky
Residence- Basin St.
Occupation- Wood Chopper
Remarks- Sarah McNease his mother lives in Harrison Co. Ky.

Account Number- 453
Name- Edward Brown
Date of Application- Sept. 10, 1867
Height and Complexion- Black 28 years old
Regiment and Company- Co. F 84h U.S.C.T.
Place of Birth- Bayou Lafourche La
Residence- Liberty St. Between Lafayette & Girod No. 205
Occupation- Laborer
Remarks- Gus Brown & Delphind Brown his brother & sister are in Bayou Lafourche La.
Signature- does not write

Account Number- 454
Name- Fraternity No. 20 Masonic Lodge
Date of Application- Sept. 18, 1867
Residence- of lodge St. Louis St. next to Exchange Alley
Remarks- See signature book for signatures of officers.

Account Number- 455

Name- Charles Ann
Date of Application- Sept. 19, 1867
Height and Complexion- Black 28 yrs. old
Father or Mother? Married?- Lucinda Ann
Name of Children- Maria & Willie Ann
Regiment and Company- Co. G 84th U.S.C.T.
Place of Birth- Baton Rouge La
Residence- Jefferson St. Austin St. near Tchoupitoulas
Occupation- Dining room Servant
Remarks- Maria 2 years old- Willie 9 months old.
Signature- yes

Account Number- 456
Name- L.J.P. Capla
Date of Application- Sept. 21, 1867
Father or Mother? Married?- Felicie Fleury Capla
Name of Children- Alfred & Lucien Capla
Place of Birth- New Orleans La
Residence- corner St. Claude & Barracks 317
Occupation- Merchant (shoe store)
Signature- yes

Account Number- 457
Name- John Birge
Date of Application- Sept. 26, 1867
Height and Complexion- Black
Father or Mother? Married?- Mary Beard
Name of Children- Andre Henderson his stepson
Regiment and Company- Co. I 1st Regt. U.S.C.T. (73rd)
Place of Birth- Baltimore Md
Residence- Gravier between Circus & St. John
Occupation- Shoeblack
Remarks- Has a stiff hand (left one) from a wound received at Port Hudson. In case of death, he wants his wife Mary Beard to get what money he may have in Bank.
Signature- does not write

Account Number- 458
Name- Mathilda Barnes
Date of Application- Sept. 28, 1867
Father or Mother? Married?- Edward Barnes
Name of Children- Edward Barnes 5 yrs. old
Place of Birth- Louisville Ky
Residence- 52 Euterpe St.
Occupation- Washer & Ironer
Remarks- No relatives living. Her husband, Edward Barnes, has authority from her to draw her money on presentation of book.
Signature- does not write

Account Number- 459
Name- James Ebar
Date of Application- Sept. 30, 1867
Height and Complexion- Black 5 feet 7 in. 24 yrs.
Father or Mother? Married?- widower
Regiment and Company- Co. F 4th U.S.C. Cavalry
Place of Birth- New Orleans La
Residence- Algiers, Orleans Parish La
Occupation- Laborer
Remarks- Sella formerly belonging to Larty Hebert his mother in Lafayette Attakapas La- his sisters name Louise & Modeste are both with their mother.
Signature- does not write

Account Number- 460
Name- William J. Lockwood
Date of Application- Oct. 3, 1867
Father or Mother? Married?- Mary Ann Lockwood
Place of Birth- Charleston S. Ca
Residence- 145 1/2 Perdido St.
Occupation- Foreman at Gasworks
Remarks- His wife Mary Ann has a daughter by the name of Victorine married to George Abbott- He has been working in the Gasworks for the last 32 years.
Signature- does not write

Account Number- 461
Name- Maria Grundy
Date of Application- Oct. 4, 1867
Height and Complexion- about 50 yrs. old

Father or Mother? Married?- widow
Name of Children- Edward Barnes & Laura Grundy
Place of Birth- Nashville Tenn
Residence- 52 Euterpe St.
Occupation- None formerly Nurse
Remarks- The first deposit is made by her son- Edward Barnes or Laura Grundy can draw deposits.

Account Number- 462
Name- Mrs. Caroline Taylor
Date of Application- Oct. 11, 1867
Height and Complexion- Black 65 years old
Father or Mother? Married?- widow of Hy Taylor
Name of Children- Julia, Rosetta & Lavinia Taylor
Place of Birth- Alexandria Va
Residence- Southwood Plantation, Ascension Parish La
Occupation- Washer & Ironer
Remarks- Her daughter Julia is empowered on presentation of book to draw either part or the whole of her deposits.

Account Number- 463
Name- Alfred Berkley
Date of Application- Oct. 14, 1867
Height and Complexion- Black 33 years old
Father or Mother? Married?- Lavinia Berkley
Name of Children- Mary & Abraham Berkley
Regiment and Company- Co. K 68th U.S.C.T.
Place of Birth- near Bardstown, Nelson Co. KY
Residence- Derbigny between Orleans & St. Ann
Occupation- Laborer
Remarks- When he was about 12 or 14 years old, he was sent from Bardstown and has never since heard from his parents.
Signature- does not write

Account Number- 464
Name- Isaac Gooe
Date of Application- Oct. 14, 1867
Height and Complexion- Black about 33 years
Father or Mother? Married?- Dicey Gooe
Name of Children- Anderson Gooe 10 yrs. old
Regiment and Company- Co. K 96th U.S.C.T. 1st Sergt.
Place of Birth- Petersburg Va
Residence- Constance St. corner Melpomene
Occupation- Laborer
Signature- yes

Account Number- 465
Name- Mary Constance Alexander
Date of Application- Oct. 15, 1867
Father or Mother? Married?- not
Name of Children- Joseph Thomas 2 years old
Place of Birth- Morganza La
Residence- 285 Gravier St.
Occupation- Washing & Ironing
Remarks- Mother's name Sarah Alexander- father's name Sandy Alexander both living at Plaquemines (upper)
Signature- does not write

Account Number- 466
Name- Baylor Cook
Date of Application- Oct. 16, 1867
Height and Complexion- Mulatto about 57 years old
Father or Mother? Married?- Nancy Cook
Name of Children- George Cook 6 mths. old
Place of Birth- King & Queen Co. Va
Residence- 256 Dryades St.
Occupation- Bricklayer
Remarks- This deposit of Mr. Baylor Cook is made for the benefit of the following named children, children of his deceased brother, Frank Cook, to wit, Virginia, Richmond, Emelia, & Richard Cook.

Account Number- 467
Name- Wm McCary

Residence- Natchez Miss.
Remarks- The deposit was made by Mr. Theodore Martin his agent duly authorized.
Signature- Theodore Martin

Account Number- 468
Name- Charles Silas Sauvinet Jr.
Date of Application- Oct. 18, 1867
Height and Complexion- White
Father or Mother? Married?- 7 years old
Place of Birth- New Orleans La
Residence- 4 corner Kerlerec & Dauphin
Occupation- going to school
Remarks- Name of father C.S. Sauvinet.

Account Number- 469
Name- John Baptiste
Date of Application- Oct. 21, 1867
Height and Complexion- Black 55 years old
Father or Mother? Married?- single
Name of Children- none
Place of Birth- Pointe Coupee La
Residence- Terpsichore, Prytania & Coliseum
Occupation- Wood Sawyer
Remarks- The first deposit was made for his a/c by Albert Parker his brother in law. In case of death John Baptiste wants the deposits to revert to his brother in law Albert Parker- Albert Parker is also authorized to draw his money on presentation of his book.

Account Number- 470
Name- Anachersis Jasper
Date of Application- Oct. 21, 1867
Height and Complexion- 5 feet 7 in. Black- 33 yrs.
Father or Mother? Married?- Nancy Turner
Name of Children- Fanny 7 years old
Regiment and Company- Co. E 96th U.S.C.T.
Place of Birth- Bayou Sarah La
Residence- Fashion Plantation St. Charles La
Occupation- Laborer
Signature- does not write

Account Number- 471
Name- Tilman Beauregard
Date of Application- Oct. 22, 1867
Height and Complexion- Dark 5 feet 10 in. 21 years old
Father or Mother? Married?- single
Regiment and Company- Co. C 78th Regt.
Place of Birth- New Orleans La
Residence- 138 Craps St. between Bagatelle & St. Anthony
Occupation- Laborer
Remarks- Enlisted on 13th Sept. 1863 in Co. C 78th U.S.C.T. under the name of John Cilicise(?)
Signature- does not write

Account Number- 472
Name- Numa Fornientin
Date of Application- Oct. 23, 1867
Height and Complexion- Light 9 years old
Place of Birth- New Orleans La
Residence- Kerlerec, Dauphin & Burgundy
Occupation- going to school
Remarks- Mother's name Eugenie Dupuy- Father's name Alexander Fornientin. (later entry) account closed by Eugenie Dupuy, Fornientin's mother. Introduced by C.S. Sauvinet.
Signature- yes

Account Number- 473
Name- Marguerite Gale
Date of Application- Oct. 26, 1867
Father or Mother? Married?- widow
Name of Children- none
Place of Birth- Eastern Shore on Comer Creek Maryland
Residence- Bienville between Robertson & Villere
Occupation- Midwife and Nurse
Remarks- Mrs. Marguerite Gale has a god child by the name of Charity Ann Maguerite Gale about 10 years old- She has no relatives living. (later entry) Eugene Joseph Thompson 5 years old- yellow John Gale can draw cousin to Marguerite.
Signature- does not write

Account Number- 474
Name- Charles Whiten
Date of Application- Oct. 28, 1867
Name of Master- He has a brother in Unity by the name of Billy Whiten 21 years old.
Height and Complexion- Dark 5 ft. 10 in. 26
Father or Mother? Married?- parents Charles & Judy
Regiment and Company- Co. A 84th U.S.C.T.
Place of Birth- Norfolk Va
Residence- Melpomene between Franklin & Liberty
Occupation- Laborer
Remarks- When he left Washington city in 1859 to come here his mother Judy Whiten was in Washington City owned by Capt. Henry Tyler.
Signature- yes

Account Number- 475
Name- Charles Hossler
Date of Application- Oct. 28, 1867
Height and Complexion- Black 18 years old
Place of Birth- Lagrange 150 miles above St. Louis Mo.
Residence- Euterpe, Benton & Howard
Occupation- Laborer
Remarks- Mother's name Milly Hossler at Lagrange Mo- left her four years ago.

Account Number- 476
Name- Ernestine Hubeau (later entry) dead
Date of Application- Oct. 29, 1867
Height and Complexion- 2 years old
Place of Birth- McDonoughville Jefferson Parish La
Residence- McDonoughville La
Remarks- Father's Name Ernest Hubeau- mother's name Mary Bacchus. Deposit made by the father E. Hubeau.
Signature- E. A. Hubeau

Account Number- 477
Name- Peter Bullard
Date of Application- Nov. 2, 1867
Father or Mother? Married?- single

Name of Children- none
Place of Birth- Trimble Co. Ky
Residence- No. 101 Franklin St.
Occupation- Laborer & Porter

Account Number- 478
Name- Benjamin Green
Date of Application- Nov. 11, 1867
Height and Complexion- Black 22 yrs. old
Father or Mother? Married?- single
Regiment and Company- 117th Ky U.S.C.T. Co. F
Place of Birth- Washington City
Residence- Dryades St. No. 63
Occupation- Waiter
Remarks- Clarissa Green his mother resides in Washington City between 6 & 4th streets on the island- has a brother by the name of James Green.
Signature- yes

Account Number- 479
Name- Mary Letitia Ford
Date of Application- Nov. 12, 1867
Father or Mother? Married?- Moon Charles John
Name of Children- none
Place of Birth- Baton Rouge City La
Residence- Common & Franklin corner
Occupation- Sick nurse
Remarks- Mary Ricks & Orlena Celestine Ross her nieces- Henry West can draw.
Signature- yes

Account Number- 480
Name- John Hodges
Date of Application- Nov. 13, 1867
Height and Complexion- White
Regiment and Company- 1st U.S.I. White Co. B
Place of Birth- Cairo Ill
Residence- Jackson Barracks
Occupation- Soldier
Remarks- A.C. Hodges his father lives in Alexandria Co. Ill near Cairo- mother dead.
Signature- yes

Account Number- 481
Name- Peter Dull

Date of Application- Nov. 15, 1867
Height and Complexion- White
Father or Mother? Married?- single
Name of Children- none
Regiment and Company- Co. A 1st U.S. Infantry
Place of Birth- Monticello Lafayette Co. Wisconsin
Residence- Commercial Hotel
Occupation- Soldier
Remarks- Mary J. Dull his mother resides in Lafayette Co. Wisconsin.
Signature- yes

Account Number- 482
Name- Nelson Adams
Date of Application- Nov. 18, 1867
Name of Master- Brother's name Alexander, Grant Waterman & George Waterman all in Desoto.
Height and Complexion- 20 years old
Regiment and Company- Co. I 39th U.S.C.I.
Place of Birth- Desoto Parish La
Residence- Camp at Greenville
Occupation- Soldier
Remarks- Sister's name Frances Edward at Desoto- Mary Waterman his mother lives in Desoto Parish La- Father's name Charles Edwards died at Desoto in 1865.
Signature- does not write

Account Number- 483
Name- Michael Walsch
Date of Application- Nov. 18, 1867
Father or Mother? Married?- single
Regiment and Company- Co. B 1st Infantry
Place of Birth- Co. Limerick Ireland
Residence- Commercial Hotel
Occupation- Soldier
Remarks- No relatives at all.
Signature- yes

Account Number- 484
Name- Lucy Johnson
Date of Application- Nov. 19, 1867
Height and Complexion- 72 years old
Father or Mother? Married?- widow of Joseph Johnson
Name of Children- none
Place of Birth- Milady Manor Baltimore Co. Md
Residence- Bienville Villere & Robertson
Occupation- none now- but sells cakes
Remarks- Ben Johnson- 16 yrs. old is not her son, but she adopted him- is now in St. James Parish- Margaret Gayle came in the office with her.
Signature- does not write.

Account Number- 485
Name- Andrew Gregory
Date of Application- Nov. 19, 1867
Father or Mother? Married?- Mary Gregory
Name of Children- none
Regiment and Company- Co. A 39th U.S.C.I.
Place of Birth- Edentown N. Ca
Residence- Greenville Barracks
Occupation- Soldier
Remarks- His mother Maria Gregory resides in Montgomery Ala.
Signature- yes

Account Number- 486
Name- John Shoenocker
Date of Application- Nov. 19, 1867
Regiment and Company- Co. G 39th U.S.C.I.

Account Number- 487
Name- Samuel Nelson
Date of Application- Nov. 20, 1867
Height and Complexion- Black
Regiment and Company- Co. I 39th U.S.C.T.
Place of Birth- 20 miles above Shreveport La Greenwood
Residence- Camp at Greenville
Occupation- Soldier
Remarks- Deposited by Henry Worthen Hospital Stewart 39th U.S.C.I.
Signature- does not write

Account Number- 488
Name- David Barnett
Date of Application- Nov. 23, 1867
Father or Mother? Married?- Lysa Barnett

Name of Children- None
Place of Birth- Greensburg, Greene Co. Ky
Residence- St. Louis, Dorgenois & Broad
Occupation- Wagon Diver
Remarks- His mother Nancy Barnett lives in Greene Co. Ky- Sisters Jenny Barnett & Fanny Barnett are also in Green Co. Ky- Joe Barnett his also there.
Signature- yes

Account Number- 489
Name- John Fortier
Date of Application- Nov. 30, 1867
Height and Complexion- White
Father or Mother? Married?- Louisa Thompson
Name of Children- none
Place of Birth- New Orleans, La
Residence- Enghien St., No. 130
Occupation- Shoe Maker
Signature- yes

Account Number- 490
Name- Joseph E. Hollond
Date of Application- Dec. 2, 1867
Height and Complexion- Black
Father or Mother? Married?- Sarah Ann Hollond
Name of Children- none
Regiment and Company- Co. I 74th U.S.C.T.
Place of Birth- Monticello Co. Va
Residence- 232 Poydras near Clara
Occupation- Cooper
Signature- yes

Account Number- 491
Name- Mary Ann Forest
Date of Application- Dec. 3, 1867
Height and Complexion- Black
Father or Mother? Married?- Joseph Forrest
Name of Children- none
Place of Birth- Winchester Va
Residence- Jackson St. No.105
Occupation- Staying at home
Remarks- Her husband is coach smith by trade. Twenty five years ago she left her mother Priscilla West at Boomillville.
Signature- yes

Account Number- 492
Name- Miami Philips
Date of Application- Dec. 5, 1867
Height and Complexion- Yellow
Name of Children- Robert Brown
Residence- Nashville Tenn
Remarks- This deposit was made by Mr. Robert Brown for transfer to Miami Philips in Nashville Tenn. Transfer No. 492 issued.

Account Number- 493
Name- Katharine Harper
Date of Application- Dec. 9, 1867
Remarks- Transfer from Mobile Ala.

Account Number- 494
Name- Mollie Walker
Date of Application- Dec. 16, 1867
Father or Mother? Married?- single
Place of Birth- Franklin St. Mary La
Residence- 438 Melpomene St.
Occupation- Seamstress
Remarks- This deposit was made for her by Hiram Carter- she will come to give her descriptive list- Name of mother Patsy Walker in Franklin, La.
Signature- does not write

Account Number- 495
Name- Houston Reedy
Date of Application- Dec. 19, 1867
Father or Mother? Married?- Harriet Wilhelmina Reedy
Name of Children- Harriet Louisa, Cassana, A.J. Reedy
Place of Birth- De Ralk Co. Tenn
Residence- Galveston Texas
Occupation- Minister (Missionary)
Remarks- Louisa White his mother resides in McMinville Warren Co. Tenn.
Signature- yes

Account Number- 496
Name- Mrs. C.C. Bodreau
Date of Application- Dec. 23, 1867
Father or Mother? Married?- C.C. Bodreau

Place of Birth- New Orleans La
Residence- St. Ann No. 213
Occupation- Her husband Mr. C.C. Bodreau is Sergt. at Arms Board of Alderman.
Remarks- She has a niece by the name of Foedora Hecand whom she and her husband have adopted. Mr. C.C. Bodreau has power on his own signature and presentation of the book to draw all deposits.
Signature- C.C.Bodreau

Account Number- 497
Name- Rachel Bradley
Date of Application- Dec. 27, 1867
Father or Mother? Married?- Clintin Williams
Name of Children- Charley Williams 19 yrs. old
Place of Birth- Opelousas La
Residence- Carondelet at Mr. Wilson Baronne & Gravier
Occupation- Washer & Ironer
Remarks- Does not live with husband- children Rose Lee & Maudier dead- Father died in Opelousas when she was young- mother in Parish St. Landry about 7 years ago. Brothers Jim in N.O. & William on Bayou Boeuf sister Lizzie widow of Ch. Washington with Rachel & Nancy wife of ___ in N.O.
Signature- do not write

Account Number- 498
Name- William Henry Johnson
Date of Application- Jan. 4, 1868
Height and Complexion- Black 46 years old
Father or Mother? Married?- Sophia Johnson
Name of Children- Winters Johnson 14 yrs. old
Place of Birth- Marengo Caroline Co. Va
Residence- 174 Liberty St.
Occupation- House Painter
Remarks- Sister's name Aimee Johnson believes she is in the state of Alabama.
Signature- does not write

Account Number- 499

Name- Frank Smith
Date of Application- Jan. 7, 1868
Height and Complexion- Black 24 years old
Father or Mother? Married?- Mary Smith
Name of Children- none
Regiment and Company- Co. T 96th Regt.
Place of Birth- Kentucky
Residence- Palmyra St. No. 89
Occupation- Laborer
Signature- yes

Account Number- 500
Name- Richard Lewis
Date of Application- Jan 7, 1868
Height and Complexion- 21 years old Dark Brown
Father or Mother? Married?- not
Regiment and Company- Co. H 68th U.S.C.T.
Place of Birth- Lincoln Co. 15 miles west of Danville Ky
Residence- Carrollton La
Occupation- Laborer
Remarks- Sarah Lewis his sister is in Lincoln Co. Ky- no mother or father.
Signature- yes

Account Number- 501
Name- Manuel Jackson
Date of Application- Jan. 7, 1868
Height and Complexion- Dark Griff about 25 yrs.
Father or Mother? Married?- not
Name of Children- none
Regiment and Company- Co. B 96th U.S.C.T.
Place of Birth- St. John Parish La on Valtin Marmillion Plantation
Residence- Carrollton
Occupation- Laborer
Remarks- His father Lewis Jackson lives in the vicinity of the city does not know where- Clara Skinner his sister lives on the Metairie Ridge.
Signature- does not write

Account Number- 502
Name- Sanders McLain
Date of Application- Jan. 8, 1868

Name of Master- left Richmond 30 years ago came to Tuckapaw Franklin- came to N.O. in 1863
Height and Complexion- 5 ft. 6 in. Brown
Father or Mother? Married?- Charlotte McLain parents Harris & Lydy Brown.
Name of Children- Julius 16, Susan 12, Sally 8, Fanny 3 & Sandey 6 mos.
Regiment and Company- Co. G 10 U.S.C.Art'y
Place of Birth- Richmond Va
Residence- Millandon's Plantation Jefferson Parish
Occupation- Laborer
Remarks- Mother died 7 yrs. ago- father dead 30 ago years here- Brothers Chapman at Millandron's place, Fred in Franklin, Edwin in Bayou La Fouche, Collin don't know where Ben, Davy, Joshua & Abram all dead- Sister Delsy wife of Hembry Jones dead, Lydy dead, Susan wife of Phil Giles in Tenn.- children Griffin, Jesse, & Lydy all dead.
Signature- yes

Account Number- 503
Name- Michael Forrest
Date of Application- Jan. 9, 1868
Father or Mother? Married?- Priscilla King Forrest
Name of Children- Panilus Forrest about 6 yrs. old
Regiment and Company- Co. I 78th U.S.C.T. private
Place of Birth- Stanley Co. N. Ca
Residence- Bayou Lafourche John Lyall's Plantation
Occupation- Laborer
Remarks- This amt. was deposited for him by Mr. John Lyall- he will come at a future day to give his descriptive list.
Signature- x

Account Number- 504
Name- William Washington
Date of Application- Jan. 9, 1868
Height and Complexion- about 55 yrs. old Dark Griff
Father or Mother? Married?- Candiss Washington
Name of Children- Becky, Sandy & Edmond Washington
Place of Birth- Leesburg Va
Residence- Lockport Bayou Lafourche La with Mr. Lyall
Occupation- Farming
Remarks- He has four more children besides those named- youngest one about 2 mos. Money deposited by Mr. Lyall.

Account Number- 505
Name- Thomas J. Durant
Date of Application- Jan. 11, 1868
Height and Complexion- Descriptive list of Elizabeth Middleton
Name of Children- Henrietta & Rosa Langston
Place of Birth- New Orleans La
Residence- Gasquet 35
Occupation- Seamstress
Remarks- This deposit of $100. made by Mr. T.J. Durant through Mr. Benedict, is made and received with the condition to pay Elizabeth Middleton colored the sum of $1. per week- the first payment to take place on date of deposit.

Account Number- 506
Name- Charlotte Augustin
Date of Application- Jan 11, 1868
Height and Complexion- Black 26 years old
Father or Mother? Married?- Simon Augustin
Name of Children- Mary & Eve Augustin
Place of Birth- T. Roman Plantation St. James La
Residence- corner Claiborne & Calhoun Carrollton
Occupation- Washer & Ironer
Remarks- no relative living
Account Number- 507
Name- James York
Date of Application- Jan. 13, 1868
Height and Complexion- Black about 60 yrs. old
Regiment and Company- Co. E 96th U.S.C.T.
Place of Birth- Eastern Shore Maryland
Residence- Metairie Ridge Jefferson Parish

Occupation- Laborer
Remarks- Rhody, Esther, Jacob & Mark York- were left about twenty years ago by him in Eastern Shore Maryland.

Account Number- 508
Name- Charley Williams
Date of Application- Jan. 14, 1868
Height and Complexion- Brown 19 years old
Place of Birth- Grand Coteau La
Residence- corner Baronne & Gravier
Occupation- Cook at Cassidy's
Remarks- C. Williams is a cripple- had his back bone broken when he was 6 years old- his mother's name Rachel Bradley.

Account Number- 509
Name- Charles Smith
Date of Application- Jan 14, 1868
Height and Complexion- White
Father or Mother? Married?-
Place of Birth- New York City
Residence- Old Levee St. No. 6
Occupation- Carpenter
Remarks- No relatives whatever.
Signature- yes

Account Number- 510
Name- Susan Gross
Date of Application- Jan. 16, 1868
Name of Master- Mother's name Patsy Walker lives in St. Mary's Parish- Father's name William Walker died about 20 years ago in St. Mary's Parish La- Bothers Joshua, Bromwell & Zachariah Walker- the first in the city- the second in Algiers- don't know where the last one is-
Father or Mother? Married?- widow of Charles Gross
Name of Children- Walker 17, Clara 15 & Ida 7
Place of Birth- Franklin La
Residence- Derbigny between Cypress & Julia
Occupation- Washer & Ironer
Remarks- This amount was deposited for her a/c by Elder Thos. Stubbs of 1st African Baptist Church. Elder Stubbs can draw.

Signature- x

Account Number- 511
Name- James Washington Daniel
Date of Application- Jan. 21, 1868
Height and Complexion- Black 54 yrs. old
Father or Mother? Married?- Leana Daniel
Name of Children- Annie, Washington & Ben Daniel
Place of Birth- Smithfield Co VA
Residence- Gretna Jefferson La
Occupation- No Particular Trade
Remarks- His only relative, his sister Laura resides in Gretna.
Signature- does not write

Account Number- 512
Name- Edward Hunt
Date of Application- Jan.22, 1868
Height and Complexion- 32 yrs. 5ft.9 1/2in. Light Brown
Father or Mother? Married?- Mary Hunt
Name of Children- Edward Hunt 6 mos. old
Regiment and Company- Co. D 48th U.S.C.T.
Place of Birth- Monroe Co. Georgia
Residence- 132 Perilliat St.
Occupation- Carpenter
Remarks- When he left Monroe Co. about 18 years ago he left two sisters by the name of Sarah & Elisa Hunt.
Signature- does not write

Account Number- 513
Name- Thomas Leaton
Date of Application- Jan 27, 1868
Height and Complexion- White
Father or Mother? Married?- single
Regiment and Company- Post Band N.O.
Place of Birth- London England
Residence- Erato St. Sailors Home
Occupation- Musician
Remarks- Miss Maria Walker his sister lives Laura House Lewishamhill London England
Signature- yes

Account Number- 514

Name- John Butler
Date of Application- Jan 27, 1868
Height and Complexion- Black 37 years old
Father or Mother? Married?- Sarah Butler
Name of Children- none
Regiment and Company- 7th La vols. Co A
Place of Birth- Prince George Co. Maryland
Residence- No. 30 Prieur between Perdido & Poydras
Occupation- Cook
Remarks- His uncle Mr. Wm. Harris one of our depositors resides in this city.
Signature- does not write

Account Number- 515
Name- James F. Asher
Date of Application- Jan 29, 1868
Father or Mother? Married?- single
Place of Birth- Baltimore Md
Residence- corner Canal & Rampart with Gen. Graham
Occupation- Body Servant
Remarks- Father's name Wm. Asher- mother Felice Asher maiden name Gray.
Signature- does not write

Account Number- 516
Name- James Alphonse
Date of Application- Feb. 1, 1868
Height and Complexion- about 41 yrs. yellow 5ft. 8in. Black eyes
Father or Mother? Married?- Mary Alphonse
Name of Children- Theresa, Mary & Gustave Alphonse
Regiment and Company- Co. A 96th U.S.C.T. Sergeant
Place of Birth- Richmond Va
Residence- 25 Music St. 3rd Dist.
Occupation- Laborer
Remarks- Courtney Robin his mother was living 28 yrs ago in Richmond- time at which he left.
Signature- yes

Account Number- 517
Name- Rev. Samuel S. Miner
Date of Application- Feb. 3, 1868
Height and Complexion- 50 yrs. old Black
Father or Mother? Married?- Anna Jane
Name of Children- none
Place of Birth- Flemingsville, Fleming Co. Ky
Residence- St. James Parish La Locoue's Plantation
Occupation- School Teacher
Signature- yes

Account Number- 518
Name- Gustave Jackson
Date of Application- Feb. 5, 1868
Name of Master- Father's name Andrew Jackson died in N.O. a long time ago. Mother's name Celia- died here can't recollect- on Common St. between Arcies & St. John.
Height and Complexion- Black 22 yrs old
Father or Mother? Married?- single
Place of Birth- New Orleans La
Residence- Clio St. between Appollo & Bacchus
Occupation- Waiter
Remarks- No father nor mother living has a brother by the name of Simms Jackson in this city.
Signature- x

Account Number- 519
Name- Sergt. William Burton
Date of Application- Feb. 5, 1868
Height and Complexion- 25 yrs. old Brown
Regiment and Company- Sergt. Co H 39th U.S.C.T.
Place of Birth- Sumner Co. Tenn.
Residence- Fort Washita Indian Territory now in garrison at ship below Island Miss.
Occupation- Soldier
Remarks- Father's name Joe Burton- was in Nashville Tenn. when he left 18 yrs. ago- Eliza his mother died about 15 years ago either in Miss. or La- No sisters nor brothers.
Signature- yes

Account Number- 520
Name- Andrew Gregory

Date of Application- Feb. 8, 1868
Signature- yes

Account Number- 521
Name- Alice Morgan Lopez
Date of Application- Feb. 8, 1868
Height and Complexion- 24 yrs. old
Father or Mother? Married?- Frederick Lopez
Name of Children- Emma Lopez 3 yrs. old
Regiment and Company- 10th H.y. Arty. U.S.C.
Place of Birth- New Orleans La
Residence- 283 Gravier St.
Occupation- Plasterer
Remarks- Renette Alexander his mother resides with him.
Signature- yes

Account Number- 522
Name- Reuben Brown
Date of Application- Feb. 10, 1868
Height and Complexion- 46 yrs. old Black
Father or Mother? Married?- Maria Brown
Name of Children- none of his own
Regiment and Company- Co. H 80th U.S.C.T.
Place of Birth- Wilmington Co. N. Ca
Residence- Rampart between Spain & Piety 3rd Dist.
Occupation- Laborer- Cook by profession
Remarks- Has two step children- a boy about 9 yrs. old named James Edington - and a girl 13 yrs. old Harriet Edington.
Signature- does not write

Account Number- 523
Name- Daniel Askins
Date of Application- Feb. 10, 1868
Height and Complexion- 45 yrs.old Black
Father or Mother? Married?- Caroline Askin
Regiment and Company- 10th H'y Arty. Co. M
Place of Birth- Eastern Shore Talbot Co. Md
Residence- 4 miles from Houma

Terrebonne La
Occupation- Laborer
Remarks- His mother Susan & father Jerry Askin were both living in Talbot Co.- Fairview Plantation, belonging to Ander Skinner 24 years ago. Book lost Aug. 21, 1872.
Signature- yes

Account Number- 524
Name- Mrs. Susan A. Green
Date of Application- Feb. 14, 1868
Father or Mother? Married?- widow of Richard A. Green
Name of Children- Henry, Luda & Gardner Green
Place of Birth- Pendelton Co. South Ca
Residence- 31 Claiborne St.
Occupation- Midwife
Signature- yes

Account Number- 525
Name- Sarah Brown
Date of Application- Feb. 21, 1868
Father or Mother? Married?- single
Place of Birth- Richmond Va
Residence- Bienville St. No. 107
Occupation- House Keeper
Remarks- Has a sister by the name of Fannie Brown residing in Richmond Va.
Signature- does not write

Account Number- 526
Name- Honore Simon
Date of Application- Feb. 24, 1868
Height and Complexion- 27 yrs 5ft.10in. Dark
Father or Mother? Married?- Pauline Simon
Name of Children- none
Regiment and Company- Co. A Corpl. 84th
Place of Birth- St. James Parish La
Residence- 347 Moreau St.
Occupation- Laborer
Remarks- Morris, Mathieu & Caroline Simon are in St. James Parish-
Signature- does not sign

Account Number- 527
Name- Eliza Hale

Date of Application- Feb. 25, 1868
Father or Mother? Married?- widow of Ambrose Hale late Sergeant Co. E 87th U.S.C.T.
Name of Children- none
Place of Birth- Richmond Va
Residence- corner Chestnut & Peters Algiers La
Occupation- Washer woman
Remarks- Has no relatives excepting one cousin Lucy Brown in Madisonville La.
Signature- does not write

Account Number- 528
Name- Mitchell Long
Date of Application- Feb. 27, 1868
Father or Mother? Married?- Sarah Ann Long
Name of Children- none
Regiment and Company- Private Co. A 84th U.S.C.T.
Place of Birth- St. John the Baptist Parish
Residence- N. Vickners Plantation Edgards Post Office
Occupation- Laborer
Remarks- "Special Deposit"
Signature- does not sign

Account Number- 529
Name- Ned Williams
Date of Application- Mar. 3, 1868
Height and Complexion- 36 years old
Father or Mother? Married?- Sophia Williams
Name of Children- Ned Williams 1 year 7 mths. old
Regiment and Company- Private Co. K 84th U.S.C.T.
Place of Birth- Arithmetic Va
Residence- St. Charles Parish Good Hope Plantation
Occupation- Laborer
Remarks- Father's name was Ned Williams Jetter when he left Va his father was living he can't remember the name of the Co. Had also a sister named Jane- He came in Louisiana with the US troops.
Signature- x

Account Number- 530
Name- Miami Philip
Date of Application- Mar. 4, 1868
Height and Complexion- yellow
Father or Mother? Married?- Robert Brown
Residence- Nashville Tenn.
Remarks- This deposit is made by Mr. Robert Brown for immediate transfer to her in Nashville Tenn. Transfer Card No. 530 issued.

Account Number- 531
Name- Alexander Dumas
Date of Application- Mar. 6, 1868
Father or Mother? Married?- Maria Simms Dumas
Name of Children- Alexander, Charlotte Harriet & Aimee Dumas
Place of Birth- New Orleans La
Residence- St. James St. 118
Occupation- Porter in a Commission House
Signature- yes

Account Number- 532
Name- Robert H Isabelle
Date of Application- Mar. 6, 1868
Father or Mother? Married?- Jamesetta E. Isabelle
Regiment and Company- 2nd La vols. Co. H 2nd. Lt.
Place of Birth- Bayou Chicot St. Landry
Residence- 98 Franklin St.
Occupation- None
Signature- yes

Account Number- 533
Name- William Edwards
Date of Application- Mar. 10, 1868
Height and Complexion- 26 Brown
Father or Mother? Married?- single
Name of Children- none
Regiment and Company- Co. I 78th U.S.C.T. Corpl.
Place of Birth- Parish of St. Martin
Residence- . New St. Benard Genius & Josephine
Occupation- Carpenter
Remarks- Mother's name Zelphie Edwards she now resides with brother's

name Prosper Berard- sister Mrs. Francis Charle & Mrs. Octave Riefel. Father died at Newberry when he was a little boy.
Signature- yes

Account Number- 534
Name- Philip Phine
Date of Application- Mar. 10, 1868
Father or Mother? Married?- single
Name of Children- none
Regiment and Company- U.S.N. Land man "Potomac"
Place of Birth- Woodville Miss.
Residence- Julia 421 between Magnolia & Claiborne
Occupation- Sailor
Remarks- No father or mother living. Has four sisters, Gracey, Barbara, Prescilla Phine are residing in Woodville Miss.
Signature- x

Account Number- 535
Name- John Parker
Date of Application- Mar. 10, 1868
Father or Mother? Married?- single
Name of Children- none
Regiment and Company- 115th Ky U.S.C.T.
Place of Birth- Harden Co. Ky
Occupation- Waiter on Steamer Frank Pargord
Remarks- Father & mother dead- his sister Jane Parker resides in Louisville on Walnut St. between Jackson & Hancock
Signature- x

Account Number- 536
Name- Hillare Zenon
Date of Application- Mar. 13, 1868
Height and Complexion- 5ft. 7in. Griffe Complexion
Father or Mother? Married?- Marie Nicholas
Name of Children- Emile Zenon 7 yrs. old
Regiment and Company- Private Co. F 96th U.S.C.T.
Place of Birth- St. Martinsville La
Residence- Union between Craps & Greatman 32
Occupation- Laborer
Remarks- Mother & father both dead has two sisters- one Victorine & Modeste Zenon both in New Orleans.
Signature- x

Account Number- 537
Name- Patrick McNalley
Date of Application- Mar. 14, 1868
Height and Complexion- White
Father or Mother? Married?- single
Name of Children- none
Regiment and Company- Co. I 1st U.S. Regulars
Place of Birth- County Kerry Ireland
Residence- Jackson Barracks N.C.
Occupation- Soldier
Remarks- Mrs. Margaret McNalley his mother is living in Co. Kerry Ireland.
Signature- yes

Account Number- 538
Name- Ester Brown
Date of Application- Mar. 14, 1868
Name of Master- Father's name Epham Bowland- died at Lone Star when I was a small girl my stepfather's name is Napoleon Jena.
Father or Mother? Married?- widow of Lewis Brown
Place of Birth- Lone Star Plantation Parish St. Charles
Residence- Parish St. Charles Eugene Ory's Plantation
Remarks- Mother's name is Nancy Jena- three brothers and one sister- James Miller, Arthur Bowland, Madison Bowland & Caroline Trotter.
Signature- yes

Account Number- 539
Name- Sergt. Silas Ware
Date of Application- Mar. 16, 1868
Name of Master- Father's name William Ware - died when he was a boy- mother's name Wennsota died in Lancaster Ky.
Height and Complexion- 24 yrs. old
Father or Mother? Married?- Charlotte Thomas
Name of Children- none him-

Regiment and Company- Co B 39th U.S.S.A.
Place of Birth- Garrett Co. Ky
Residence- Ship Island Station Miss.
Occupation- Soldier- formerly Co. H 116th U.S.C.T.
Remarks- Brother's name George Washington half brother in Lancaster Ky. Deposit made by Col. N. Vedder Paymaster U.S.S.A. May 24, 1869 By consolidation Silas Ware is now Corporal Co. G 25th U.S.I. stationed at Jackson Barracks.
Signature- yes

Account Number- 540
Name- William Russell
Date of Application- Mar. 16, 1868
Height and Complexion- Yellow
Father or Mother? Married?- single
Regiment and Company- Co. I 39th U.S.S.T.
Place of Birth- Savannah Georgia
Residence- Ship Island Station Miss.
Occupation- Steward Sea faring man
Remarks- Deposit made by Col. N. Vedder- Paymaster U.S.S.A.
Signature- yes

Account Number- 541
Name- John Hodges
Date of Application- Mar. 17, 1868
Signature- yes

Account Number- 542
Name- Samuel Roberts
Date of Application- Mar. 17, 1868
Height and Complexion- White
Regiment and Company- Co. B 1st U.S. Infty.
Place of Birth- Greenfield Hancock Indiana
Residence- Commercial Hotel Barracks
Occupation- Soldier
Remarks- Margaret Roberts his mother, Walter S. Roberts his father are living in Hancock Co. Indiana.
Signature- yes

Account Number- 543
Name- Nicholas Walker
Date of Application- Mar. 17, 1868
Height and Complexion- Black
Father or Mother? Married?- single
Name of Children- none
Regiment and Company- Co. E 117th U.S.C.T.
Place of Birth- Briggs Plantation Brunswick Co. Va
Residence- New Basin next to Jackson Depot
Occupation- Laborer at the Jackson R.R. Co.
Remarks- Caroline Briggs his mother, Henderson Walker his father live in Brunswick Co. Va.
Signature- x

Account Number- 545
Name- James Wilson
Date of Application- Mar. 19, 1868
Height and Complexion- 5ft. 7in. Dark
Father or Mother? Married?- single
Name of Children- none
Regiment and Company- Co. H 84th U.S.C.T.
Place of Birth- St. Helena Parish La
Residence- near Amite City St. Helena Parish
Occupation- Farmer
Remarks- Sister's name Winnie & Sarah Jennings his mother live with him- father is dead- Henry & Frank Jennings are half brothers of his and live with him.
Signature- x

Account Number- 544
Name- Mary H. Griffin
Date of Application- Mar. 19, 1868
Father or Mother? Married?- single
Place of Birth- New Orleans La
Residence- 158 Gasquet St. N.O.
Occupation- Midwife, Nurse
Signature- does not write

Account Number- 545
Name- James Carter
Date of Application- Mar. 20, 1868
Father or Mother? Married?- Josephine Seymour Carter
Name of Children- Louisa & Timothy Carter

Regiment and Company- Cook on U.S.S. Glasgow
Place of Birth- New Orleans La
Residence- Canal between Carondelet & Baronne
Occupation-Privy Cleaner
Remarks- Mother and father dead- no relatives besides.
Signature- yes

Account Number- 547
Name- Moses Frazier
Date of Application- Mar. 21, 1868
Height and Complexion- has a heavy mark on the left cheek
Father or Mother? Married?- single
Regiment and Company- Co. H 78th U.S.C.T.
Place of Birth- Lexington Ky
Residence- corner Magazine & Calliope
Occupation- Laborer
Remarks- Capt. Bockee was in command of his Company. Have no relation but a sister-in-law, who is a widow her name is Mary Jane Frazier.
Signature- yes

Account Number- 548
Name- Gloster Hill
Date of Application- Mar. 21, 1868
Height and Complexion- 28 years old
Father or Mother? Married?- Emily Hill
Name of Children- none
Regiment and Company- 99th U.S.C.T. 1st Sergt. K Co.
Place of Birth- Ascension Parish La 9 miles above Donaldsonville
Residence- at Henry Doyle's Plantation near Donaldsonville
Occupation- Carpenter
Remarks- Mother & father dead- has four brothers Adam Harris, Abner Hill, Aaron Hill, Anderson Bryan- Abner Hill is in this city the other three are with Gloster Hill.
Signature- yes

Account Number- 549
Name- Giles Anderson
Date of Application- Mar. 21, 1868
Height and Complexion- Black

Father or Mother? Married?- Rosetta Anderson his wife
Name of Children- 2 children girls
Regiment and Company- Co. C 96th U.S.C.T.
Place of Birth- Rowan Lomity Saulsbury South Carolina
Residence- on Short St. Carrollton Parish of Jefferson La
Occupation- Baker
Remarks- His children's name Elyza & Emily- not other relation.
Signature- does not write

Account Number- 550
Name- Cezar Brown
Date of Application- Mar. 23, 1868
Height and Complexion- 5ft. 5in. Black
Father or Mother? Married?- widow
Name of Children- William Brown 7 yrs. old
Regiment and Company- Co. D 84th U.S.C.T.
Place of Birth- Terrebonne Parish La
Residence- Algiers La
Occupation- Deck hand on Steamboat
Remarks- His wife Sarah Jane Walker mother of his son William died four years ago. Has only one brother by the name of Ben Brown in Terrebonne Parish.
Signature- x

Account Number- 551
Name- David McConnell
Date of Application- Mar. 24, 1868
Father or Mother? Married?- single
Regiment and Company- Quarter Master Sergeant of the 39th U.S.T.
Place of Birth- St. James Parish La
Residence- Station at Ship Island Miss.
Occupation- Soldier
Remarks- Has a father living whose name is Cesar Seldon- mother living Caroline Seldon.
Signature- yes

Account Number- 552
Name- Amelia Davis
Date of Application- Mar. 25, 1868
Father or Mother? Married?- wife of Francis A. Davis

Place of Birth- New Orleans La
Residence- 203 Franklin between Lafayette & Girod
Occupation- Hairdresser
Remarks- Has a brother named Gabriel Joseph.
Signature- x

Account Number- 553
Name- Louisa Dorsey alias Pauline Dozier
Date of Application- Mar. 26, 1868
Height and Complexion- Black
Father or Mother? Married?- widow of John Dorsey Co. I 74th
Name of Children- five children
Place of Birth- Parish of Plaquemines La
Residence- Derbigny St. between Kerlerec & Columbus No. 258
Occupation- Washer woman
Remarks- Her children's name are Marie, Joseph, Nelda, Adelaide & Georgiana Dorsey.
Signature- x

Account Number- 554
Name- James Lewis
Date of Application- Mar. 26, 1868
Father or Mother? Married?- Rebecca Lewis
Name of Children- Wm Henderson & Ellen Lewis
Place of Birth- Lexington Holmes Co. Miss.
Residence- Sixth between St. Patrick & St. Denis
Occupation- Baggage Wagon Driver
Remarks- About 12 years ago he left his mother Ellen Johnson in Lexington Texas- also left his bother Anderson and his sister Louisa at the same place.
Signature- x

Account Number- 556
Name- Moses Briggs
Date of Application- Mar. 27, 1868
Father or Mother? Married?- Malinda Briggs
Name of Children- none
Place of Birth- New Orleans La
Residence- Derbigny between Julia & Cypress
Occupation- Bricklayer
Remarks- Mother's name Patsy Briggs lives on Sixth between St. Denis & Patrick- father's name Moses Briggs. Marthe & Rebecca Briggs his sisters are living with their mother.
Signature- yes

Account Number- 557
Name- Eulalie Verret
Date of Application- Mar. 28, 1868
Father or Mother? Married?- single
Name of Children- none
Place of Birth- about 3 miles above the Convent in St. James Parish
Residence- Girod between Baronne & Philippa
Occupation- Cake Vendress
Remarks- Has a sister by the name of Mary Vassern Cantrelle- In case of any accident she declares that the money this day deposited belongs to Marie Louise Jean Berg, who resides on Julia St. between Carondelet & Baronne.
Signature- x

Account Number- 557
Name- Samuel Brooks
Date of Application- Mar. 30, 1868
Father or Mother? Married?- single
Name of Children- none
Regiment and Company- 6th U.S. Hy. Arty. Colored 1st. Duty Sergeant
Place of Birth- Richmond Va
Residence- Lafayette between Baronne & Carondelet
Occupation- Cook
Remarks- Mother's name Eliza Haley- dead- father's name Bill Brooks- dead- Patsy Ann Brooks & Delph Brooks brother and sister are living in Richmond Va. Samuel Brooks is a stranger in this city on his way to Richmond.
Signature- x

Account Number- 558
Name- Harriet Henry
Date of Application- Mar. 31, 1868
Father or Mother? Married?- widow of Wm. Henry late private Co. G 96th regt.

C.T. her parents Jim Taylor & Celia Dossey
Name of Children- Mary Agnes, Mary Emma (dead) & Richard Henry
Place of Birth- St. Mary's Co. Md
Residence- Parapet (Camp) Jefferson Parish
Occupation- Seamstress
Remarks- Brothers Jim, Sam, Joe, Phil, & Charles all in Md. Eleven years ago when she left Maryland her father & mother Celia Dossey were living in St. Mary's co. Md. Sisters Lucinda, Cecilia, Sophy, Levy, Therison & May Eliza in Md. Child Charles Henry dead.
Signature- x

Account Number- 559
Name- Maria Johnson
Date of Application- Mar. 31, 1868
Father or Mother? Married?- Charles Johnson
Name of Children- none
Place of Birth- Carrollton La
Residence- Front St. Carrollton La
Occupation- Washer & Ironer
Remarks- This amount was deposited by her husband.

Account Number- 560
Name- Lazare Rodriguez
Date of Application- Apr. 1, 1868
Father or Mother? Married?- Mathilde Rodriguez
Name of Children- Henriette 2 years old
Regiment and Company- Capt. Co. K 7th La U.S. vols.
Place of Birth- New Orleans La
Residence- Marais between Ursulines & Hospital
Occupation- Shoemaker
Signature- yes

Account Number- 561
Name- Eliza Hale
Date of Application- Apr. 2, 1868
Remarks- See No. 527

Account Number- 562
Name- Sambo Iron
Date of Application- Apr. 3, 1868
Height and Complexion- Black
Father or Mother? Married?- Mary Iron
Name of Children- boy Sye Iron
Regiment and Company- Private Co. C 97th U.S.C.T.
Place of Birth- Christborn Parish near Charleston South Carolina
Residence- Varret Canal back of Algiers La
Occupation- Laborer, farming at present
Remarks- Two sisters Sally & Anna- one brother Paldo -living Rivertown Plantation 4 miles below Donaldsonville
Signature- x

Account Number- 563
Name- Peter Stark
Date of Application- Apr. 3, 1868
Height and Complexion- Black
Father or Mother? Married?- single
Name of Children- one boy 15 yrs. old
Regiment and Company- Co. F 97th U.S.C.T.
Place of Birth- Fairfield South Carolina 150 miles above Charleston
Residence- 236 Girod St.
Occupation- Wood Sawyer
Remarks- Wishes in case of death the money to go to his son Wire Stark
Signature- yes

Account Number- 564
Name- Primus Sweeney
Date of Application- Apr. 3, 1868
Height and Complexion- Black
Father or Mother? Married?- Polly Ann Sweeney
Name of Children- none
Regiment and Company- Co. C 97th U.S.C.T.
Place of Birth- Charleston South Carolina
Residence- Moreau St. between Marigny & Mandeville
Occupation- Laborer
Remarks- No relation.
Signature- x

Account Number- 565
Name- U. O. Krause
Date of Application- Apr. 3, 1868

Father or Mother? Married?- Mary K. Krause
Name of Children- none
Regiment and Company- Adjt. of 84th U.S.C.T.
Place of Birth- Kalamazoo Michigan
Residence- 159 Camp
Occupation- Notary Public
Signature- yes

Account Number- 566
Name- William Thomas
Date of Application- Apr. 4, 1868
Name of Master- Mrs. Amanda Lewis has been authorized by Wm Thomas to draw, whatever money she may need.
Height and Complexion- Black 26 years old
Father or Mother? Married?- Amanda Thomas
Name of Children- none
Regiment and Company- Sergt. Co. K 97th U.S.C.T.
Place of Birth- about 10 miles from Portabaro Md.
Residence- on Bienville corner Rocheblave
Occupation- Carpenter
Remarks- Left Maryland in 1860- Dolly Thomas his mother died before he left- Charles Thomas his father and Amanda Jordan his sister were living 10 miles from Portabaro Md, where he left them.
Signature- x

Account Number- 567
Name- Jackson Nelson
Date of Application- Apr. 6, 1868
Height and Complexion- 26 yrs. old
Father or Mother? Married?- single
Name of Children- none
Regiment and Company- Private Co. F 55th U.S.C.T.
Place of Birth- Springhill Arkansas
Residence- Franklin, Poydras & Perdido
Occupation- Laborer
Remarks- Ida Hales his mother is dead- his father John Kennedy is dead also- His sister Louisa Jackson lives with him- Jackson Nelson wants in case anything should happen to him that the money should go to her.
Signature- x

Account Number- 568
Name- Alpheus McCray
Date of Application- Apr. 6, 1868
Height and Complexion- 35 years old
Father or Mother? Married?- Marceline McCray
Name of Children- none
Regiment and Company- Commadore's steward on board of the U.S. Sloop Pensacola discharged from "Estrella"
Place of Birth- near Florence Alabama
Residence- Terpsichore St. 315
Occupation- Dining Room Servant
Remarks- Mother's name Jane Cook, lives at Pass Christian Miss. -father's name Henry McCray is dead.
Signature- yes

Account Number- 569
Name- Emily Wright widow of Henry Wright late private Co. I 97th
Date of Application- Apr. 7, 1868
Height and Complexion- 67 years old
Father or Mother? Married?- widow of Henry Wright
Name of Children- None
Place of Birth- Baltimore Md
Residence- Basin St. No. 105
Occupation- Washer & Ironer
Remarks- She has no relatives in this city- left Maryland 28 years ago- had left in Baltimore a brother by the name of Greenberry Harbuck- does not know if he is living.
Signature- x

Account Number- 570
Name- James Robinson
Date of Application- Apr. 7, 1868
Height and Complexion- Black
Father or Mother? Married?- single
Name of Children- no
Regiment and Company- Co. H 97th Regt. U.S.C.T.
Place of Birth- New Virginia State of Virginia
Residence- Carrollton Parish of Jefferson La

Occupation- Laborer
Remarks- No relation to his knowledge.
Signature- x

Account Number- 571
Name- Lewis Bruce
Date of Application- Apr. 7, 1868
Height and Complexion- Black
Father or Mother? Married?- Jane
Name of Children- a girl 10 months old
Regiment and Company- Co. B 97th U.S.C.T.
Place of Birth- Tchefuncta, St. Tammany Parish La
Residence- corner Melpomene & Liberty Sts.
Occupation- sailor
Remarks- His mother living in Mandeville La name Malinda- two sisters named Fine & Pheobe- three brothers named Elmond, August & Dave.
Signature- x

Account Number- 572
Name- John Francis
Date of Application- Apr. 7, 1868
Height and Complexion- Black 25 years old
Father or Mother? Married?- to Sarah Francis
Name of Children- Lucinda 1 year 2 weeks
Regiment and Company- Co. B 97th U.S.C.T.
Place of Birth- Spottsylvania Co. Md
Residence- No. 170 St. Anthony St. 3rd Dist.
Occupation- Laborer
Remarks- About 18 years when he left Spottsylvania Co. his mother Sarah Ann Hodgins was living- his father Frank Hodgins is dead.
Signature- does not write

Account Number- 573
Name- Charles L. Cooper
Date of Application- Apr. 9, 1868
Father or Mother? Married?- Flora G. Cooper
Name of Children- Forestine & Kay Cooper

Regiment and Company- 1st Lieut. 39th U.S.C.T.
Place of Birth- New York City
Residence- 167 St. Charles St.
Remarks- 1st Lieut. 39th U.S.I. AAA Gen.(?)
Signature- yes

Account Number- 574
Name- George McGuire
Date of Application- Apr. 10, 1868
Father or Mother? Married?- to Angelina Conway
Regiment and Company- Co. K 97th U.S.C.T.
Place of Birth- New Orleans
Residence- Treme St. Between St. Ann & Dumaine 133
Occupation- Bricklayer
Remarks- No relation.
Signature- x

Account Number- 575
Name- George Merritt
Date of Application- Apr. 10, 1868
Father or Mother? Married?- to Ariann Merritt
Name of Children- Sally, Charley & Fanny Merritt
Regiment and Company- Co. F 74th U.S.C.T.
Place of Birth- Greenville Co. Va
Residence- Palmyra St. near Broad
Occupation- Mattrass Maker
Remarks- His mother is living in Warren Co. Miss.
Signature- yes

Account Number- 576
Name- James Frelow
Date of Application- Apr. 11, 1868
Height and Complexion- Black
Father or Mother? Married?- to Henrietta Davis
Regiment and Company- Co. F 97th U.S.C.T.
Place of Birth- St. Mary's Parish La
Residence- New Iberia St. Martin's Parish La
Occupation- Carpenter
Remarks- Father & mother living on

Major Levi's Plantation St. Mary's Parish La- Father's name John Patterson, mother's name Adelaide Patterson- four sisters, one brother now in Army in Co. H 9th U.S.C. Cavalry.
Signature- x

Account Number- 577
Name- Michael D. Carey
Date of Application- Apr. 14,1868
Father or Mother? Married?- single
Place of Birth- Manchester England
Residence- Circus St.
Occupation- Clerk
Remarks- John Carey his father lives in Bradford, Yorkshire England.
Signature- yes

Account Number- 578
Name- James Gardner
Date of Application- Apr. 14,1868
Height and Complexion- 21 yrs. old
Father or Mother? Married?- single
Name of Children- none
Regiment and Company- Co. I 36th U.S.C.T. private
Place of Birth- Mattis Co. Va
Residence- Julia St. No. 103
Occupation- Laborer
Remarks- Maria Gardner his mother & his father Daniel Gardner are both living in Mattis Co. Va- John Gardner & Lucy Gardner his brother & sister are also living at the same place.
Signature- yes

Account Number- 579
Name- John Booker
Date of Application- Apr. 20, 1868

Account Number- 580
Name- John B. Lester
Date of Application- Apr. 20,1868
Father or Mother? Married?- single
Name of Children- Joseph Lester 12 years old
Regiment and Company- Co. C Sergt. 99th U.S.C.T.
Place of Birth- Jefferson Parish La
Residence- Louisiana Ave. Jefferson
Occupation- Gardener
Remarks- Fanchonette the mother of his boy married another man whilst he was in the army. Delia Daniel his mother lives with him in Jefferson.
Signature- yes

Account Number- 581
Name- Rudolph Harris
Date of Application- Apr. 21,1868
Height and Complexion- Black 23 years old
Father or Mother? Married?- single
Name of Children- none
Place of Birth- Vicksburg Miss.
Residence- Thalia, Appollo & Bacchus
Occupation- Dining Room Servant
Remarks- Fanny Harris mother- Ben Harris his father are living with him- Sarah Harris & Martha Field his sisters also live in this city.
Signature- can't write his name

Account Number- 582
Name- Robert Wells
Date of Application- Apr. 21,1868
Height and Complexion- Black 36 years old
Father or Mother? Married?- Minerva Wells
Name of Children- none
Regiment and Company- Sergt. Co. D 97th U.S.C.T.
Place of Birth- near Cloverport Breckinridge Co. Ky
Residence- 217 Basin St. near Girod
Occupation- Laborer
Remarks- Katherine & William Wells his father and mother and Nancy Crawford his sister when he last heard from five months ago were living in Breckinridge Ky. Wife can draw with book.
Signature- yes

Account Number- 584
Name- Catherine Little
Date of Application- Apr. 27,1868
Father or Mother? Married?- widow
Name of Children- one son George about 13 yrs.old
Place of Birth- Ireland
Residence- 205 St. Joseph St.

Occupation- Servant
Remarks- At present in the employ of Revd. Dr. J. P. Newman- she is well know by Judge Howell, R.K.

Account Number- 585
Name- Tinman Clark
Date of Application- Apr. 28,1868
Height and Complexion- Black
Father or Mother? Married?- to Fanny Clark
Regiment and Company- Co. K 96th Regt. U.S.C.T.
Place of Birth- Bayou Sara La
Residence- Franklin St. between Girod & Julia
Occupation- Laborer
Remarks- Has two sisters named Betty & Viney Clark- two brothers named Arthur & Mitchell Clark- his father's name Joe Clark, mother Becky Clark both dead.
Signature- x

Account Number- 587
Name- Newtown Quilland
Date of Application- Apr. 28,1868
Height and Complexion- 23 yrs. old
Father or Mother? Married?- Anna Walker Quilland
Name of Children- James Hervey 4 yrs. old
Regiment and Company- Co. A 39th U.S.C.T. private
Place of Birth- St. Helena Parish La
Residence- Soldier at Fort Pike
Occupation- Shoemaker
Remarks- His mother's name Susan Quilland lives at Osyka Miss. April Quilland his father is dead- Lewis & Hervey Quilland his brothers are at Osyka Miss.
Signature- yes

Account Number- 587
Name- Frank Maxwell
Date of Application- May 1,1868
Height and Complexion- Light 14 yrs. old
Father or Mother? Married?- single
Name of Children- none
Place of Birth- Texas

Residence- Girod St. No. 192
Remarks- Father's name Mr. Maxwell- stepfather Frank Robinson- mother's name Mary Robinson live on Girod St. 192.
Signature- yes

Account Number- 588
Name- Louis Cass
Date of Application- May 1,1868
Height and Complexion- Black
Father or Mother? Married?- single
Place of Birth- Port Hudson La
Residence- Carondelet St. between Third & Fourth
Occupation- work in cotton
Remarks- His mother living in Texas, Henderson Co. named Manda Brown. One brother Soloman & a sister Louisa.
Signature- yes

Account Number- 589
Name- Marceline McCray
Date of Application- May 4,1868
Father or Mother? Married?- to Alpheus McCray
Name of Children- none
Place of Birth- New Orleans La
Residence- Terpsichore St. No. 315
Occupation- Seamstress
Remarks- Mother's name Mary Duncan, resides with her- Alonzo Borel & Ambrose Borel her brothers- Clara J. Narcissa her sister are all residing in this city.
Signature- yes

Account Number- 590
Name- Robert Carter & his wife Cecilia Carter
Date of Application- May 4,1868
Name of Master- Cecilia Carter's father's name is Samuel Sheridan- mother's Maria- father in Washington Parish about 1 year ago- mother Maria lives in Covington La.
Name of Children- Joseph Hurlburt & Emma Maria Carter & Corinne married to Newton Allis
Place of Birth- Robert in Frederick Co. Va, Cecilia in Washington Parish La
Residence- 41 Cypress St.

Occupation- Robert- Teamster Cecilia- Washer & Ironer
Remarks- This record is taken both of the husband & wife the top descriptive is the husband's and the lowest the wife's.
Signature- x x

Account Number- 591
Name- John Francis
Date of Application- May, 5 1868
Remarks- See for descriptive list No. 572.

Account Number- 592
Name- William Foley
Date of Application- May 5, 1868
Height and Complexion- Black 32 years old
Father or Mother? Married?- single
Regiment and Company- Private Co. A 97th U.S.C.T.
Place of Birth- Cumberland Co. Ky
Residence- Jackson & Dryades corner
Occupation- Laborer
Remarks- No mother or father living- Sarah & Ann Thompson his sisters are in Cumberland C. Ky.
Signature- x

Account Number- 593
Name- Harriet Marshall
Date of Application- May 5, 1868
Height and Complexion- Light
Father or Mother? Married?- widow of James Marshall
Name of Children- none
Place of Birth- Wilkinson Co. Miss.
Residence- Triton Walk 203
Occupation- Washing & Ironing
Remarks- Has a sister Mary Williams resides in Columbus Texas- has a brother by the name of Morgan Moore in Woodville Miss.

Account Number- 594
Name- William Morell
Date of Application- May 5, 1868
Height and Complexion- Light 21 years old
Father or Mother? Married?- single
Name of Children- none
Regiment and Company- 138th Colored Infty.
Place of Birth- Lynchburg Va
Residence- Girod between Carondelet & St. Charles
Occupation- Page around Convention
Remarks- No father nor mother living- no relatives living- father's name was John Morell- mother's name was Mary.
Signature- cannot write

Account Number- 595
Name- Isabella Battice
Date of Application- May 5, 1868
Height and Complexion- Black 28 yrs. old
Father or Mother? Married?- widow of John Battice
Name of Children- Mary Baptiste 10 yrs. old
Place of Birth- Born in South Carolina raised in Rapides La
Residence- Dryades & Lafayette corner
Occupation- Cook
Remarks- Her mother Ledy Coleman lives in Rapides Parish on Doctor Sullivan's Plantation. Mary Baptiste can draw.
Signature- does not write

Account Number- 596
Name- Beverly Austin
Date of Application- May 5, 1868
Name of Master- Living here 8 years came from Ascension Parish.
Height and Complexion- 21 Black
Father or Mother? Married?- Single
Parents Abram & Louisa
Regiment and Company- Co. H 97th U.S.C.T.
Place of Birth- Ascension Parish La
Residence- Camp Parapet Parish of Jefferson La lives with father.
Occupation- Carpenter
Remarks- Mother died in Ascension Parish when he was about 5 yrs. old- father living Abraham Austin, one sister Minny Austin in N.O. Stepmother Milly dead. Sisters Priscilla & Irany dead.
Signature- does not write

Account Number- 597
Name- William M. Henry
Date of Application- May 8,1868
Height and Complexion- White
Father or Mother? Married?- single
Name of Children- none
Place of Birth- Havana NY
Residence- 205 St. Joseph St.
Occupation- Clergyman
Remarks- Deposited as funds pertaining to the business of the New Orleans Advocate.
Signature- yes

Account Number- 598
Name- Daniel Carter
Date of Application- May 8,1868
Height and Complexion- Black
Father or Mother? Married?- to Elyza Carter
Name of Children- none
Regiment and Company- Co. B 99th U.S.C.T.
Place of Birth- Charleston South Carolina
Residence- just above Carrollton near Hoye's Foundry
Occupation- Gardener
Remarks- Father dead, mother living named Puss Carter at Doyle's Plantation Ascension Parish Lafourche, have sister at same place named Peggy Gardner.
Signature- does not write

Account Number- 599
Name- John Alexander
Date of Application- May 8,1868
Name of Master- Mother's name Rosalie- died when he was a little baby at Waterloo Pointe Coupee- father's name Severin also dead.
Height and Complexion- Black
Father or Mother? Married?- single
Name of Children- none
Regiment and Company- Co. K 97th U.S.C.T.
Place of Birth- Baton Rouge La
Residence- 279 St. Louis St. between Robertson & Claiborne
Occupation- Laborer
Remarks- Sister named Coralie Leblanc lives in the same house as depositor. July 1- on Villere between St. Ann & Dumaine
Signature- yes

Account Number- 601
Name- Lucy Day
Date of Application- May 9,1868
Father or Mother? Married?- Widow of James Day late Private Co. B 97th U.S.C.T.
Name of Children- none
Place of Birth- Jackson Miss.
Residence- Terpsichore between White & Hercules
Occupation- Washing & Ironing
Remarks- Rachel Courtney her mother when heard from two years ago was in Iberville Parish. Joe Courtney her father when last heard from about two months ago was in Baton Rouge La. (Later Entry) Has moved to Kellysville on Mr. Fairview's place child Sarah Ann died when 6 months old. Brothers Wiley & Soloman up country, Willis- dead, sister Janey(?) sold away when a child.
Signature- x

Account Number- 600
Name- C.S. Sauvinet administrator of the Estate of Dr. A.W. Lewis
Date of Application- May 8,1868
Place of Birth- New Orleans La
Residence- corner Dauphin & Kerlerec
Occupation- Cashier Freedman's Bank
Remarks- This deposit made in the capacity of administrator to the Estate of the late Dr. A.W. Lewis.
Signature- yes

Account Number- 602
Name- Edward Babbin
Date of Application- May 11,1868
Height and Complexion- Black
Father or Mother? Married?- to Sarah Babbin
Name of Children- none
Regiment and Company- Co. A 96th U.S.C.T.
Place of Birth- Baton Rouge La
Residence- Live Oak St. City of

Jefferson
Occupation- Laborer
Remarks- Mother dead- father living in Baton Rouge La named Simon Babbin- 3 sisters, Josephine Morgan, Virginia Wallace & Phrosine Whitley.
Signature- yes

Account Number- 603
Name- David Smith
Date of Application- May 11, 1868
Height and Complexion- Black
Father or Mother? Married?- single
Name of Children- one daughter Rosalie Smith
Regiment and Company- Co. A 96th U.S.C.T.
Place of Birth- St. Landry Parish La
Residence- Canal St. Between Villere & Robertson
Occupation- Laborer
Remarks- Father & mother dead- has 2 sisters living, Sophia at Terre aux boeufs & Margaret Silas in Opelousas
Signature- does not write

Account Number- 604
Name- Patrick J. Isabelle
Date of Application- May 11, 1868
Father or Mother? Married?- single
Name of Children- none
Place of Birth- St. Landry Parish Bayou Chicot La
Residence- Freret St. between Poydras & Lafayette
Occupation- Retail Merchant
Remarks- Mother & father dead- five brothers, Thomas, Robert, Andrew, William & James Isabelle.
Signature- yes

Account Number- 605
Name- Clementine Mann
Date of Application- May 11, 1868
Height and Complexion- Black
Father or Mother? Married?- widow
Name of Children- Grandchild Sandy
Place of Birth- Pattersonville Bayou Teche
Residence- Brashear City
Occupation- Cook

Remarks- Mary, Martha & Sandy are her own daughters.
Signature- does not write

Account Number- 606
Name- John Butler
Date of Application- May 11, 1868
Height and Complexion- Black
Father or Mother? Married?- Delphine
Name of Children- two children
Regiment and Company- co. A 94th U.S.C.T.
Place of Birth- Carrollton, Jefferson Parish La
Residence- Washington St. Carrollton
Occupation- Plasterer
Remarks- Father & mother dead- one sister Mary Butler & four brothers, Zeb & Albert Butler & John Wright.
Signature- yes

Account Number- 607
Name- Basil Coursay
Date of Application- May 12, 1868
Name of Master- Left Md. about 22 years ago.
Height and Complexion- Black
Father or Mother? Married?- to Elvira- parents Jesse & Jenny
Name of Children- none
Regiment and Company- Co. K 97th U.S.C.T.
Place of Birth- Williamsport Potomac Md
Residence- 240 Dryades St.
Occupation- Slater
Remarks- All his relations were living in Maryland when he left in 1847 does not know if they are living yet has not heard from them since 1847. (later entry) Heard brothers Daniel & Adam both in Canada, sisters Maria, Ellen, Lorilla & Annie were all in Md.
Signature- does not write

Account Number- 608
Name- Henry Clay
Date of Application- May 13, 1868
Height and Complexion- Black 24 years old
Father or Mother? Married?- single
Name of Children- none

Regiment and Company- Private Co. A 97th U.S.C.T.
Place of Birth- New Orleans La raised at Bayou Goula
Residence- corner Dumaine & Villere 231
Occupation- Cooper
Remarks- Mother's name was Kasiah- father's name was William Clay- no other relatives
Signature- x

Account Number- 609
Name- Robert McIntire
Date of Application- May 13,1868
Height and Complexion- Black
Father or Mother? Married?- to Harriet Smith
Name of Children- one boy aged 22 yrs. old
Place of Birth- Eastern Shore Md.
Residence- St. Dennis St. between Washington & Sixth
Occupation- Laborer or Warehouse man
Remarks- This money is deposited as agent of Ann Chapman, minor and is not to be drawn out or any portion of it except by depositor in person.
Signature- does not write

Account Number- 610
Name- Alfred Burbank
Date of Application- May 13,1868
Height and Complexion- Black
Father or Mother? Married?- single
Regiment and Company- Co. B 99th U.S.C.T.
Place of Birth- Iberville Parish La
Residence- Iberville Parish
Occupation- Field hand
Remarks- Stepfather & mother living at Iberville Parish named Tony & Harriet Fobb. One sister Louisa Hantney- two brothers James Burbank & Joseph Butler.
Signature- yes

Account Number- 611
Name- Raphael Lange
Date of Application- May 16,1868
Name of Master- Father died in St. Mary's Parish when Raphael was small mother died before father in St. Mary's.
Height and Complexion- Black
Father or Mother? Married?- to Manette- parents John Baptiste & Eliza.
Name of Children- One boy 9 months old named Alexander.
Regiment and Company- Co. A 96th U.S.C.T.
Place of Birth- New Iberia St. Mary's Parish
Residence- Algiers Right Bank
Occupation- Laborer
Remarks- Has three sisters living- Annette in the city, Rose Attakapy(?). Marie Louise Packwood's Plantation Plaquemines Parish. One brother Richard Anderson. Children Paulin, Antoine & Lizzie dead. Sister, Victoria dead.
Signature- does not write

Account Number- 612.
Name- Mrs. C.C. Bodreau
Date of Application- May 16,1868

Account Number- 613
Name- Madison Bell
Date of Application- May 16,1868
Height and Complexion- Black
Father or Mother? Married?- to Alice
Name of Children- no children here
Regiment and Company- Co. G 7th or 97th U.S.C.T.
Place of Birth- Arundale Co. Maryland
Residence- 179 Religious St.
Occupation- Laborer
Remarks- Parents dead- no relations to his knowledge now living.
Signature- does not write

Account Number- 614
Name- F.W. Jones
Date of Application- May 18,1868
Signature- yes

Account Number- 616
Name- Emmeline Reed
Date of Application- May 19,1868
Plantation- Mrs. Long's Plantation
Height and Complexion- Black 25 yrs.

old
Name of Children- John McCoy Reed 5 yrs. old
Place of Birth- Alexandria La
Residence- Conti between Broad & Dolhinde
Occupation- Washer & Ironer
Remarks- William Reed her boy's father is now dead- he was a member of the 70th U.S.C.T. Co. D

Account Number- 615
Name- Spencer Kenner
Date of Application- May 18,1868
Plantation- Oliver Norman
Height and Complexion- 5ft. 6in. Black
Father or Mother? Married?- yes
Name of Children- Nancy
Place of Birth- Edgefield S. Ca
Residence- Marksville La
Occupation- Farmer
Remarks- Age 57 ends of 2nd & 4th fingers of left hand gone- very bald headed. This descriptive list was sent from Marksville by Amos S. Collis A.S.A.C.

Account Number- 617
Name- William Johnson
Date of Application- May 21,1868
Name of Master- Left Va when about 14.
Height and Complexion- Black
Father or Mother? Married?- to Sophie- parents William & Patsy
Name of Children- Wither Johnson about 14 yrs. old
Place of Birth- Caroline Co. Va
Residence- 174 Liberty St.
Occupation- Painter
Remarks- Mother died in Va before he left- father in Va, sisters Mary, Amy, Dicy & Judy all sold away before he was- brother Jerry dead.
Signature- does not write

Account Number- 618
Name- James Parker
Date of Application- May 22,1868
Height and Complexion- Black
Father or Mother? Married?- to Rosalie
Name of Children-Jules, Harry & the oldest Martha
Regiment and Company- Co. G 97th U.S.C.T.
Place of Birth- Culbert Co. Md
Residence- Algiers on Goslin St.
Occupation- Laborer
Signature- does not write

Account Number- 619
Name- William Morris
Date of Application- May 22,1868
Height and Complexion- Black
Father or Mother? Married?- to Juddy
Name of Children- one girl Dow 9 months old
Regiment and Company- Co. A 99th U.S.C.T.
Place of Birth- Nashville Tenn.
Residence- on Bayou Lafourche Berteau's Place
Occupation- Farmer
Remarks- No relations that he knows of.
Signature- does not write

Account Number- 620
Name- Henry Camille
Date of Application- May 25,1868
Height and Complexion- Black
Father or Mother? Married?- single
Regiment and Company- Co. K 96th U.S.C.T.
Place of Birth- Pendelton Dist. South Carolina raised in Miss.
Residence- Lyon St. between Live Oak & Laurel Jefferson City
Occupation- Laborer
Remarks- Does not know if he has any relation living when he left Mississippi twenty-three years ago he had a sister & brother living there then never heard from them since.
Signature- x

Account Number- 621
Name- William Colbird
Date of Application- May 25,1868
Height and Complexion- Black 29 yrs. old
Father or Mother? Married?- Hannah Colbird
Name of Children- none

Regiment and Company- Private Co. D 92nd U.S.C.T.
Place of Birth- District of Columbia on Gustson(?) Hill
Residence- corner Washington & Appollo
Occupation- Cook
Remarks- Ten years before the war he left the district. Maria & Sandy Colbird his father & mother were living there- his brother Peter Colbird was also living there.
Signature- x

Account Number- 622
Name- George Brown
Date of Application- May 25,1868
Height and Complexion- Light 32 yrs. old
Father or Mother? Married?- Malvina Brown
Name of Children- none
Regiment and Company- Private Co. A 92nd U.S.C.T.
Place of Birth- Green Co. Georgia
Residence- Pointe Coupee Parish La Van Eckel's place
Occupation- Steam boating
Remarks- His mother Lucinda he has not seen for fifteen years and supposes she is in Texas- his brother Alfred is with her.
Signature- yes

Account Number- 623
Name- Robert Smith
Date of Application- May 25,1868
Height and Complexion- Black 30 yrs. old
Father or Mother? Married?- single
Name of Children- none
Regiment and Company- Co. F 97th U.S.C.T.
Place of Birth- Green Co. North Carolina
Residence- corner Caracaloo & Poland
Occupation- Laborer
Remarks- Olive Smith his mother, Robert Smith his father- Simon & Wright Smith his brothers were living in Green Co. North Carolina when he left nine years ago.
Signature- x

Account Number- 624
Name- Jasper Johnson
Date of Application- May 26,1868
Height and Complexion- Black
Father or Mother? Married?- single
Regiment and Company- Co. E 96th U.S.C.T.
Place of Birth- Naples, Maryland
Residence- 148 Franklin St.
Occupation- Laborer
Remarks- Mother & father dead-about ten years ago when he left he had three brothers, Abraham,Henry & Levi and one sister Ellen Johnson.
Signature- does not write

Account Number- 625
Name- Thomas Leason
Date of Application- May 26,1868
Remarks- See No. 513
Signature- yes

Account Number- 626
Name- Wm. F. Lynch
Date of Application- May 27,1868

Account Number- 627
Name- Nancy Randolph
Date of Application- May 28,1868
Height and Complexion- Black
Father or Mother? Married?- single
Name of Children- no children
Place of Birth- Richmond Va
Residence-   First St. Carrollton
Occupation- Cook & Washing
Remarks- Her only child was Robert Randolph who was a soldier in Co. B 97th U.S.C.T. and this money is the bounty back pay of Robert Randolph deceased. Ellen Jackson born Newcastle Ky- age 25 yellow- husband Nat Jackson- children all dead- occupation washing- father's name Edmund Owens mother Peggy Owens dead. (later entry) Ellen Jackson dead. Jessy Pero can draw in case of death- father Paul, mother Magaritte, sister Matildie Pero age 5.
Signature- does not write

Account Number- 628
Name- Wilson Clark

Date of Application- May 28, 1868
Height and Complexion- 21 yrs. old
Father or Mother? Married?- Mary Johnson
Name of Children- none
Regiment and Company- Corporal Co. K 96th U.S.C.T.
Place of Birth- Donaldsonville La
Residence- Donaldsonville La
Occupation- House Painter
Remarks- Phebe Landry his mother lives with him- Steven Clark his father died when he was a child- Jim Clark & John Narice his brothers are also in Donaldsonville La.
Signature- yes

Account Number- 629
Name- John Baker
Date of Application- May 29, 1868
Name of Master- Works for Mr. Spencelbuy on Mr. Marshall's Place two miles above Camp Parapet
Height and Complexion- Black 29 yrs. old
Father or Mother? Married?- single
Name of Children- none
Regiment and Company- Co. C 99th U.S.C.T. Private
Place of Birth- Baltimore Md.
Residence- Short St. near Courthouse Carrollton
Occupation- Laborer
Remarks- Hannah & John Baker his father & mother were in Baltimore, Maryland when he left as a young boy- has no other relatives that he knows of.
Signature- x

Account Number- 630
Name- Laura Johnson
Date of Application- June 1, 1868
Height and Complexion- Black 27 yrs. old
Father or Mother? Married?- single
Name of Children- Jenny Jackson 1 yr. 7 mths. old
Place of Birth- Charleston S. Ca
Residence- Triton Walk at Mrs. Smith's place
Occupation- Cook & Washer woman

Remarks- Her child's father's name is John Jackson- his parents Peggy Scantling & Abraham Scantling they left Charleston about the same time Laura did, a year before the war but they were carried to Missouri with Mr. Benj. Dudon(?).

Account Number- 631
Name- James F. Mc Daniel
Date of Application- June 1, 1868
Plantation- Houma La
Height and Complexion- Black 5ft. 5 1/2 in.
Father or Mother? Married?- yes Muriel McDaniel
Place of Birth- Miss.
Residence- Houma La
Occupation- Laborer
Remarks- No check unless certified to be of the Freedman's Bureau

Account Number- 632
Name- Isaac Washington
Date of Application- June 1, 1868
Father or Mother? Married?- Isabella Washington
Name of Children- Riley Washington 7 yrs. old
Place of Birth- Carroll Co. Mo.
Residence- corner Thalia & Annunciation
Occupation- Barber
Remarks- Annie Davidson his mother lives in St. Louis Mo.- Eliza, Hannah & Margaret Jackson are in St. Louis.
Signature- x

Account Number- 633
Name- John Roberts
Date of Application- June 1, 1868
Name of Master- Had one child by name of Romeo who died when 9 days old.
Height and Complexion- Brown
Father or Mother? Married?- to Anna Kettle
Name of Children- none
Regiment and Company- Co. C Sergt. 99th U.S.C.T.
Place of Birth- Butler Co. Alabama
Residence- Thalia between Bacchus & Dryades 271

73

Occupation- Stonemason
Remarks- Raised in Wilcox Co. Alabama- no relations living known to him.
Signature- yes

Account Number- 634
Name- Madison McBride
Date of Application- June 1, 1868
Name of Master- Came from Va when 19 to N.O. then to Tuckapaw Co. lived there 5 yrs. then came back to N.O.
Height and Complexion- nearly 50 Dark Brown
Father or Mother? Married?- single (later entry) wife Patsy parents Stephen & Sally
Name of Children- two daughters
Regiment and Company- Co. H 97th U.S.C.T.
Place of Birth- Richmond Va
Residence- Algiers La
Occupation- Blacksmith
Remarks- Daughters Elmire 15 and Alzere 16- wife was sent away during the war- she is in Cincinnati- mother died before he came from Va- father in Va 60 miles from Richmond in Orange Co.- brother Marcus (dead)-sister Betsy wife of William Tolliver at Orange C.H.- sister Susan same place.
Signature- x

Account Number- 635
Name- Thomas J. Hill
Date of Application- June 2, 1868
Height and Complexion- Black
Father or Mother? Married?- single
Place of Birth- Nashville Tenn.
Residence- 141 Perdido St. between Howard & Liberty
Occupation- Laborer
Remarks- Father dead- mother's living with him named Jane Calhoun a brother Robert Robertson
Signature- yes

Account Number- 636
Name- Rosa Young
Date of Application- June 2, 1868
Height and Complexion- Black

Father or Mother? Married?- widow- parents Henry & Betsy
Name of Children- Robert
Place of Birth- across the Lake Bonforica Parish St. Tammany
Residence- Basin St. between Julia & Girod St.
Occupation- Washer woman
Remarks- Her husband Robert Young private Co. D 86th U.S.C.T. died whilst in the service- her boy is Robert- five sisters living here in this city. Father die up coast long time ago- Mother died in N.O. 2 yrs. ago- sister Mary wife of Isaac Bradford & Bagiligue wife of Chaney _____ & Margaret wife of Phillis Fishon & Katish wife of Capt. Luke Durfee.
Signature- x

Account Number- 637
Name- Sixth St. M.E. Church
Date of Application- June 2, 1868
Remarks- This money is deposited as belonging to the congregation by William C. Johnson, and is not to be drawn but by himself or Rev. Henry Green.
Signature- yes

Account Number- 638
Name- Aleck Garrison
Date of Application- June 3, 1868
Name of Master- Father's name Henry Hanson died when he was an infant mother's name Philis died before the father.
Height and Complexion- Black
Father or Mother? Married?- single
Regiment and Company- Co. D 92nd U.S.C.T. Private
Place of Birth- Parish of Iberville
Residence- Eureka's Plantation Iberville Parish
Occupation- Farming
Remarks- Father & mother dead- 2 brothers one named Harris Garrison living at the same place- the other Wilson Hanson lives in Pointe Coupee.
Signature- x

Account Number- 639

Name- D.E. Barr
Date of Application- June 3,1868
Signature- yes

Account Number- 640
Name- Wesley G. Morell
Date of Application- June 3,1868
Height and Complexion- Dark Chestnut 5ft 2 1/2 in
Father or Mother? Married?- both
Regiment and Company- Co. E 39th U.S. Infantry Private
Place of Birth- Kentess Ga Breed Phil. Pa
Residence- 1444 South Seventh St. Philadelphia Pa
Occupation- Studying or Schooler
Remarks- If I should die you will please to send my 15$ or any other amount that is due me to Sarah Bracy 1444 S. Seventh St. Phil. Pa- in garrison at Ship Island.
Signature- yes

Account Number- 641
Name- Susan O'Hare
Date of Application- June 3,1868
Father or Mother? Married?- to Patrick O'Hare
Place of Birth- Charleston S. Ca
Residence- Parish of Terrebonne La
Remarks- She knows nothing about any relation whatsoever.
Signature- does not write

Account Number- 642
Name- Richard Wilson
Date of Application- June 5,1868
Height and Complexion- 33 yrs. old
Father or Mother? Married?- Martha A. Wilson
Name of Children- John P. & Edward Lee Wilson
Regiment and Company- waited on Major Fredberg of Canby's staff
Place of Birth- Kennerville Parish of Jefferson La
Residence- 475 Rampart St.
Occupation- Porter at Dieter & Goldstein
Remarks- Mother's name Peggy Wilson- resides at Franklin St.

Signature- yes

Account Number- 643
Name- Edward Fields
Date of Application- June 6,1868
Remarks- see record No. 116

Account Number- 644
Name- Jackson Sheppard
Date of Application- June 8,1868
Height and Complexion- Black
Father or Mother? Married?- to Sarah Ann Hays
Regiment and Company- Co. H 97th Regt. U.S.C.T.
Place of Birth- St. James Parish
Residence- Common St. between Broad & White
Occupation- Sampling Cotton
Remarks- Father & mother dead- three bothers Thomas, Julien & Rubin Sheppard- one sister Rossette.
Signature- x

Account Number- 645
Name- Joe Clark
Date of Application- June 8,1868
Height and Complexion- Black
Father or Mother? Married?- to Emma
Regiment and Company- Co. I 96th U.S.C.T. Private
Place of Birth- Baltimore Md
Residence- Carrollton, Jefferson Parish
Occupation- Carpenter
Remarks- Father & mother dead- one brother Harrison Carter living in Carrollton on Washington St.
Signature- does not write

Account Number- 646
Name- Alexander Davis
Date of Application- June 9,1868
Height and Complexion- 5ft 4in. Dark Complexion
Father or Mother? Married?- Martha Stewart Davis
Name of Children- Martha Stewart 1 year 3 mths. old
Regiment and Company- Co. B 99th U.S.C.T. Private
Place of Birth- McCall's Plantation

Ascension Parish La
Residence- Howard between Thalia & Erato St.
Occupation- Whitewasher
Remarks- Mother & father dead- his brother Willis Wooden is in this city- his sister Arice Wooden is at Donaldsonville La.
Signature- x

Account Number- 647
Name- Charlotte Woods
Date of Application- June 9,1868
Father or Mother? Married?- widow of Edward Woods
Name of Children- Henry Woods 15 years old
Place of Birth- Woodford Co. Kentucky (Versailles)
Residence- Louisville Ky 10th St. between Walnut & Chestnut
Occupation- Chambermaid
Remarks- Mother's name was Susan Casmer- father's name Lewis Casmer- both dead- brother's name Merritt Casmer in Woodford Co.-sister Jemima Casmer in Lexington Ky.
Signature- x

Account Number- 648
Name- John B. Theodore
Date of Application- June 10,1868
Height and Complexion- 40 yrs. old Black
Father or Mother? Married?- single
Name of Children- Rosalie Theodore 18 yrs. old
Regiment and Company- Co. A 99th U.S.C.T.
Place of Birth-at Peter Becknell's Plantation St. John the Baptist La
Residence- at Mien Veuve's Plantation St. John the Baptist's Post Office
Occupation- Laborer
Remarks- Mother's name Rosalie Alexis lives at Mr. Peter Becknell's Plantation. His true name is John B. Alexis but when he enlisted he went in as John B. Theodore.
Signature- x

Account Number- 649
Name- William Robertson
Date of Application- June 12,1868
Height and Complexion- Black
Regiment and Company- Co. A 99th U.S.C.T.
Place of Birth- New Orleans Lake Pontchartrain
Residence- Custom House St. between Villere & Robertson
Occupation- Laborer
Remarks- Father living corner of Galvez & Perdido named Dudley Robertson- mother living with father named Sally Robertson- brother Manuel-two sisters Agnes Smith & Maria Robertson.
Signature- yes

Account Number- 650
Name- David Nash
Date of Application- June 12,1868
Height and Complexion- Black
Father or Mother? Married?- single
Regiment and Company- Co. B 99th U.S.C.T.
Place of Birth- New Orleans La
Residence- 257 Gravier St. near Basin
Occupation- Sailor
Remarks- Father dead mother living in Madisonville St. Tammany Parish named Susan Cloth, a brother named Sam Day lives with mother.
Signature- yes

Account Number- 651
Name- George Mitchell
Date of Application- June 13,1868
Height and Complexion- Black 26 yrs. old
Father or Mother? Married?- single
Name of Children- none
Regiment and Company- When in the army was mustered in as George Washington Co. F 96th U.S.C.T. Sergt. he now assumes his right name.
Place of Birth- St. Tammany Parish La
Residence- Madisonville St. Tammany Parish La
Occupation- Laborer
Remarks- Mother's name Mary Dicey is now living in St. Tammany Parish La-

brother's name Paul, sisters Jane & Louisa Mitchell are all living in St. Tammany Parish.
Signature- x

Account Number- 652
Name- Henry T. Grandpre
Date of Application- June 13,1868
Father or Mother? Married?- single
Name of Children- none
Regiment and Company- U.S.C.T.
Place of Birth- New Orleans La
Residence- 1st Street corner Howard 4th Dist.
Occupation- Teacher- Private School
Remarks- Charlotte Shelburn his mother- Theophite Grandpre his father both dead.
Signature- yes

Account Number- 653
Name- Charles Davis
Date of Application- June 15,1868
Height and Complexion- Black
Father or Mother? Married?- to Lucian Davis
Name of Children- one girl 9 yrs. old
Regiment and Company- Co. H 92nd U.S.C.T.
Place of Birth- Tallahassee Florida
Residence- Jacob & Lamon's Plantation Ascension Parish 1 mile from Donaldsonville
Occupation- Field hand
Remarks- Father named Castillo Davis lives on Richard McCall's Plantation mother named Patience lives same place- 2 sisters Rhyna lives in Carrollton La & Peggy who lives with parents.
Signature- x

Account Number- 654
Name- Harris Garrison
Date of Application- June 15,1868
Height and Complexion- Black
Father or Mother? Married?- Melly Garrison
Regiment and Company- Co. H 92nd U.S.C.T.
Place of Birth- Iberville Parish on Bayou Goula

Residence- Eureka's Plantation Iberville Parish
Occupation- Field hand
Remarks- Father & mother dead, 3 brothers, Aleck Garrison with Harris, Wilson Hennison at Point Coupee & Lorenzo Dow at Raccourci.
Signature- x

Account Number- 655
Name- Jackson Wilson
Date of Application- June 15,1868
Father or Mother? Married?- Ellen Armstead
Regiment and Company- Co. A 68th U.S.C.T.
Place of Birth- St. Louis Co. Missouri
Residence- St. Mary St. Carrollton La
Occupation- Laborer
Remarks- Parents John & Elyza Wilson, 3 brothers Charley, Isaac & Perry are all in St. Louis Missouri, a sister Mary Wilson living with parents.
Signature- x

Account Number- 656
Name- John Brooks
Date of Application- June 17,1868
Height and Complexion- Black 5ft 6in
Father or Mother? Married?- single
Name of Children- none
Regiment and Company- Co. C 99th U.S.C.T. Private
Place of Birth- Donaldsonville La
Residence- at Mr. Robert Baron's Plantation below Donaldsonville La
Occupation- Laborer
Remarks- Harriet Brooks his mother- Aleck Brooks his brother and Crecy Ann Tucker his sister all live at the same place.
Signature- x

Account Number- 657
Name- Michael Gordy
Date of Application- June 17,1868
Height and Complexion- Black
Father or Mother? Married?- Margaret
Regiment and Company- Co. A 97th U.S.C.T.
Place of Birth- St. Mary Parish La

Residence- Custus Plantation Jefferson Parish right bank
Occupation- Field Hand
Remarks- Father & mother dead- one brother Henry Butler in Gretna Jefferson Parish.
Signature- x

Account Number- 658
Name- Joseph Custis
Date of Application- June 17, 1868
Height and Complexion- Black
Father or Mother? Married?- single
Name of Children- one girl 1 month old
Regiment and Company- Co. C 92nd U.S.C.T.
Place of Birth- Woodville Miss.
Residence- Hewitt's Plantation Ascension Parish La
Occupation- Laborer
Remarks- Father & mother dead 3 sisters, Roddy Parker, Malvina, Emma 2 living at Hewitt the other at Charles Kock's Plantation Ascension Parish with a brother Berry Custis.
Signature- x

Account Number- 659
Name- Charles Barrie
Date of Application- June 17, 1868
Plantation- McCall's Assumption Parish
Height and Complexion- Black 5ft 6 1/2in
Father or Mother? Married?- Melly Barrie
Name of Children- none
Regiment and Company- Corporal Co. A 92nd U.S.C.T.
Place of Birth- on McCall's Plantation Assumption Parish
Residence- on McCall's Plantation
Occupation- Carpenter
Remarks- Julia & Charles Barrie his parents live with him. Carris Barrie his brother and six sisters are with him.
Signature- x

Account Number- 660
Name- Levins Steward
Date of Application- June 20, 1868
Height and Complexion- Black
Father or Mother? Married?- single
Regiment and Company- Co. H 92nd U.S.C.T.
Place of Birth- Ascension Parish
Residence- Home Place Ascension Parish
Occupation- Field Hand
Remarks- Father dead- mother named Holday Briscoe- sister Margaret Steward both live on Home Place.
Signature- x

Account Number- 661
Name- Cornelius Bright
Date of Application- June 20, 1868
Height and Complexion- Light
Father or Mother? Married?- to Alice Fontenett
Name of Children- 1 girl 1 year old
Place of Birth- Norfolk Va
Residence- Washington Ave. & Girod St. 3rd Dist.
Occupation- Bricklayer
Remarks- Father & mother dead- brother George Mallony living in St. Martinserle Attakapas. July 7, 1868 Cornelius Bright gives authorization to his wife to draw whatever money he has as a balance.
Signature- x

Account Number- 662
Name- Hannah Walker
Date of Application- June 22, 1868
Father or Mother? Married?- Lewis Walker
Name of Children- none
Place of Birth- Yazoo City Miss.
Residence- Sixth St. corner Dryades
Occupation- Washer woman
Remarks- This money was given to Hannah Walker by her aunt Annie Bell. Father & mother dead- sisters Mary Bawley & Rhody Glover are living on Beelake Plantation in Yazoo Co. Miss.
Signature- x

Account Number- 663
Name- Isaac Hyatt
Date of Application- June 22, 1868
Height and Complexion- 8 yrs. old
Father or Mother? Married?- Mother's name Sarah Hooker- Father's name Dick Hyatt

Place of Birth- New Orleans La
Residence- Sixth St. corner Dryades
Occupation- School Boy
Remarks- This deposit was made for his a/c by his aunt Annie Bell.

Account Number- 664
Name- Charles Galley
Date of Application- June 22, 1868
Height and Complexion- Black 27 years old
Father or Mother? Married?- Emmeline Washington Galley
Name of Children- William Galley 6 months old
Regiment and Company- Co. E 99th U.S.C.T. Corporal
Place of Birth- St. John the Baptist Parish La
Residence- corner of Annunciation & Erato St.
Occupation- Carpenter
Remarks- Nelly Thomas his mother lives on Erato St. between Magazine & Camp- father is dead- Adeline & Emilia Galley his sisters are living with their mother.
Signature- yes

Account Number- 665
Name- Alexander Robinson
Date of Application- June 24, 1868
Father or Mother? Married?- widow (later entry) married Jan. 4, 1871 to Harriet Champ
Place of Birth- Baltimore Md
Residence- 441 Josephine St.
Occupation- Cotton Weigher
Remarks- Had a little girl, Nelly Ann was kidnapped some two years ago does not know where she is. Spencer Alexander is authorized to draw the same only in case of death which he must give proof. Spencer Alexander lives on Fourth St. between St. Dennis & St. Patrick. Wife can draw.
Signature- yes

Account Number- 666
Name- Albert Malard
Date of Application- June 24, 1868
Height and Complexion- Light

Father or Mother? Married?- to Mary Coralie Couvestie(?)
Name of Children- Laura 2mths. old
Place of Birth- New Orleans La
Residence- 134 St. Peter St.
Occupation- Jeweler
Remarks- Father & mother dead- 3 sisters Ernestine, Angelina, Alice & 3 brothers Arthur, Ernest, Fracois all living in Mexico.
Signature- yes

Account Number- 667
Name- Frederick Green
Date of Application- June 24, 1868
Height and Complexion- Black
Father or Mother? Married?- single
Name of Children- 1 boy 2 months old
Regiment and Company- Co. I 92nd U.S.C.T.
Place of Birth- St. Mary Parish La
Residence- corner of Monroe & Berger St. Algiers La
Occupation- Laborer
Remarks- Father living same place named Lange Green- mother Mary Green- seven brothers Thomas, Henry, Daniel, Alexander, Sam, Joseph, Celestin- 2 sisters Lizzie & Celestine.
Signature- x

Account Number- 668
Name- John Edmond
Date of Application- June 25, 1868
Father or Mother? Married?- to Charlotte Maurey
Name of Children- 2 girls
Regiment and Company- Co. B 6th La. Vols.
Place of Birth- New Orleans La
Residence- Barracks St. between Bourbon & Dauphine No. 93
Occupation- Carpenter
Remarks- Father dead, mother living with him named Laurence- children Mary Lorenza 3 yrs. old & Julia 13 yrs. old.
Signature- x

Account Number- 669
Name- Field Williams
Date of Application- June 30, 1868

Name of Master- Father's name Philus Williams died in Ft. Adams Miss. when Field was a small boy- mother's name Charlotte died at Ft. Adams Miss.
Height and Complexion- Black
Father or Mother? Married?- to Vina
Name of Children- 1 boy about 4 yrs. old named Philus (later entry) Washington
Place of Birth- Natchez Miss.
Residence- Marcelin Peyrous Plantation St. John the Baptist Parish
Occupation- Cooper
Remarks- Has no other relations living known to him- has a half brother by the name of Abraham Dyer does not know where he is. (later entry) Since he first deposited he found two of his daughters Celeste and Celie Williams both in Ft. Adams Miss.
Signature- x

Account Number- 670
Name- Mirtile Auguste
Date of Application- July 1, 1868
Father or Mother? Married?- single
Place of Birth- New Orleans La
Residence- 381 Love St. between Columbus & St. Anthony
Occupation- Collector- Brokers
Remarks- Father, Francois Auguste living on Burgundy St. near Barracks- mother dead- one brother Laurent Auguste- one sister Hermina Auguste.
Signature- yes

Account Number- 671
Name- Nathan Goodman
Date of Application- July 1, 1868
Name of Master- (later entry) Left N.C. in 1862- came here in 1863
Height and Complexion- about 23 Brown
Father or Mother? Married?- single (later entry) wife Molly Smith parents James Rook & Emmy
Regiment and Company- Co. C 2nd U.S.C.T.
Place of Birth- Chewoane Co. North Carolina
Residence- at Headquaters B.R.F. & A.L.
Occupation- Soldier

Remarks- He is now in Co. E 39th on detached service at Headquaters B.R.F. & A.L.- mother died in N.C. about 3 yrs. ago- father living in Gates Co. North Ca named James- brother Bolin - half sister Sarah Brinkley both in Hampton Va- brother Quentan (dead).
Signature- yes

Account Number- 672
Name- R.K. Diossy
Date of Application- July 2, 1868
Height and Complexion- White
Father or Mother? Married?- to Sarah E. Diossy
Name of Children- Eva
Place of Birth- New York
Residence- 205 St. Joseph St.
Occupation- Preacher
Signature- yes

Account Number- 673
Name- Abram Williams
Date of Application- July 3, 1868
Height and Complexion- Black 5ft 8in 30 yrs. old
Father or Mother? Married?- Charlotte Williams
Name of Children- had 3 children all dead
Regiment and Company- Corporal Co. G 92nd U.S.C.T.
Place of Birth- Iberville Parish John Gallix Plantation
Residence- Eureka Plantation Iberville Parish
Occupation- Laborer
Remarks- Parents Charles & Sallie Williams both dead- sister Martha Williams lives with him on Eureka Plantation.
Signature- x

Account Number- 674
Name- Stephen Coates
Date of Application- July 3, 1868
Height and Complexion- Black
Father or Mother? Married?- to Angeline Coates
Name of Children- 2 children 1 boy 1 girl
Regiment and Company- Co. I 92nd U.S.C.T.

Place of Birth- Yazoo Co. Miss.
Residence- 170 Tchoupitoulas St. between Julia & St. Joseph
Occupation- Waiter
Remarks- Mother dead- father he has not seen for five years does not know where he is- has brothers & sisters but doesn't know where they are.
Signature- yes

Account Number- 675
Name- Henry Mitchell
Date of Application- July 7,1868
Father or Mother? Married?- to Pelagie Marie
Regiment and Company- Co. D 99th U.S.C.T.
Place of Birth- New Orleans La
Residence- corner Columbus & Roman St.
Occupation- Porter in Cotton Brokers Office
Remarks- Father dead- mother, Pauline living on St. Philip between Robertson & Villere- 1 brother Alfred Paillerse- 3 sisters Syvanie, Aspasie & Celeste.
Signature- x

Account Number- 676
Name- Moses Briggs
Date of Application- July 8,1868
Remarks- see descriptive list No. 556

Account Number- 677
Name- Virginia Sanders
Date of Application- July 8,1868
Father or Mother? Married?- single
Place of Birth- Bird Spring Mountain Co. Va
Residence- at Marines Hospital Common St.
Occupation- "Nurse"
Remarks- Mother, Nancy Sanders when last of was in Va no brothers or sisters known to her- July 9, 1869 now lives on Magazine between Julia & St. Joseph mother is in Washington D.C.
Signature- x

Account Number- 678
Name- Charles W. Hays
Date of Application- July 9,1868
Height and Complexion- White
Father or Mother? Married?- single
Place of Birth- Hanover Germany
Residence- 39 Gasquet St.
Occupation- Clerk
Remarks- Father dead- mother, Margaret- 3 sisters Anna, Getchie, Rebecca all living in Germany.
Signature- yes

Account Number- 679
Name- William Cobb
Date of Application- July 11,1868
Height and Complexion- Black
Father or Mother? Married?- to Mary Cobb
Regiment and Company- Co. C 84th U.S.C.T. Sergt.
Place of Birth- Kingston, North Carolina
Residence- corner of Fourth & Dryades St.
Occupation- Carpenter
Remarks- Father dead- left mother in N.C. about 10 years ago doesn't know if she is living. Left 2 brothers also Daniel & Henry Cobb.
Signature- yes

Account Number- 680
Name- Joseph Stevenson
Date of Application- July 11,1868
Name of Master- Was raised in Logan Co. Ky came to N.O. about 20 years ago.
Height and Complexion- Black 70
Father or Mother? Married?- to Daphne parents Wilby & Christina
Place of Birth- Davidson Co. Tenn
Residence- Palmyra St. below Broad
Occupation- Drayman
Remarks- Father & mother dead- no brothers or sisters that he knows of. Has a brother in law Andrew Davis on Palmyra St. below Broad (later entry) never saw his father- mother left him in Davidson Co. Tenn. had a sister taken away with his mother when he was 10 years old.
Signature- x

Account Number- 681
Name- Benjamin Davis

Date of Application- July 13,1868
Name of Master- Born in King William Co. raised same place- father named Davis died 5 yrs ago in Va.
Height and Complexion- Black
Father or Mother? Married?- single
Regiment and Company- Co. B 39th U.S.C.T. formerly Co. K 36th U.S.C.T.
Place of Birth- King William Co. Va
Residence- Ship Island with his 39th Regt. Co. B
Occupation- Soldier
Remarks- Father & mother dead mother's name Milly died 4 years ago in Va- Apr. 27, 1869 he now belongs to the 25th U.S.I. Co. G Private.
Signature- x

Account Number- 682
Name- George Windsor
Date of Application- July 15,1868
Height and Complexion- Black
Father or Mother? Married?- single
Regiment and Company- Co. A 96th U.S.C.T.
Place of Birth- Richmond Va
Residence- Felicity Rd. between Clara & Willow St.
Occupation- Laborer
Remarks- Father & mother dead has no relations know to him.
Signature- x

Account Number- 683
Name- William Lackey and his wife Jane Lackey
Date of Application- July 16,1868
Height and Complexion- Light 31 years old
Father or Mother? Married?- Jane Lackey
Name of Children- none
Place of Birth- Alexandria La
Residence- 369 Carondelet St.
Occupation- Laborer
Remarks- No father nor mother- 18 years ago his sister Rosina Brooks was living at Alexandria La does not know where she is now.
Signature- x

Account Number- 684
Name- Addison Carter
Date of Application- July 14,1868
Height and Complexion- Yellow
Father or Mother? Married?- single
Regiment and Company- Co. I 1st. U.S.C.T.
Place of Birth- Northumberland Co. Va
Residence- St. James Parish on Francois Roelies(?) Plantation
Occupation- Farming
Remarks- Father dead- mother, Juddy Carter living in Washington D.C.- one brother Malchior Carter lives there too- four sisters, Charlotte, Manda, Esther & Delphine Carter.
Signature- yes

Account Number- 685
Name- William Jones
Date of Application- July 17,1868
Height and Complexion- Black 5ft 4 1/2in
Father or Mother? Married?- to Susanne
Name of Children- Susanne 1 1/2 yrs. old
Regiment and Company- Co. B 92nd U.S.C.T.
Place of Birth- Savannah Georgia
Residence- Goodchildren between Marigny & Elysian Field
Occupation- Laborer
Remarks- Father & mother dead- no relation known to him living
Signature- x

Account Number- 686
Name- John Lewis
Date of Application- July 17,1868
Height and Complexion- Black 5ft 8in
Father or Mother? Married?- single
Regiment and Company- Corporal Co. C 96th U.S.C.T.
Place of Birth- Camp Parapet near Carrollton La Jefferson Parish
Residence- Carrollton Jefferson Parish
Occupation- Farming
Remarks- Father dead- mother Lucy Jackson lives in N.O. on corner Marigny & Moreau St. 3rd. Dist.- 3 sisters, Josephine, Clarice & Phroline all living with mother- no brothers all dead.

Signature- x

Account Number- 687
Name- Charles H. Hailey
Date of Application- July 18, 1868
Name of Master- Lived in Nashville 5 or 6 years- to Natchez Miss. then to N.O.- Sent here as a present in Fall of 1856.
Height and Complexion- about 32 Light
Father or Mother? Married?- Eulalie Hailey parents Henry & Silvy
Name of Children- Charles (dead)
Place of Birth- Virginia
Residence- Ursulines St. 120
Occupation- News dealer on Steamboat Tom Jasper
Remarks- Never saw father- Sylvy Hailey his mother was in Murray Co. Tenn. 17 or 18 years ago. Does not now if his mother is living or not.
Signature- yes

Account Number- 688
Name- Curtis Benford
Date of Application- July 18,1868
Height and Complexion- Black 37 years old
Father or Mother? Married?- single
Place of Birth- on Chattahoochie River Dekalb Co. Ga.
Residence- corner Lafayette & Miro
Occupation- Gardener
Remarks- His parents Jemima & Phed Benford were living 18 yrs. ago- Jemima in Gordon Co.- does not know where his father is- Clark Benford his brother is in the city.
Signature- x

Account Number- 690
Name- Henry Adams
Date of Application- July 20,1868
Plantation- born at Mrs. Jane Ferguson's
Height and Complexion- Black 45 yrs. old
Father or Mother? Married?- Elizabeth Adams
Name of Children- none
Place of Birth- Mrs. Jane Ferguson's Plantation Adams Co. Miss.

Residence- 243 Thalia between Bacchus & Appollo
Occupation- Fire Hand at the Gasworks
Remarks- Father died in 1856 in Miss.- mother died in 1860 in Miss.- Alexander Adams, his brother lives in Jefferson Co. Miss. May 25 1869- he now resides corner Magazine & Gaienne over Mr. Thos. Hailey's store.
Signature- x

Account Number- 689
Name- Evaline Taylor
Date of Application- July 18,1868
Name of Master- I.V.
Height and Complexion- Light
Father or Mother? Married?- Henry Taylor died about 7 years ago
Name of Children- George Franklin 19 yrs. old
Place of Birth- Hinds Co. Miss
Residence- Union between Philippa & Baronne
Occupation- Cooking, Washing & Ironing
Remarks- Jim Byass in Vicksburg is her father- mother Barbain Byass in Vicksburg- brother Alfred Anderson in Hinds Co.- May 19, 1869 Eveline resides now on Frenchman St. between Love & Craps 3rd. Dist.
Signature- x

Account Number- 691
Name- Green Slaughter
Date of Application- July 20,1868
Height and Complexion- Black
Father or Mother? Married?- to Catherine Jackson
Name of Children- 2 girl 1 boy
Regiment and Company- I Co. 92nd U.S.C.T.
Place of Birth- Jasper Co. Georgia
Residence- Parish St. James on Alexis Ferrier Plantation
Occupation- Field hand
Remarks- Father dead- left mother in Georgia in 1859- doesn't know if she is living- also left sisters Lucy & Mary and brother Daniel.
Signature- yes

83

Account Number- 692
Name- Thomas County
Date of Application- July 20, 1868
Height and Complexion- Black 33 yrs. old
Father or Mother? Married?- Celina County
Name of Children- Lucy, George & Emma County
Regiment and Company- Private Co. D 70th U.S.C.T.
Place of Birth- Maryland (doesn't know where)
Residence- Algiers La, Second St. close to Peters St.
Occupation- Laborer on Canal St. Ferry
Remarks- Pox Marked- Harry County his father resides in Alexandria La- mother dead- brother Frederic County & sister Betsy County living with father on Dr. Clark's Plantation 4 miles above Alexandria La. Special Deposit No. 7.
Signature- yes

Account Number- 693
Name- Ephraim Maherty
Date of Application- July 20, 1868
Height and Complexion- Black
Father or Mother? Married?- to Mathilda
Name of Children- Elina 5 months old
Regiment and Company- Co. D 92nd U.S.C.T.
Place of Birth- Florence, Franklin Co. Ala.
Residence- Magnolia's Plantation Parish St. James
Occupation- Farming
Remarks- Parents Ben Maherty & America Bill living in St. James Parish- sisters Minerva, Melly, Carolina & Parelly.
Signature- x

Account Number- 694
Name- Tony Smith
Date of Application- July 20, 1868
Height and Complexion- Black 30 yrs. old
Father or Mother? Married?- Patience Smith
Name of Children- Adam, Lincoln &

Emberly Smith
Regiment and Company- Corporal Co. D 99th U.S.C.T.
Place of Birth- St. John the Baptist Parish
Residence- Hope Plantation St. John the Baptist Parish
Occupation- Laborer
Remarks- Parents Anthony & Melinda Smith- brothers Thomas & Moses Smith and sister Mary Smith all live on the same plantation he does.
Signature- yes

Account Number- 695
Remarks- See No. 527

Account Number- 696
Name- Mrs. Zelphire Edwards
Date of Application- July 23, 1868
Father or Mother? Married?- widow
Name of Children- 2 boys 2 girls
Place of Birth- St. Martinsville Parish St. Martin
Residence- New St. Bernard No. 51 3rd Dist.
Occupation- Washer woman
Remarks- This money is deposited by her son William Edwards- he can draw.
Signature- William Edwards

Account Number- 697
Name- Stephen Humphrey
Date of Application- July 23, 1868
Height and Complexion- Black
Father or Mother? Married?- to Susan
Name of Children- 3 girls-Daphne, Era & Mary
Regiment and Company- U.S.C.T.
Place of Birth- Prince George Co. Md
Residence- Mansfield Desoto Parish
Occupation- Member of Legislature - House of Representatives
Remarks- Mother dead does not know if his father is living or not hasn't seen him for 19 years.
Signature- yes

Account Number- 698
Name- Isaac A. Abbott
Date of Application- July 23, 1868

Height and Complexion- White 25 years old
Father or Mother? Married?- single
Regiment and Company- Ensign U.S.N. on Glasgow
Place of Birth- Provincetown Mass.
Residence- Vidalia La
Occupation- Member of State Legislature
Remarks- His parents Francis & Melinda Abbott reside in Provincetown Mass.
Signature- yes

Account Number- 699
Name- Milton Morris
Date of Application- July 24,1868
Height and Complexion- Black
Father or Mother? Married?- Lucy Ann Richardson
Place of Birth- Howard Co. Missouri
Residence- Donaldsonville La
Occupation- Member House Of Rep. Legislature 1868
Signature- yes

Account Number- 700
Name- Julia Foley
Date of Application- July 25,1868
Height and Complexion- White
Father or Mother? Married?- widow
Place of Birth- New Orleans La
Residence- 103 St. John St.
Remarks- Father & mother dead- 1 brother John. Stepbrother.
Signature- yes

Account Number- 701
Name- George H. Ziegler
Date of Application- July 28,1868
Height and Complexion- White
Father or Mother? Married?- single
Regiment and Company- 43rd Infantry 1st. Lieut.
Place of Birth- Philadelphia Penn.
Residence- 230 St. Charles
Occupation- U.S.A.
Remarks- Father & Mother dead- brother George K. Ziegler President Bank of Commerce Philadelphia.
Signature- yes

Account Number- 702
Name- Johnson Reed
Date of Application- July 29,1868
Father or Mother? Married?- to Maria Reed
Name of Children- Elyzabeth 8yrs. old
Place of Birth- Burtee Co. N. Ca
Residence- Girod St. between Bagatelle & St. Anthony St. 3rd. Dist.
Occupation- Minister
Signature- yes

Account Number- 703
Name- Abner Hill
Date of Application- July 31,1868
Father or Mother? Married?- single
Name of Children- Joe Hill 4 yrs. old
Regiment and Company- Co. G 96th U.S.C.T.
Place of Birth- Ascension Parish
Residence- 234 Girod St. corner Dryades
Occupation- Servant
Remarks- Father & mother dead- brothers Yosty(?), Arron, Adam Harris & Anderson Brant
Signature- yes

Account Number- 70
Name- George Green
Date of Application- Aug. 4,1868
Height and Complexion- Light 32 yrs. old
Father or Mother? Married?- Margaret Robertson
Name of Children- none
Place of Birth- New Orleans La
Residence- Clara between Hevin & Poydras
Occupation- Drayman
Remarks- Mother's name Diana Braxton lives with him- sister Louisa Blye- May pay to his wife on presentation of book.
Signature- x

Account Number- 705
Name- George Moore
Date of Application- Aug. 4,1868
Height and Complexion- Black
Father or Mother? Married?- single
Regiment and Company- Co. B 36th U.S.C.T.

Place of Birth- Carter Co. N. Carolina
Residence- Appollo St. Between St. Mary & Felicity Rd.
Occupation- Laborer
Remarks- Father & mother dead- sister in N. Ca named Roddy.
Signature- x

Account Number- 706
Name- Peter Carter
Date of Application- Aug. 5,1868
Height and Complexion- Black 31 yrs. old
Father or Mother? Married?- single
Regiment and Company- Co. H 4th Hvy. Arty. U.S.A. Colored
Place of Birth- Dixon Co. Tenn.
Residence- Marine Hospital
Occupation- Engineer
Remarks- Parents Peter & Mathilda both dead. Mellie & John Carter his brother & sister are both living near Bowlery Green, little place near Clarksville Tenn, 50 miles from Nashville- Stewart Co.- In case of death wishes his sister Mellie to get what money he may have on deposit.
Signature- x

Account Number- 707
Name- John Lord
Date of Application- Aug. 5,1868
Height and Complexion- Black 28 yrs. old
Father or Mother? Married?- Rosalie Lord
Name of Children- Francis (Frank) 6 yrs. old, Jenny, Rose & Milly
Regiment and Company- Co. K 92nd U.S.C.T.
Place of Birth- Washington City D.C.
Residence- Widow Tareaud's Plantation St. James Parish
Occupation- Laborer
Remarks- Brother & sister Frank & Sarah Lord.
Signature- x

Account Number- 708
Name- Benjamin Brown
Date of Application- Aug. 5,1868
Height and Complexion- Black
Father or Mother? Married?- single
Name of Children- Henry Jackson 9 yrs. old
Regiment and Company- Co. K 84th U.S.C.T.
Place of Birth- Baton Rouge La
Residence- Carrollton, Jefferson Parish
Occupation- Gardener
Remarks- Father & mother dead- two brothers Joseph & Edward- one sister Poiner all living in Baton Rouge. B. Brown is going to marry Margaret Hatchet- and directs that whenever she presents his book what money she asks be paid to her, as she asks.
Signature- x

Account Number- 709
Name- Joseph Dever
Date of Application- Aug. 5,1868
Height and Complexion- Brick Red
Father or Mother? Married?- single
Regiment and Company- Co. K 84th U.S.C.T.
Place of Birth- West Baton Rouge
Residence- Corner Mandeville & Craps St.
Occupation- Laborer
Remarks- Father, Nathaniel Dever & mother, Jennie are living in West Baton Rouge- no brothers or sisters.
Signature- x

Account Number- 710
Name- Edmund Button
Date of Application- Aug. 5,1868
Height and Complexion- Black
Father or Mother? Married?- single
Name of Children- none
Regiment and Company- Private Co. A 97th U.S.C.T.
Place of Birth- King & Queen Co. Va
Residence- corner Fourth & Shaw Carrollton
Occupation- Laborer
Remarks- 13 years ago he left his parents Davy & Lucy Badrop in King & Queen Co. Va- has a brother somewhere in Texas by the name of Randall Taliaferro.
Signature- x

Account Number- 711
Name- Mrs. Angele Celestin
Date of Application- Aug. 6,1868
Place of Birth- New Orleans La
Residence- 287 Marias St. (old number)
Occupation- Houskeeper
Remarks- This money was deposited by Jos. L. Londe.
Signature- does not write

Account Number- 712
Name- Revd. J.P. Newman
Date of Application- Aug. 7,1868

Account Number- 713
Name- Thomas Hunter
Date of Application- Aug. 7,1868
Height and Complexion- Colored Black eyes 5ft 7in
Regiment and Company- Private Co. C 20th U.S.C.T.
Place of Birth- Abbeville Dist. South Ca.
Residence- 453 Gravier
Occupation- Blacksmith
Remarks- No relatives whatever living to his knowledge.
Signature- x

Account Number- 714
Name- John Williams
Date of Application- Aug. 7,1868
Height and Complexion- Black 52 yrs. old
Father or Mother? Married?- Mellie Williams
Name of Children- none
Regiment and Company- Private Co. H 97th U.S.C.T.
Place of Birth- Culpepper Va
Residence- 118 Johnson St.
Occupation- Deckhand on a River Steamboat
Remarks- Has no relatives living is entirely alone in this world
Signature- x

Account Number- 715
Name- Thomas Burns
Date of Application- Aug. 7,1868
Height and Complexion- Black 5ft 5in Black eyes

Father or Mother? Married?- Jane Burns
Name of Children- none
Regiment and Company- Private Co. F 84th U.S.C.T.
Place of Birth- Richmond Va
Residence- Houma Parish of Terrebonne La
Occupation- Farmer- Laborer
Remarks- Robert, Julia Ann & Sara Burns his brother and sisters were left by him in Richmond Va, 20 yrs. ago.
Signature- x

Account Number- 716
Name- Arthur Wilson
Date of Application- Aug. 7,1868
Father or Mother? Married?- single
Regiment and Company- Co. F 84th U.S.C.T.
Place of Birth- St. James Parish La
Residence- 287 Delord St. N.O.
Occupation- works in a Distillery
Remarks- Parents living on Delord St. named Arthur & Charlotte Bentson- 3 sisters, Milly, Charlotte & Sylvania- 1 brother, John.
Signature- x

Account Number- 717
Name- Claiborn Cannon
Date of Application- Aug. 8,1868
Height and Complexion- Black
Father or Mother? Married?- Emilia
Name of Children- Mary Jane 1 8/12 yrs. old
Regiment and Company- Sergt. Co, B 92nd U.S.C.T.
Place of Birth- Marksville Avoyelles Parish La
Residence- Fishers Landing Pointe Coupee
Occupation- Laborer
Remarks- Fathers name Isaac Burns & mother Martha Burns both dead- no sisters or brothers- no other living relatives. Jan. 3, 1870- has a boy Steven now 9 months old.
Signature- yes

Account Number- 718
Name- William Finney

Date of Application- Aug. 10,1868
Height and Complexion- 56 yrs. old
Father or Mother? Married?- Louisa Finney
Name of Children- Hortense & Camille Finney
Place of Birth- Richmond Va
Residence- Custom House St. No. 190
Occupation- School Teacher
Remarks- Has a brother Armstead Finney- no other relatives that he knows of.
Signature- yes

Account Number- 719
Name- James Bennett
Date of Application- Aug. 10,1868
Plantation- Eureka Plantation
Height and Complexion- 26 yrs. old Black
Father or Mother? Married?- Jane Brooks
Name of Children- none
Regiment and Company- Private Co. H 92nd U.S.C.T.
Place of Birth- East Feliciana La
Residence- Bayou Gonlas Iberville Parish La
Occupation- Laborer
Remarks- Charley, Ben & Lively Bennett are his children by his first wife Ellen Bennett- all together he had ten children from Ellen, five died.
Signature- x

Account Number- 720
Name- Nathan James / Nathaniel Bonaparte
Date of Application- Aug. 12,1868
Name of Master- Left Tenn. when 6 yrs. old & went to Holmes Co. Miss- there 5 yrs. then to Bayou Lafourche La- came to N.O. in Nov. 1862
Height and Complexion- Bright Colored
Father or Mother? Married?- parents Jacob & Eliza- wife Sarah Jane Riley
Name of Children- Jacob 6 months old
Regiment and Company- Co. D 75th U.S.C.T.
Place of Birth- Rutherford Co. Tenn.
Residence- Bagatelle corner Gaienne 3rd Dist.
Occupation- Carpenter
Remarks- Father & mother, Jacob & Eliza James living with him- 3 brothers Alfred, Burrell in city & Frank missionary in Lafourche- sister Harriet E. Halloway dead. His wife authorized to draw.
Signature- yes

Account Number- 721
Name- Walter Todd
Date of Application- Aug. 14,1868
Height and Complexion- Black
Father or Mother? Married?- single
Regiment and Company- Co. A 10th U.S.C.T.
Place of Birth- Brashear City La
Residence- Gretna, Jefferson Parish
Occupation- laborer
Remarks- Father dead- mother Prescilla Todd lives in Brashear City- 1 sister, Elyzabeth- 1 brother, Thomas Todd
Signature- x

Account Number- 722
Name- James H. Johnson
Date of Application- Aug. 15,1868
Father or Mother? Married?- single
Regiment and Company- Co. B 39th U.S.I.
Place of Birth- Washington D.C.
Signature- does not write

Account Number- 723
Name- William Porter
Date of Application- Aug. 15,1868
Father or Mother? Married?- single
Regiment and Company- U.S.N. Steamer Tennessee
Place of Birth- Newark New Jersey
Residence- 243 Thalia St. between Appollo & Bacchus
Occupation- Police Officer
Remarks- Father dead- mother , Becky was living when he last heard of about 3 years ago.
Signature- yes

Account Number- 724
Name- Mrs. Julia Ann Brown
Date of Application- Aug. 17,1868

Father or Mother? Married?- Alexander Brown
Name of Children- Daniel Lewis 6 yrs. old
Place of Birth- Richmond Va
Residence- Lafayette corner Locust
Occupation- Keeping house
Remarks- Father, A.W. Lewis- mother, Judy Lewis- has a brother Edwin W. Lewis in Richmond Va.
Signature- yes

Account Number- 725
Name- Joseph Gustaff
Date of Application- Aug. 17,1868
Father or Mother? Married?- to Mary Pitchen
Name of Children- Joseph, 4 years old
Regiment and Company- Co. C 92nd U.S.C.T.
Place of Birth- Opelousas, Parish St. Landry
Residence- 3 miles from Barry's Landing Opelousas
Occupation- Farming
Remarks- Father dead, mother,Clementine Jones living in Opelousas- brother Joseph Laud.
Signature- x

Account Number- 726
Name- Hatcher Ferguson
Date of Application- Aug. 17,1868
Height and Complexion- Black
Father or Mother? Married?- single
Regiment and Company- Co. A 10th Heavy Arty.
Place of Birth- Charleston S.Ca
Residence- St. Thomas St. corner Bracy Alley
Occupation- Cooper
Remarks- Father dead, mother Melinda was living in Charleston when he left 15 yrs. ago.
Signature- x

Account Number- 727
Name- Solomon R. Moses
Date of Application- Aug. 18,1868
Remarks- See descriptive list No. 328
Signature- yes

Account Number- 728
Name- Joe Davis
Date of Application- Aug. 18,1868
Father or Mother? Married?- single
Father John died when he was a small boy- mother Nelly died in Va when he was very young.
Place of Birth- King & Queen City Va
Residence- corner Hospital & Gallatin St.
Occupation- Laborer
Remarks- Parents dead- no other relations known to him. Brothers John & Moses and sisters Martha & Milly were in Va 25 years ago when he left.
Signature- does not write

Account Number- 730
Name- Benjamin Lewis
Date of Application- Aug. 27,1868
Father or Mother? Married?- Rosetta
Regiment and Company- Co. E 68th Missouri
Place of Birth- Montgomery Co. Ky
Residence- 272 Poydras between Basin & Franklin
Occupation- Steam boating
Remarks- Parents Carolina & Edmond were living in Ky about 3 years ago when he last heard- sisters Sarah Adeline & Mary. His wife Rosetta is authorized by him to draw with this book money that may be here to his credit.
Signature- x

Account Number- 731
Name- Sydney Byrd
Date of Application- Sept. 2,1868
Father or Mother? Married?- single
Place of Birth- Columbus Miss.
Residence- Common between Carondelet & Baronne
Occupation- Steward at Hawkins Saloon
Remarks- Lucy Byrd his mother lives at Columbus, Miss.- father John Byrd is in Jackson Miss.- sisters Louisa Topp, Elizabeth & Victoria Byrd all in Columbus, Miss.
Signature- yes

Account Number- 732

Name- Jordan Summer
Date of Application- Sept. 3,1868
Height and Complexion- Black
Father or Mother? Married?- single
Regiment and Company- U.S.N.S. Calhoun
Place of Birth- Perry Co. Miss.
Residence- corner St. Joseph & St. Charles
Occupation- waiter on U.S. Officer
Remarks- Parents Ralph & Elzie Summer- brothers Orton, Pleasant, Tom, Ephraim & Peter- hasn't heard from them since seven years ago. He left some in Perry Co., Jasper Co., & Clark Miss.
Signature- x

Account Number- 733
Name- John Benjamin Esnard
Date of Application- Sept. 4,1868
Regiment and Company- 5th La 60 day Regt.
Place of Birth- New Orleans La
Residence- Jeannerette St. Mary's Parish
Occupation- Member of the Legislature
Remarks- The first deposit was made by T. Esnard, his brother.
Signature- yes

Account Number- 734
Name- Benjamin Dyer
Date of Application- Sept. 4,1868
Father or Mother? Married?- single
Regiment and Company- Co. K 99th U.S.C.T.
Place of Birth- New Orleans La
Residence- Mt. Houma Plantation Ascension Parish
Occupation- Farming
Remarks- Father dead- mother, Ellen Dyer living at the same place with him.
Signature- yes

Account Number- 735
Name- Richard H. Taylor
Date of Application- Sept. 4,1868
Father or Mother? Married?- single
Regiment and Company- Co. A 39th U.S.I. late Co. A 2nd U.S.C.T.
Place of Birth- King & Queen City, Va
Residence- Detached Services Head Quarters in N.O.
Occupation- Soldier Co. A 39th U.S.I.
Remarks- Parents Humphrey & Polly (?) Taylor both living in Richmond Va.
Signature- yes

Account Number- 736
Name- Allen Harris
Date of Application- Sept. 5,1868
Name of Master- Lost his right arm at Liverpool Height Miss.
Height and Complexion- Black
Father or Mother? Married?- Margaret Harris
Regiment and Company- Co. K 47th U.S.C.T. Private
Place of Birth- Williamsburg, Va
Residence- Corner Love & Frenchman No. 128
Occupation- Carpenter
Remarks- (written in later) wife Louisa Harris can draw with book- Mother's name Sarah Harris- Father's name Abbinter Harris left them in 1849 at Goodrich's Landing La.- never heard of them since. Whenever Mary Ann Gibbs will present the book- the sum of ten dollars may be paid to her each time.
Signature- yes

Account Number- 737
Name- Lewis Hancock
Date of Application- Sept. 7,1868
Height and Complexion- Black
Father or Mother? Married?- single
Name of Children- 1 boy 2 years old Alfred Daniel Hancock
Regiment and Company- U.S.N.S. Kennebec
Place of Birth- Lynchburg Va
Residence- Felicity Rd, corner of Willow
Occupation- Steward
Remarks- Father named Lewis Hancock living in Alexandria Va- mother dead, 1 brother named George W. Hancock living also in Alexandria Va- in case of death the money is to go to Alfred Daniel Hancock my son.
Signature- yes

Account Number- 738
Name- Clara Kilgore
Date of Application- Sept. 7, 1868
Place of Birth- New Orleans La
Residence- 205 Baronne St. between Julia & Girod
Occupation- Sell Coffee
Remarks- money deposited by Rachel Bradley

Account Number- 739
Name- John Battice
Date of Application- Sept. 7, 1868
Height and Complexion- Black about 60 years old
Father or Mother? Married?- Marie Agnes
Name of Children- Augustin, Rafael & Adele Battice
Regiment and Company- U.S.C.T. 96th E Co.
Place of Birth- Bonner Carre La
Residence- Home Place Plantation St. James Parish La
Occupation- Laborer
Remarks- He works on Home Place with W. Valerien Choppin in the Parish of St. James- If his son Augustin presents his pass book he is authorized to draw by me.
Signature- x

Account Number- 740
Name- Caleb Jones
Date of Application- Sept. 7, 1868
Height and Complexion- Black about 51 years old
Father or Mother? Married?- Becky Jones
Regiment and Company- U.S.C.T. 96th Private Co. D
Place of Birth- Eastern Shore Maryland
Residence- 160 Franklin St. between Perdido & Poydras
Occupation- Wood Sawyer
Remarks- Edward Jones his son by Lucy Jones is now on False River La- by his present wife Becky he has no children- Lucy Jones is now dead.
Signature- x

Account Number- 741
Name- Allen Crawford
Date of Application- Sept. 8, 1868
Height and Complexion- Black 25 years old
Father or Mother? Married?- single
Name of Children- none
Regiment and Company- formerly Private C Co. 36th U.S.C.T.
Place of Birth- Beaufort Co. North Ca
Residence- Camp at Ship Island Miss.
Occupation- Sergeant Co. E 39th U.S. Infantry C'd
Remarks- Jenny Crawford his mother and Milly Crawford his sister- his mother lives in little Washington N. Ca, and his sister in Newbern.
Signature- yes

Account Number- 742
Name- Lafayette Carr
Date of Application- Sept. 9, 1868
Height and Complexion- 5ft. 5 in. Brown
Father or Mother? Married?- Charlotte Carr
Name of Children- none
Regiment and Company- Private Co. G 51st U.S.C.T.
Place of Birth- Harrison Co. Ky
Residence- corner Magnolia & Gravier
Occupation- Dining Room Servant
Remarks- Lewis Carr his father was living in Harrison Co. Ky 15 yrs. ago when he left that place- mother's name Emily Carr she is dead. His wife is empowered part or the whole of his deposits (Nov. 6, 1868)
Signature- yes

Account Number- 743
Name- Eliza Jefferson
Date of Application- Sept. 9, 1868
Father or Mother? Married?- widow of John Jefferson late of D co. 75th U.S.C.T.
Name of Children- none
Place of Birth- Baton Rouge La
Residence- Erato between Magazine & Constance No. 109
Occupation- Washer & Ironer
Remarks- John her father and Hannah

her mother are dead- Anthony Peter her brother when she last saw him about 15 years ago was living on Bayou Lafourche La. June 2, 1869- Eliza now resides on Magazine St. between Erato & Gaienne Streets.
Signature- x

Account Number- 744
Name- Henry Carter
Date of Application- Sept. 9, 1868
Father or Mother? Married?- Ellen Carter
Name of Children- 4 girls & 1 boy
Regiment and Company- Co. H 75th U.S.C.T.
Place of Birth- New Orleans
Residence- St. Ann St. between Burgundy & Rampart Streets
Occupation- Laborer
Remarks- Titine, Caroline, Ellsey, Rose are the girls names, boy named Anthony- mother dead father named Anthony Carter living on Bayou Lafourche.
Signature- x

Account Number- 745
Name- Robert H. Isabelle
Date of Application- Sept. 11, 1868
Remarks- See No. 532
Signature- yes

Account Number- 746
Name- William Hollman alias Barrow
Date of Application- Sept. 11, 1868
Height and Complexion- 5ft. 3 Brown
Father or Mother? Married?- Milly Barrow
Name of Children- Sarah 1yr. & 4 mos. old
Regiment and Company- Musician Co. G 92nd U.S.C.T.
Place of Birth- Terrebonne Parish La
Residence- Terrebonne Station, Woodworth Plantation
Occupation- Laborer
Remarks- Mother's name Nancy Chambers lives with him- his sisters and brothers all live with him- A.J. Brown, Maria Chambers & America Brown.
Signature- x

Account Number- 747
Name- Augustus Ridley
Date of Application- Sept. 12, 1868
Height and Complexion- Black
Father or Mother? Married?- single
Name of Children- none
Regiment and Company- Private Co. K 74th U.S.C.T.
Place of Birth- Jasper Co. Ga
Residence- Starkhouse Plantation below English Turn
Occupation- Farmer
Remarks- Father's name Charles Ridley mother's name Isabella- sister's name Ann, Jane & Eliza Ridley were all living in Jasper Co. two years ago before the rebellion broke, at which time he came here. June 14, 1869- Ridley now lives at Bayou Lafourche- Mr. Batchess place.
Signature- x

Account Number- 748
Name- Benjamin Jones
Date of Application- Sept. 14, 1868
Height and Complexion- Black- blind of left eye
Father or Mother? Married?- single
Regiment and Company- Co. A 10th Heavy Artillery
Place of Birth- Raymond South Ca
Residence- Villere St. Algiers
Occupation- Laborer
Remarks- Do not remember nothing about his father, his mother living in Yazoo Co. Miss. her name is Alpha- 1 brother living at the same place named Willis Thompson.
Signature- x

Account Number- 749
Remarks- See No. 678
Signature- yes

Account Number- 750
Name- Robert P. Smith
Date of Application- Sept. 17, 1868
Height and Complexion- White
Father or Mother? Married?- single
Name of Children- none
Regiment and Company- Co. D 1st U.S. Infantry

Place of Birth- Newburgh Beaver Co. Penn.
Residence- on Detached Service at Head Quarters
Occupation- Soldier
Remarks- Name of mother Esther Carnes resides at North Salem Guernsey Co. Ohio- The proper name of Smith is Robert P. Smith- but on enlisting an error was made by the enlisting office and his name was set down as Robert C. Smith.
Signature- yes

Account Number- 751
Name- Samuel Hinkling
Date of Application- Sept. 18, 1868
Height and Complexion- Black
Father or Mother? Married?- single
Name of Children- 3 children in Tenn.
Regiment and Company- Co. F 51st U.S.C.T.
Place of Birth- Williamson Co. Middle Tenn.
Residence- Corner of Conti & Galvez Streets
Occupation- Contractor on the Levee
Remarks- Father and mother dead- no relation known to him- James, Smith & Sam is the name of his children in Tenn.
Signature- x

Account Number- 752
Name- Minter Holland
Date of Application- Sept. 18, 1868
Height and Complexion- Brown 34 yrs. old
Father or Mother? Married?- widow of Coleman Holland Private Co. C 99th U.S.C.T.
Name of Children- none
Place of Birth- Georgetown District of Columbia
Residence- on Tchefunshe River between Madison & Covington at W Hands Iron Foundry
Occupation- Washer & Ironer
Remarks- Mother's name Susan Graham- dead- father's name Sam Graham- was in Georgetown about 22 years ago when she was sold away from that place.
Signature- x

Account Number- 753
Name- Andrew Gregory
Date of Application- Sept. 23, 1868
Height and Complexion- 21 Light
Father or Mother? Married?- Father Mackey- mother Maria- wife Mary
Regiment and Company- Co. A 39th U.S.C.T.
Place of Birth- Edenton N.C.
Remarks- See record No. 485 (taken Feb. 17, 1869) about 5 yrs. old when he left N.C. came to Montgomery Ala. there until 1861- father died in Edenton N.C. before Andrew was 1 yr.. old- mother in New Orleans- brothers James in Montgomery Ala. & George dead- has a child in Montgomery Ala. was not married.
Signature- yes

Account Number- 754
Name- Henry Seldon
Date of Application- Sept. 23, 1868
Regiment and Company- Quarter Master Sergt. 39th U.S. Infantry
Residence- Station Ship Island Miss.
Remarks- See record No. 551 Henry Seldon (his true name) has an a/c under the name of David McConnell.

Account Number- 755
Name- Charles Mitchell
Date of Application- Sept. 25, 1868
Height and Complexion- Black 5 ft. 9 in
Father or Mother? Married?- Ellen Mitchell
Name of Children- Doria & James Henry Mitchell
Regiment and Company- 1st Sergt. Co. B 75th U.S.C.T.
Place of Birth- Madisonville St. Tammany Parish
Residence- corner Perdido & Clara
Occupation- Fireman in Gas House Co.
Remarks- Kitty Mitchell, mother dead- Charles Mitchell, father dead- Isabella & Alfred his sister and brother reside in the 3rd District of the city.
Signature- yes

Account Number- 756
Name- Charles Stansbury
Date of Application- Sept. 25, 1868
Height and Complexion- Black
Father or Mother? Married?- Elyza Stansbury
Name of Children- Henry & Henrietta
Regiment and Company- Co. C 97th U.S.C.T.
Place of Birth- Baltimore, Maryland
Residence- corner First & Liberty
Occupation- Drayman
Remarks- do not know of any relation living.
Signature- x

Account Number- 757
Name- Andrew Blackson
Date of Application- Sept. 28, 1868
Height and Complexion- Black about 16 yrs. old
Residence- Orphan's Home St. Mary's Parish La
Occupation- Servant
Remarks- The first deposit was made for Andrew Blackson by Rev. R.K. Diossy.

Account Number- 758
Name- Samuel J. Reynolds
Date of Application- Sept. 29, 1868
Height and Complexion- Dark Brown 21 yrs. old
Father or Mother? Married?- single
Name of Children- none
Regiment and Company- Sergt. Co. H 39th U.S.Infantry
Place of Birth- Vincennes Indiana
Residence- Garrison at Ship Island Miss.
Occupation- Soldier
Remarks- Father's name John P. Reynolds- mother's name Delia Reynolds- brother's name Jason Joseph- his father and brother are living in Vincennes- mother is dead. By consolidation is now May 31, 1869 of Co I 25th U.S. Infantry.
Signature- yes

Account Number- 759
Name- John Thomas
Date of Application- Oct. 1, 1868
Height and Complexion- Black 22 yrs. old
Father or Mother? Married?- single
Name of Children- none
Regiment and Company- Corporal Co. E 39th U.S.C.T.
Place of Birth- Fredericksburg Va
Residence- Garrison at Ship Island Miss.
Occupation- Soldier- Jan. 25, 1870 discharged from Co. F 25th U.S. Infantry
Remarks- Mother's name Esther- Father George Thomas- father is dead- mother lives in Fredericksburg Va- no other relatives.
Signature- yes

Account Number- 760
Name- J.J. McMyler
Date of Application- Oct. 3, 1868
Height and Complexion- White
Father or Mother? Married?- single
Place of Birth- Westport Mayo Co. Ireland
Residence- 177 1/2 Poydras St.
Occupation- Store Keeper
Signature- yes

Account Number- 761
Name- William Duncan
Date of Application- Oct. 5, 1868
Height and Complexion- Yellow
Father or Mother? Married?- Caroline Duncan
Name of Children- 3 girls
Regiment and Company- Co. K 92nd U.S.C.T.
Place of Birth- Richmond Va
Residence- Philip St. between St. Denis & Dryades
Occupation- Laborer
Remarks- His wife is authorized to draw as himself- girl's name Fanny, Maria, Lizzie- father & mother dead, one sister in New Orleans named Maria Ross. Book said to be lost- Mrs. Burg residing on Philip between St. Denis & Dryades - gives him a very good character.
Signature- x

Account Number- 762
Name- Max Beer

Date of Application- Oct. 6, 1868
Height and Complexion- White 15 yrs. old
Place of Birth- Ingenheim Bavaria
Residence- at Kern & Fellman 108 Baronne St.
Occupation- Clerk in a Dry Goods Store
Remarks- Mother's name Mrs. Beer dead- father's name Moses Beer living in Ingenheim- brother's name Henry Beer.
Signature- yes

Account Number- 763
Name- Daniel Lowry
Date of Application- Oct. 8, 1868
Height and Complexion- Black
Father or Mother? Married?- Father Beverly- mother Mary- wife Mathilda
Name of Children- Phillis about 2 yrs. old
Regiment and Company- Co. F 75th U.S.C.T.
Place of Birth- Jefferson Co. Va
Residence- Homer St. Algiers
Occupation- Steam boating
Remarks- Does not know whether his parents are living- his brother Tom Lowry died about 2 months ago. (added later) baby 3 weeks old- children Peter & John dead- sister Arrena in Va & Rebecca dead.
Signature- x

Account Number- 764
Name- Frederic Regand alias Cook
Date of Application- Oct. 9, 1868
Height and Complexion- Black 26 yrs old
Father or Mother? Married?- Mary Toussaint
Name of Children- none
Regiment and Company- Private Co. B 75th U.S.C.T.
Place of Birth- New Orleans
Residence- corner St. Paul & Poydras
Occupation- Cooper
Remarks- His right name is Frederic Cook but when he enlisted he did it under the name of Frederic Regand
Signature- yes

Account Number- 765
Name- Henderson Wright
Date of Application- Oct. 9, 1868
Height and Complexion- Black
Father or Mother? Married?- Father Thomas Wright- mother Virginia- mother died when he was about 2 yrs. old- father left him when he was 5 yrs. old -don't know where he is- wife Julia Ann
Name of Children- 1 girl 4 yrs old
Regiment and Company- Corpl. Co. K 46th U.S.C.T.
Place of Birth- Richmond Va
Residence- 337 Tchoupitoulas St. between Erato & Thalia Streets
Occupation- Carpenter
Remarks- Mother dead- no relation known to him. He was born on the way from Richmond to Kentucky- was raised in Tenn- and came to La 3 yrs. ago.
Signature- yes

Account Number- 766
Name- Peter Boreland
Date of Application- Oct. 9, 1868
Height and Complexion- Light brown 28 yrs. old
Father or Mother? Married?- single
Name of Children- none
Regiment and Company- Co. A 39th U.S.Infantry
Place of Birth- Jersey City NJ
Residence- Garrison Ship Island Miss.
Occupation- Priv. in 39th Infantry Co. A
Remarks- Father's name Peter Boreland - mother's name Lavina Boreland - brothers William & Robert all in Richmond Va- sister Margaret Boreland don't know where she is. Forwarded for deposit by Rev. D.E. Barr Chaplain 39th U.S.I. (Sept. 22 1869) is now in Co.K 25th U.S.I.- messenger to Ship Island Miss.
Signature- yes

Account Number- 767
Name- Johnson Reed
Date of Application- Oct. 13, 1868
Remarks- Cert. of Deposit No. 16- See descriptive list No. 702

Account Number- 768
Name- H. T. Florey

Date of Application- Oct. 14, 1868
Height and Complexion- White
Place of Birth- Illinois
Residence- Vicksburg Miss.
Signature- yes

Account Number- 769
Name- Daniel Jones
Date of Application- Oct. 16, 1868
Remarks- Feb. 5, 1870- Daniel Jones came and introduced his wife, Susan Jones- she was born in Iberville Parish- 24 yrs. old yellow complexion- father's name Eli Jones dead- mother's name Caroline Washington- brother Eli Johnson in city- sister Mathilda Washington in city-See record No. 382- Daniel Jones authorizes he to draw money with his book as well as himself.
Signature- x

Account Number- 770
Name- William Johnson
Date of Application- Oct.16, 1868
Height and Complexion- Black 47 yrs. old
Father or Mother? Married?- Margaret Edwards
Name of Children- Mary Jane 10, Emily 8, Edward 3 & Francis Johnson 11mos.
Place of Birth- Wheeland Ky
Residence- 258 Calliope St.
Occupation- Drayman
Remarks- Father was left in Ky- Came to this city about 34 years ago- left his mother Emily (Milly) Johnson at Louisville Ky- she died 17 or 18 years ago in Louisville
Signature- yes

Account Number- 771
Name- Joseph Edwards
Date of Application- Oct. 16, 1868
Height and Complexion- Black 26
Father or Mother? Married?- Single- Father John Archy- mother Susan- step father Dick Frederick
Regiment and Company- Co. H 97th U.S.C.T.
Place of Birth- Col. Butler's Plantation Iberville Parish La

Residence- Col. Butler's Plantation Iberville Parish La
Occupation- Speculation
Remarks- Lost his right arm in the war- mother & father dead has two brothers- Milton Green living in New Orleans the other living with him named Daley Smith- Father died on Col. Butler's place when he was a child- mother died on same place about 15 years ago- step father died before mother at same place.
Signature- x

Account Number- 772
Name- Jeffery Goulon
Date of Application- Oct. 16, 1868
Height and Complexion- Black 29 years
Father or Mother? Married?- single
Name of Children- none
Regiment and Company- Private Co. E 73rd U.S.C.T.
Place of Birth- New Orleans
Residence- 100 Ursulines St.
Occupation- Laborer
Remarks- Mother's name Estelle- lives in St. James Parish at Mr. Leblanc's- brother's name Colin Goulon- lives in this city.
Signature- x

Account Number- 773
Name- Anderson Randall
Date of Application- Oct. 19, 1868
Height and Complexion- Yellow
Father or Mother? Married?- Rosine Curan
Name of Children- none
Regiment and Company- Cook in 4th Kty. Cavalry
Place of Birth- Lagrange Georgia
Residence- 2 South St.
Occupation- Cook
Remarks- See No. 323
Signature- x

Account Number- 774
Name- Augustin James
Date of Application- Oct. 19, 1868
Height and Complexion- Black
Father or Mother? Married?- Mary Antoinette Jean

Name of Children- 2 sons 1 daughter
Regiment and Company- Co. H 7th La Infantry Ord. Sergt.
Place of Birth- New Orleans
Residence- History St. between Craps & Greatman Streets No. 212
Occupation- Painter
Signature- yes

Account Number- 775
Name- Marie Antoinette James
Date of Application- Oct. 19, 1868
Father or Mother? Married?- Augustin James
Name of Children- Joseph 18, Elizabeth 15 & Samuel 4
Place of Birth- New Orleans La
Residence- Kerlerec between Dauphin & Burgundy
Occupation- Dress Maker
Remarks- Father's name John- died about 12 years ago- mother's name Laure Dupre- died here about 20 years ago.
Signature- x

Account Number- 776
Name- Joseph Augustin James
Date of Application- Oct. 19, 1868
Height and Complexion- 17 yrs. old
Place of Birth- New Orleans La
Residence- Kerlerec between Dauphin & Burgundy
Occupation- Painter
Remarks- Son of Augustin James
Signature- yes

Account Number- 777
Name- Charles Henry Hailey and Eulalie Hailey
Date of Application- Oct. 20, 1868
Remarks- See descriptive list No. 687- See record for Eulalie Hailey
Signature- yes

Account Number- 778
Name- Celestin Davis
Date of Application- Oct. 20, 1868
Height and Complexion- Yellow 24 yrs. old
Father or Mother? Married?- Thomas Davis Sergt. Co. G 9th U.S. Cavalry
Name of Children- Rachel & Evariste Davis
Place of Birth- New Orleans La
Residence- Benson between 1st & 2nd
Occupation- Seamstress & Hairdresser
Remarks- Rachel Groves her mother lives with her.
Signature- x

Account Number- 779
Name- John Harris
Date of Application- Oct. 22, 1868
Plantation- Chicot Pass Attakapas
Height and Complexion- Black
Father or Mother? Married?-
Father Manuel- mother Arena
Name of Children- John Henry 18, Andrew James 22, George W. Harris 15, & Irena 20
Regiment and Company- Co. A 10th Heavy Artillery
Place of Birth- Richmond Va
Residence- No. 8 Toulouse St.
Occupation- Peddler
Remarks- Left Richmond and has been here 23 years- Has no wife living- Andrew James, Irena & John Henry are children of Rachel- George Washington child of Elizabeth- Parents died in Va thinks mother died first- brother Emanuel in N.O. sister Ann Rebecca in Va- brothers George & Dekeeser & sisters Mary & Martha dead.
Signature-yes

Account Number- 780
Name- F. Blackwell
Date of Application- Oct. 23, 1868
Remarks- Deposited on Cert. of deposit by Capt. H.H. Pierce USA Supt. Bureau of Education

Account Number- 781
Name- L. Hunter
Date of Application- Oct. 23, 1868
Remarks- Deposited on Cert. of deposit by Capt. H.H. Pierce USA Supt. Bureau of Education

Account Number- 782

Name- Julius Abrahamsen
Date of Application- Oct. 23, 1868
Remarks- Deposited on Cert. of deposit by Capt. H.H. Pierce USA Supt. Bureau of Education

Account Number- 783
Name- Charles Brown
Date of Application- Oct. 27, 1868
Height and Complexion- Black
Father or Mother? Married?- Melia Brown
Name of Children- Eveline Brown
Regiment and Company- Co. D 97th U.S.C.T.
Place of Birth- Sampson City N.C.
Residence- George Walker's Sawmill St. Mary's Parish
Occupation- Laborer
Remarks- Left mother & father 16 years ago in North Carolina doesn't if they are living- have no relation in this state known to him.
Signature- x

Account Number- 784
Name- William Holliday & Sarah Brooks Holliday
Date of Application- Oct. 27, 1868
Height and Complexion- 43 years old
Father or Mother? Married?- Sarah Brooks Holliday
Name of Children- Lucy, Mary, Spenser, Celina & Emma Holliday
Place of Birth- Queen Ann Co. Md
Residence- 68 Liberty between Gravier & Commons
Occupation- Drayman
Remarks- Sarah Brooks was born in Washington DC- age 30- husband William Holliday- children see above- father John Brooks- she left him in Washington when she was a child- mother's name Kitty Brooks was also left in Washington at the same time. Both husband and wife can draw all moneys deposited in their names. Sarah Brooks is authorized by her husband William to withdraw whatever money of his she may want.
Signature- x x

Account Number- 785
Name- Charles C. Doughty
Date of Application- Oct. 28, 1868
Height and Complexion- Black about 65 years old
Father or Mother? Married?- Patience Lowry
Name of Children- none
Place of Birth- King & Queen Co. Va
Residence- corner Roman & Columbus
Occupation- Minister of the Gospel
Remarks- Revd. Doughty wishes that his wife should be paid whatever money she might want to draw, even the whole balance on deposit, although it would be done by himself.
Signature- yes

Account Number- 786
Name- Thomas Jefferson
Date of Application- Nov. 4, 1868
Place of Birth- 2 miles below Napoleonville Bayou Lafourche
Residence- Julia corner Roman St.
Remarks- Thomas Jefferson is 19 years old, the money is deposited by his father, not be drawn without his consent.
Signature- Nicholas Jefferson

Account Number- 787
Name- Henry Duest
Date of Application- Nov. 4, 1868
Height and Complexion- White
Place of Birth- Cincinnati Ohio
Residence- 93 Perdido St.
Occupation- Clerk corner Rampart & Thalia
Remarks- Mother's name Catharnia Duest lives with him at 93 Perdido St.
Signature- yes

Account Number- 788
Name- D.C. Starkes
Date of Application- Nov. 6, 1868
Height and Complexion- Light 26 years old
Father or Mother? Married?- single
Place of Birth- Mobile Ala.
Residence- 32 St. Charles St.
Occupation- Waiter at Rivers Club
Remarks- Milly Blunt his mother lives in

Mobile- father's name Douglas Starkes is dead- has one brother by the name of Seward Jones.
Signature- yes

Account Number- 789
Name- Milah Hubbard
Date of Application- Nov. 11, 1868
Height and Complexion- Black
Father or Mother? Married?- single
Regiment and Company- Co. D 99th U.S.C.T.
Place of Birth- Wilkinson Co. Miss.
Residence-Golden Grove St. James Parish
Occupation- Field hand
Remarks- His mother Sallie lives in Wilkinson Co. Miss.- father Peter Hubbard lives in the same county- one brother named Wallow- one sister Jenny
Signature- x

Account Number- 790
Name- F.G. Llorens
Date of Application- Nov. 12, 1868
Father or Mother? Married?- single
Name of Children- none
Place of Birth- New Orleans La
Residence- corner Union & Urquhart
Occupation- Clerk at Auditors office
Remarks- Deposited for Mr. Llorens a/c by Jos Presas Esq.

Account Number- 791
Name- Revd. John Turner
Date of Application- Nov. 12, 1868
Father or Mother? Married?- Mary E. Turner
Name of Children- Susan V. Robertson
Place of Birth- Frederick Co. Md
Residence- corner St. Bernard & Robertson
Occupation- Minister
Signature- yes

Account Number- 792
Name- William R. Harris
Date of Application- Nov. 12, 1868
Remarks- See No. 90
Signature- yes

Account Number- 793
Name- Adolph Zemar
Date of Application- Nov. 12, 1868
Father or Mother? Married?- Lavinia Zemar
Place of Birth- New Orleans La
Residence- Johnson between Poydras & Perdido
Occupation- Cotton Sampler
Remarks- Mother's name Adele Begger- she lives in Jefferson City.
Signature- yes

Account Number- 794
Name- Revd. M. M. Clark
Date of Application- Nov. 13, 1868
Father or Mother? Married?- Eliza Clark
Name of Children- Ellsworth, Charles & 4 others
Place of Birth- Sussex Co. Delaware
Residence- 94 Basin St.
Occupation- Minister & physician
Signature- yes

Account Number- 795
Name- William Butler
Date of Application- Nov. 16, 1868
Height and Complexion- Black
Father or Mother? Married?- Father William- mother Hannah- wife Nancy Butler
Name of Children- William Butler Jr. 11, Thomas dead
Place of Birth- Charleston S.C.
Residence- 107 Lafayette St.
Occupation- Cooper
Remarks- Parents dead-father died before he came- mother died after- brother Thomas sold before William was- one sister Melia Davis living in Charleston S.C. - William has been here nearly 21 years.
Signature- yes

Account Number- 796
Name- Foster Bradley
Date of Application- Nov. 18, 1868
Height and Complexion- Black
Father or Mother? Married?- Lizzie Bradley
Regiment and Company- Co. D 68th

U.S.C.T.
Place of Birth- Callaway Co. Missouri
Residence- Front St. Carrollton
Occupation- Laborer
Remarks- Left Missouri in 1863- father Joe Bradley & mother Caroline live in Callaway Co.- has five brothers William, Joe, John, Dud, George and two sisters Charity & ?.
Signature- x

Account Number- 797
Name- Henry Bell
Date of Application- Nov. 18, 1868
Remarks- See No. 422

Account Number- 798
Name- John A. Nelson
Date of Application- Nov. 21, 1868
Height and Complexion- Dark 33 years old
Father or Mother? Married?- Clemenci Nelson
Regiment and Company- Private Co. F 73th U.S.C.T.
Place of Birth- New Orleans La
Residence- 238 Rampart St. corner Girod
Occupation- Baker
Remarks- His wife Clemenci has two children Numa & Emile- from another party.
Signature- x

Account Number- 799
Name- Joseph Clark
Date of Application- Nov. 23, 1868
Height and Complexion- Black
Father or Mother? Married?- Emma Clark
Regiment and Company- Private Co. I 96th U.S.C.T.
Place of Birth- Baltimore Md
Residence- Burdette St. Carrollton
Occupation- Plasterer
Remarks- Father named Lewis Clark- mother named Felice both living in Baltimore- one brother William Clark living in N.O.- one sister Elizabeth living in Baltimore.
Signature- x

Account Number- 800
Name-Benjamin Miles
Date of Application- Nov. 24, 1868
Height and Complexion- Dark
Father or Mother? Married?- Maria Young
Name of Children- Henry Miles 1 year old
Place of Birth- Greenville S.C.
Residence- corner Johnson & Perdido Sts.
Occupation- Laborer
Remarks- Father Henry Miles living in Charleston S.C.- mother Becky living in Greenville S.C.- brothers John, Barney & William- sister Sarah in S.C.
Signature- x

Account Number- 801
Name- Robert P. Smith
Date of Application- Nov. 26, 1868
Remarks- See descriptive list No. 750
Signature- yes

Account Number- 802
Name- Timothy Skelley
Date of Application- Nov. 27, 1868
Height and Complexion- White 22 years old
Father or Mother? Married?- single
Name of Children- none
Regiment and Company- Co. E 34th U.S.Infantry
Place of Birth- Wismade Ireland
Residence- Brooklyn NY
Occupation- Gardener
Remarks- Mother Ellen Skelley resides in Brooklyn.
Signature- yes

Account Number- 803
Name- Michael Gaule
Date of Application- Nov. 27, 1868
Height and Complexion- White 30 years old
Father or Mother? Married?- single
Regiment and Company- Co. E 34th U.S. Infantry
Place of Birth- Tipperary Ireland
Residence- 86 Girod St.
Occupation- Sailor
Remarks- His mother Mary Gaule resides

Carrickon Su(?) Co. Tipperary.
Signature- yes

Account Number- 804
Name- H.H. Pierce
Date of Application- Nov. 28, 1868
Height and Complexion- White
Father or Mother? Married?- Maggie E. Pierce
Name of Children- none
Regiment and Company- Capt. 1st, Infantry U.S.A.
Place of Birth- Northampton Mass
Residence- City
Occupation- Genl. Supt. Education in La
Signature- yes

Account Number- 805
Name- Mrs. E. M. Menard
Date of Application- Nov. 28, 1868
Father or Mother? Married?- J.W. Menard
Name of Children- Willis Tirrell Menard
Place of Birth- Kingston Jamaica
Residence- Perdido between Galvez & Johnson
Occupation- None
Signature- yes

Account Number- 806
Name- Henry Mitchell
Date of Application- Dec. 1, 1868
Residence- Prieur St. between Ursulines & St. Philip
Remarks- See descriptive list No. 675
Signature- x

Account Number- 807
Name- Henry Bell
Date of Application- Dec. 2, 1868
Height and Complexion- Black 45 years old
Father or Mother? Married?- Mother Mary- wife Mary Bell
Name of Children- Henry, Martha, Gus & Georgiana Christina
Regiment and Company- Co. F 73rd U.S.C.T.
Place of Birth- Washington DC
Residence- Miro St. between Common & Gravier

Occupation- House work
Remarks- Came from Washington in the Mexican War- never saw father- mother died in Washington after he left-Benjamin & Gus Bell his brothers are in this city- brother Anthony in Washington- sisters Mary & Rachel dead- children (4) dead not named.
Signature- x

Account Number- 808
Name- Benjamin Bell
Date of Application- Dec. 2, 1868
Height and Complexion- Black 33 years old
Father or Mother? Married?- Mother Polly- never heard father's name- wife Eliza Bell
Name of Children- none
Regiment and Company- Co. F 73rd U.S.C.T.
Place of Birth- Washington DC
Residence- 254 Lafayette
Occupation- Porter
Remarks- Never saw his father- mother died when he was 10- has two brothers in this city Henry & Gus- sisters Mary & Eliza both dead- see Henry Bell above.
Signature- yes

Account Number- 809
Name- George Johnson
Date of Application- Dec. 3, 1868
Height and Complexion- Black
Father or Mother? Married?- Louisa Carter
Name of Children- Clara 8 yrs. old
Regiment and Company- Co. D 73rd U.S.C.T.
Place of Birth- Williamsburg Va
Residence- Derbigny St. between Julia & Cypress
Occupation- Driving a Wagon
Remarks- Do not know if father James Johnson is living- mother Betsy is living in Williamsburg- one sister Eliza Johnson- three brothers Daniel, William & James.
Signature- yes

Account Number- 810

Name- Edmund Dancer
Date of Application- Dec. 4, 1868
Height and Complexion- Black 55 years old
Father or Mother? Married?- Mary Dancer
Name of Children- none
Regiment and Company- Private Co. D 70th U.S.C.T.
Place of Birth- Halifaxtown N.C.
Residence- corner Poydras & Broon
Occupation- Carpenter
Remarks- Father's name Charles Dancer, I left him in NC when I was a little boy- Agar Hagwood, his mother he heard from two months ago - she was at Alexandria, Red River La.
Signature- yes

Account Number- 811
Name- Isiah Bradley
Date of Application- Dec. 4, 1868
Height and Complexion- Black 35 years old
Father or Mother? Married?- single
Name of Children- none
Regiment and Company- Sergt. Co. F 68th U.S.C.T.
Place of Birth- Shelby Co. Ky
Residence- Greenville Jefferson Parish
Occupation- Laborer
Remarks- Taken from Kentucky to Missouri when he was about 13 years old- after Isaac was taken to Missouri his mother was sold away- Nancy Bradley mother dead
Dorsey Bradley his father died in Kentucky- brother David Sandford died up Red River- Isaac enlisted in Petter Co. at Cordalia Mo.- lived before that at Cambridge Salene Co. Mo.
Signature- x

Account Number- 812
Name- Nelson Chillis
Date of Application- Dec. 5, 1868
Height and Complexion- Black about 23 years old
Father or Mother? Married?- single- mother Amy
Name of Children- none
Regiment and Company- Private Co. B 78th U.S.C.T.
Place of Birth- Bayou Teche St. Mary's Parish La
Residence- corner Melpomene & St. Thomas
Occupation- Laborer, Levee Hand
Remarks- Mother died in 1863 in Bayou Lafourche- Father Nelson Chillis is in Baton Rouge La- sister Laura McFerlane lives corner Josephine & Franklin- sisters Keziah & Katy in city- Sister Sally in St. Mary's Parish- sister Dinah dead- Brothers Jim & Matt in St. Mary's Parish
Signature- x

Account Number- 813
Name- William Nelson
Date of Application- Dec. 7, 1868
Height and Complexion- Black 45 years old
Father or Mother? Married?- Lysa Nelson
Name of Children- none
Regiment and Company- 3rd Sergt. Co. D 70th U.S.C.T.
Place of Birth- North Carolina- raised in La
Residence- Broad St. corner Poydras
Occupation- driving Cotton Wagon, afloat
Remarks- Mary Dancer, Lysa Gordon & Rachel Gordon his sisters all living in this city.
Signature- x

Account Number- 814
Name- William May
Date of Application- Dec. 8, 1868
Height and Complexion- Yellow 53 years old
Father or Mother? Married?- Harriet May
Place of Birth- Richmond Va
Residence- Laurent between Josephine & St. Andrew
Occupation- Drayman
Remarks- Has a stepson Edward Anderson
Signature- x

Account Number- 815

Name- Philip Packer
Date of Application- Dec. 8, 1868
Height and Complexion- Black 37 years old
Father or Mother? Married?- Mary Packer
Name of Children- Thomas 3 months
Regiment and Company- Co. G 47th U.S.C.T.
Place of Birth- Spottsylvania Co. Va
Residence- Gravier St. between Claiborne & Derbigny
Occupation- Laborer- Blacksmith by trade
Remarks- George Henry Packer his brother is here- Patsy Jane & Mildred Ann Packer his sisters who were left by him in Spottsylvania Co. Va about 13 years ago. Feb. 22, 1870 now resides on Salon between Rampart & Dryades
Signature- yes

Account Number- 816
Name- George A. Stallwood
Date of Application- Dec. 8, 1868
Height and Complexion- White 24 years old
Father or Mother? Married?- single
Name of Children- none
Regiment and Company- Co. D 34th U.S. Infantry
Place of Birth- Brooklyn NY
Residence- city
Occupation- none just discharged
Remarks- Henry Stallwood his father resides in Brooklyn NY.
Signature- yes

Account Number- 817
Name- Eliza Antoinette Branch
Date of Application- Dec. 8, 1868
Height and Complexion- Black
Father or Mother? Married?- Father Meajor- mother Edey- husband George
Place of Birth- Northampton Co. NC
Residence- corner Girod & Basin Streets
Occupation- Washer woman
Remarks- Been out here near 23 years- father died in NC when she was 6 yrs. old- mother Edey living in Northampton NC- brothers Green Branch & Jack Branch both living in NC- sister Harriet went to the "Western Countries" when Eliza was a little girl- sister Malvina dead.
Signature- x

Account Number- 818
Name- Richard Dunn
Date of Application- Dec. 8, 1868
Height and Complexion- Bright 22 years old
Father or Mother? Married?- single
Regiment and Company- Private Co. F 78th U.S.C.T.
Place of Birth- New Orleans La
Residence- Common between Claiborne & Willow
Occupation- Laborer
Remarks- Father William Dunn- mother Delia Dunn.
Signature- yes

Account Number- 819
Name- John Fitzgerald
Date of Application- Dec. 8, 1868
Height and Complexion- Dark 25 years old
Father or Mother? Married?- Father Jim- mother Matilda- wife Josephine
Name of Children- Julia 8 years old
Regiment and Company- Chf. Musician 50th U.S.C.T.
Place of Birth- New Orleans
Residence- 177 Calliope St.
Occupation- Blacksmith
Remarks- Father died in Natchez Miss about 14 yrs. ago- mother died there about 7 years ago- brother George in La- sister Violet Amelia dead.
Signature- yes

Account Number- 820
Name- David Cosby
Date of Application- Dec. 9, 1868
Height and Complexion- Black 44 years old
Father or Mother? Married?- Father Frank- mother Sarah- wife Mary Jane Cosby
Name of Children- none
Regiment and Company- Co. D 73th U.S.C.T.

Place of Birth- Smith Co. Dixon's Pains Tenn
Residence- 245 Conti St.
Occupation- Cooper
Remarks- Left Tenn. 25 or 26 years ago- Parents in Tenn.- brothers Washington & Madison in Tenn.- Sisters Matilda & Amy- one child died before he was born.
Signature- yes

Account Number- 821
Name- Jean Bertrand alias Batron
Date of Application- Dec. 10, 1868
Height and Complexion- Dark about 28 years old
Father or Mother? Married?- Charlotte Abram
Name of Children- Denis, Eugenie, Marie & Bertrand
Regiment and Company- Co. C 77th U.S.C.T.
Place of Birth- St. Bernard Parish La
Residence- 15 Barracks St.
Occupation- Carpenter
Remarks- Made. Auguste his mother resides corner Marais & St. Bernard St.
Signature- x

Account Number- 822
Name- Henry Buford
Date of Application- Dec. 10, 1868
Height and Complexion- Yellow 46 years old
Father or Mother? Married?- Ellen Buford
Name of Children- none
Regiment and Company- Co. C 46th U.S.C.T.
Place of Birth- Pulaski Tenn.
Residence- 96 Gaienne St.
Occupation- Laborer
Remarks- Father Raswall Buford & mother Aime Buford are living in Pulaski Tenn.
Signature- x

Account Number- 823
Date of Application- Dec. 10, 1868
Remarks- See No. 672
Signature- yes

Account Number- 824-825-826
Blank

Account Number- 827
Name- Jean Victor
Date of Application- Dec. 11, 1868
Father or Mother? Married?- Henriette
Regiment and Company- Co. E 74th U.S.C.T.
Place of Birth- New Orleans La
Residence- corner Bagatelle & Greatman Sts.
Occupation- Coach driver
Remarks- Father & mother dead has only one sister Rosa Claude living in New Orleans
Signature- x

Account Number- 828
Name- Victor Cheneau
Date of Application- Dec. 11, 1868
Height and Complexion- Black 26
Father or Mother? Married?- Father Lewis- mother Mary Jennie- wife Philomene Dalbz
Name of Children- Henry about 2 years old & Anatole 3 months
Regiment and Company- Co. E 73rd U.S.C.T.
Place of Birth- New Orleans
Residence- 100 Congress between Love & Craps
Occupation- Shoemaker
Remarks- Father died here 19 years ago- mother Mrs. Louis Cheneau living in the city 3rd Dist.- 2 sisters Marie & Cecile- brother Anatole dead.
Signature- yes

Account Number- 829
Name- Jacob Smith
Date of Application- Dec. 11, 1868
Height and Complexion- Black
Father or Mother? Married?- Father Green- mother Luconda- single
Regiment and Company- Musician Co. F 97th U.S.C.T.
Place of Birth- Natchez Miss.
Residence- corner Liberty & Perdido Sts.
Occupation- Shoemaker
Remarks- Came here about 4 years

before the war- Father drown in Natchez when he was a little boy- mother died in New Orleans in 1862- 2 sisters Roxanne wife of Ferdinand Rubere & Barbry Green living in this city- brother Cicero Harris living on Laurel St. City of Jefferson Parish of Jefferson- brothers Lee & Emanuel dead- sisters Clara, Louisa & Gracy dead.
Signature- x

Account Number- 830
Name- Simon Giles
Date of Application- Dec. 12, 1868
Height and Complexion- Black
Father or Mother? Married?- Jane
Name of Children- Louisa & George
Regiment and Company- Co. B 78th U.S.C.T.
Place of Birth- Clay Co. Missouri
Residence- corner Palmyra & Roman Sts.
Occupation- Fireman at Gas Works
Remarks- Fathers name Joseph Giles died in Missouri time of first cholera- mother's name Aby she died a week after her husband- one brother John Giles lives in Leavenworth City Kansas
Signature- x

Account Number- 831
Name- Pryor Lewis
Date of Application- Dec. 14, 1868
Height and Complexion- Black
Father or Mother? Married?- Father Peter- mother Phoebe- wife Sarah Lewis
Regiment and Company- Co. E 70th U.S.C.T.
Place of Birth- Rapides Parish La
Residence- 445 Julia St.
Occupation- Laborer
Remarks- First wife Mary dead- father died in Rapides Parish 30 years ago- mother died there about 28 years ago- sister Uassala in city- Kitty living in Madisonville St. Tammany Parish- brother Reuben living in this city- children Adam, Peter, Lewis & Kitty all dead- wife's children George & William- half brother Aleck Forbush lives in Bayou St. Louis.

Signature- x

Account Number- 832
Name- James Lewis
Date of Application- Dec. 18, 1868
Height and Complexion- Black 24 years old
Father or Mother? Married?- Mary Lewis
Name of Children- Emma 3 months
Regiment and Company- Private Co. E 39th U.S.Infantry
Place of Birth- Greenville Jefferson Parish La
Residence- at Ship Island
Occupation- Sawyer
Remarks- Father William Lewis & mother Esther both dead- Money deposited for James Lewis' account by N. Winehill- discharged 19th Sept. 1869 from Co. F 25th U.S. Infantry.
Signature- yes

Account Number- 833
Name- Horace Whally
Date of Application- Dec. 18, 1868
Height and Complexion- Yellow
Father or Mother? Married?- Monique
Name of Children- Leontine & Horace
Place of Birth- Iberville Parish
Residence- St. Mary St. between St. Charles & Prytania Sts.
Occupation- Carpenter
Remarks- Father & mother dead- 3 sisters Catherine, Clementine & Anna all living in New Orleans- on sister Martha in Iberville.
Signature- yes

Account Number- 834
Name- Georgia Riley
Date of Application- Dec. 21, 1868
Father or Mother? Married?- Father Hermes Cripps- mother Mary Lewis- husband John Riley
Place of Birth- New Orleans
Residence- 159 Perdido St.
Occupation- Music Teacher
Remarks- Father died in New Orleans 3 years ago- mother living in New Orleans- sister Hortense Cripps in city- brother Charles Cripps in city- sister Cora Corbin

dead.
Signature- yes

Account Number- 835
Name- David Anderson
Date of Application- Dec. 22, 1868
Height and Complexion- White
Father or Mother? Married?- single
Regiment and Company- Co. D 15th U.S. Infantry
Place of Birth- Pittsburgh Penn
Residence- St. Charles St. at Fred's
Occupation- Laborer
Remarks- Father & mother dead- sister Ellen Anderson- brother John Anderson both living in Pittsburgh.
Signature- yes

Account Number- 836
Name- Thomas Berry
Date of Application- Dec. 22, 1868
Height and Complexion- White
Father or Mother? Married?- single
Regiment and Company- Co. D 15th U.S. Infantry
Place of Birth- Wermaid Ireland
Residence- St. Charles St. at Fred's
Occupation- Cutter
Remarks- Father dead- mother Ellen- brother James Berry both living in NY.
Signature-yes

Account Number- 837
Name- Female Benevolent Association of La.
Date of Application- Dec. 23, 1868
Residence- Place of meeting St. James Chapel on Roman St. between Customhouse & Bienville
Remarks- see record of officers following 1017.
Mary Lewis-Chairman
P. Hopkins-President
Mary A. Fox-Secretary
Mrs. Cornish- Treasurer
Drafts to be made on exhibition of power to do so according to charter or by-laws- money can be drawn by the President, Treasurer, and Secretary or by order signed by the three
Signature- Mary Lewis

Account Number- 838
Name- Terence Wolfe
Date of Application- Dec. 24, 1868
Height and Complexion- White 16 years old
Father or Mother? Married?- Father Terence Sr.- mother Julia- stepmother Mary-single
Place of Birth- New Orleans
Residence- 426 Barome St.
Occupation- Clerk
Remarks- Mother dead- sister Julia- 2 stepsisters Anna & Jane- brother Francis dead- sisters Anna, Jane & Elizabeth dead.
Signature- yes

Account Number- 839
Name- Henry Williams
Date of Application- Dec. 28, 1868
Height and Complexion- Dark Brown 28 has scar on left cheek
Father or Mother? Married?- Father Primus Winley- mother Louisa- wife Charity
Place of Birth- Miggs Co. Ga- raised in Ga- lived in Mobile Ala. 2 yrs.
Residence- corner Beauregard & Conception (later entry) corner Dryades & Jewitt Sts.
Occupation- Laborer
Remarks- He can write his name- transferred from Mobile- Left Georgia 7 years before war- sister Flora A. Winley & brother Zeke Winley both in Tuskega Ala.- (later entry) Father in Ga sold away when Henry was small-mother died before Henry can remember- sister Flora wife of Frank Hunter.
Signature- yes

Account Number- 840
Name- George Reed
Date of Application- Dec. 28, 1868
Height and Complexion- Black
Father or Mother? Married?- single
Regiment and Company-Co. C 39th U.S. Infantry just discharged formerly of Co. K 81st U.S.C.T.
Place of Birth- Chickasaw Co. Miss
Residence- 61 Burgundy St.

Remarks- Father Ransom Reed living in Chickasaw Co.- mother dead- sister Emily Dorse- brother Priest Leary living in Chickasaw Co.
Signature- yes

Account Number- 841
Name- Mrs. J. B. Goland
Date of Application- Dec. 28, 1868
Father or Mother? Married?- widow
Name of Children- Rosette Bacchus about 35 yrs. old
Place of Birth- New Orleans La
Residence- St. Joseph between Carondelet & St. Charles
Occupation- Nurse
Remarks- First deposit made for her a/c by Mr. William B. Russell.
Signature- x

Account Number- 842
Name- Hannah Quilland
Date of Application- Dec. 29, 1868
Height and Complexion- Black 20 yrs. old
Father or Mother? Married?- Newton Quillard
Place of Birth- Louisville Ky
Residence- Derbigny between Cypress & Julia
Occupation- Cooking, Washing & Ironing
Remarks- Grandmother's name Hannah Walker.
Signature- x

Account Number- 843
Name- H. T. Florey
Date of Application- Dec. 29, 1868
Height and Complexion- White
Place of Birth- Illinois
Residence- Vicksburg Miss
Remarks- see No. 768
Signature- yes

Account Number- 844
Name- Felix Montegut
Date of Application- Dec. 31, 1868
Height and Complexion- Dark
Father or Mother? Married?- Marie Ferrand
Name of Children- Felicie, Alphonsine & Michel
Place of Birth- New Orleans
Residence- 394 Love St. between St. Anthony & Bagatelle Sts.
Occupation- Bricklayer
Remarks- Father & mother dead- 1 sister Marie Montegut
Signature- yes

Account Number- 845
Name- Peter McWilliams
Date of Application- Dec. 31, 1868
Father or Mother? Married?- single
Place of Birth- St. , Mary's Parish
Residence- Euterpe St. (?) between Baronne & Carondelet
Occupation- Steam boating
Remarks- Becky Handy his mother is living with him- Mar. 19, 1870 is now on Steamer Frank Payand- (later entry) mother Becky Hazelup 363 Jackson- Jan. 19, 1874 can pay to mother
Signature- x

Account Number- 846
Name- Mrs. M. Burchard
Date of Application- Jan. 2, 1869
Height and Complexion- White
Father or Mother? Married?- J.M. Burchard
Name of Children- Willy, Loulou & Jenny
Place of Birth- Covington Canton Co. KY
Residence- 181 Camp St.
Signature- yes

Account Number- 847
Name- Charles T. Roe
Date of Application- Jan. 2, 1869
Height and Complexion- White 11 yrs. old
Place of Birth- Kinderhook NY
Residence- 197 Lafayette St.
Occupation- going to school
Remarks- Son of Mrs. Jane Roe
Signature- yes

Account Number- 848
Name- Susan Marshall
Date of Application- Jan. 2, 1869
Father or Mother? Married?- Father Jim Harkins- mother Delia- widow of John

Marshall late Co. I 84th U.S.C.T.
Place of Birth- Maryland
Residence- Custom House between Prieur & Roman
Occupation- Washing
Remarks- Came from Maryland when she was small- husband dead- she lives at Mr. Slater's house- servant- father died in Bayou Lafourche when she was a little girl- mother died same place before he father's child Francis died- brother Tom in Bayou Lafourche- brothers Charles & Jack dead.
Signature- x

Account Number- 849
Name- Nancy Melinda Banwoode
Date of Application- Jan. 4, 1869
Height and Complexion- Mulatress about 26 yrs. old
Father or Mother? Married?- Walker Banwoode
Place of Birth- Red River born in the village of Plaisance
Residence- 368 St. Andrew St.
Occupation- Cook
Remarks- Mother Nancy lives in Camp Parapet- father Pierre Lacour a white man- Deposit made by Mr. R. Seig at whose place she is a cook- sister's name Louisa in this city lives with her- Louisa has a daughter Henriette Gardner- "She was raised by the Cartaner family"
Signature- x

Account Number- 850
Name- Hannah Walker
Date of Application- Jan. 4, 1869
Remarks- Aug. 17, 1870 am now living at corner 3rd & Bacchus St.- Lewis Walker my husband died on June 20, 1870- in case of accident or sickness Hannah Walker wants her aunt Annie Bell to draw or inherit her deposits- See No. 662- this book issued to replace book 662 which was burnt 3 months ago at the fire on 6th St. corner Dryades.

Account Number- 851
Name- James H. Johnson
Date of Application- Jan. 4, 1869
Remarks- See No. 722
Signature- yes

Account Number- 852
Name- Isaac Washington
Date of Application- Jan. 4, 1869
Remarks- See No. 632

Account Number- 853
Name- Marie Lacorbiere
Date of Application- Jan. 4, 1869
Height and Complexion- 4 yrs. old Light Comp.
Place of Birth- New Orleans
Residence- Roman between Hospital & Ursulines
Remarks- Daughter of Victor & Rosa Lacorbiere- first deposit by V. Lacorbiere.

Account Number- 854
Name- Uranie Lacorbiere or Warburg
Date of Application- Jan. 4, 1869
Height and Complexion- 8 yrs. old Light
Place of Birth- New Orleans
Residence- Roman between Hospital & Ursulines
Remarks- Daughter of Daniel & Josephine Warburg- first deposit by V. Lacorbiere.

Account Number- 855
Name- Paul Trevigne
Date of Application- Jan. 4, 1869
Height and Complexion- 7 yrs. old.
Place of Birth- New Orleans
Residence- 155 Columbus St.
Occupation- Scholar
Remarks- Son of Paul & Hortensia Trevigne- first deposit by Mr. Trevigne.

Account Number- 856
Name- Charles Nerestan Trevigne
Date of Application- Jan. 4, 1869
Height and Complexion- 10 months old.
Place of Birth- New Orleans
Residence- 155 Columbus St.
Remarks- Son of Paul & Hortensia Trevigne- first deposit by Mr. Trevigne.

Account Number- 857

Name- Alexandre Wale
Date of Application- Jan. 5, 1869
Height and Complexion- White
Father or Mother? Married?- single
Place of Birth- New Orleans
Residence- St. Peter at Rampart & Burgundy
Occupation- Typograph
Remarks- No Father or mother- sister Angele Couvertie born Wale.
Signature- yes

Account Number- 858
Name- Isaac A. Abbott
Date of Application- Jan. 5, 1869
Remarks- See No. 698
Signature- yes

Account Number- 859
Name- Oliver Russell
Date of Application- Jan. 6, 1869
Height and Complexion- Black 33 yrs. old
Father or Mother? Married?- Louisa Russell
Regiment and Company- Co. A 60 day volunteers 7th Regt. U.S.C.T.
Place of Birth- Norfolk Va
Residence- Melpomene between Magnolia & Locust
Occupation- Painter
Remarks- No relatives
Signature- x

Account Number- 860
Name- Isaac Wilson
Date of Application- Jan. 8, 1869
Height and Complexion- Black 64 yrs. old
Father or Mother? Married?- Father Jack- mother Amy-single
Name of Children- none
Place of Birth- York Co. Va
Residence- 62 Garquet St.
Occupation- Porter in offices- works at 59 Carondelet
Remarks- Left Va about 46 or 47 years ago- came to NO- is to be married to Jane Kimball- sisters Milly, Lettis & Nancy Wilson are somewhere in Va- brother John Shield Wilson when he last heard from him about 8 years ago was at Fortress Monroe- brothers Patrick & Jim both dead.
Signature- yes

Account Number- 861
Name- Wilhelm Bostram
Date of Application- Jan. 9, 1869
Height and Complexion- White
Father or Mother? Married?- single
Name of Children- none
Place of Birth- Stockholm Sweden
Residence- Algiers, Orleans La
Occupation- Steersman on Boarothe Vigens (?)
Signature- yes

Account Number- 862
Name- William Jarvis
Date of Application- Jan. 9, 1869
Height and Complexion- Black 21 years old
Father or Mother? Married?- single
Name of Children- none
Place of Birth- Bayou Lafourche on Mr. Sabatier's Plantation
Residence- Bellechatte Plantation Plaquemines
Occupation- Farmer
Remarks- Father James Jarvis- mother Maky Jarvis are living at Bayou Lafourche.
Signature- x

Account Number- 863
Name- Robert Poindexter
Date of Application- Jan. 9, 1869
Height and Complexion- 47 years old
Father or Mother? Married?- Mathilda Poindexter
Name of Children- none
Regiment and Company- Co. F 78th U.S.C.T.
Place of Birth- Sullivan Co. Tenn
Residence- Assumption Parish
Occupation- State Senator
Signature- yes

Account Number- 864
Name- Edward Major
Date of Application- Jan. 11, 1869

Remarks- See No. 205

Account Number- 865
Name- Rose Caroline Dubois
Date of Application- Jan.11, 1869
Height and Complexion-
6 1/2 months old
Place of Birth- New Orleans
Residence- 335 Craps or Burgundy, Kerlerec & Caplanside
Occupation- Sucking
Remarks- Father Etienne Dubois Jr. can draw- mother Henriette Dubois- first deposit made by Etienne Dubois Sr.

Account Number- 866
Name- Joseph Bruce
Date of Application- Jan. 11, 1869
Height and Complexion- Black 20 yrs. old
Father or Mother? Married?- single
Name of Children- none
Regiment and Company- Co. G 4th U.S.C. Calvary
Place of Birth- Attakapas La
Residence- 162 Dryades Washington & 6th Sts.
Occupation- Steam boating
Remarks- No other relative but one uncle Etienne Broussard.
Signature- x

Account Number- 867
Name- Paul Joseph
Date of Application- Jan. 11, 1869
Name of Master- Mr. J.B. Sauvenet
Height and Complexion- Black 67 yrs. old
Father or Mother? Married?- Father Joseph Smith- mother Silvy- wife Hannah
Name of Children- Joe 13, Pauline 9, Adele 16 & Delphine 17
Regiment and Company- Co. B 74th U.S.C.T.
Place of Birth- Petersburg Va
Residence- Corner Caracaloo & Royal
Occupation- works at Leason's Daguerestypist
Remarks- Came here in 1815- father died in Petersburg about 40 years ago- mother died there- children dead Victor, Joseph, John & Paul- sisters Hannah widow of John in city & Mary wife of Thomas in city.
Signature- x

Account Number- 868
Name- Paul Trevigne Sr.
Date of Application- Jan. 11, 1869
Height and Complexion- Light 40 yrs.old
Father or Mother? Married?- Hortensia Trevigne
Name of Children- Paul & Simeon Nerestan
Place of Birth- New Orleans La
Residence- 155 Columbus
Occupation- Editor of New Orleans Tribune
Signature- yes

Account Number- 869
Name- Simeon Nerestan Trevigne
Date of Application- Jan. 11, 1869
Height and Complexion- 10 months old.
Place of Birth- New Orleans
Residence- 155 Columbus St.
Remarks- Son of Paul & Hortensia Trevigne- first deposit by Mr. Trevigne.

Account Number- 870
Name- Kate Gardner
Date of Application- Jan. 12, 1869
Height and Complexion- White 26 years old
Father or Mother? Married?- widow
Name of Children- none
Place of Birth- Limmerick Ireland
Residence- Common between Circus & St. John
Occupation- Seamstress
Remarks- Honora Gleason her mother is a resident of this city.
Signature- yes

Account Number- 871
Name- Joseph Washington Burns
Date of Application- Jan. 15, 1869
Height and Complexion- Black 26 years old
Father or Mother? Married?- single
Name of Children- none
Place of Birth- New Orleans

Residence- corner 4th & Laurel
Occupation- Servant of J.P. Hagan
Remarks- James Burns his father lives in Algiers- brothers Emile & James Burns- Selvine & Mary Ann his sisters- Mary Ann in NY.
Signature- yes on Mar. 1, 1873

Account Number- 872
Name- A.L. Chesse
Date of Application- Jan. 16, 1869
Father or Mother? Married?- Rosa Esnard
Place of Birth- New Orleans
Residence- corner Burgundy & Kerlerec
Occupation- Merchant Tailor
Signature- yes

Account Number- 873
Name- Edward Fields
Residence-corner 1st & St. Patrick
Remarks- See record No. 116
Signature- yes

Account Number- 874
Name- Edward Crump
Date of Application- Jan. 19, 1869
Height and Complexion- Yellow
Father or Mother? Married?- single
Regiment and Company- Co. G 50th U.S.C.T.
Place of Birth- New Orleans
Residence- corner 3rd & Prytania
Occupation- Private Servant
Remarks- Father Jack Crump- mother Mary Crump both living in New Orleans- brothers William & John- sisters Fanny & Mary all living here.
Signature- yes

Account Number- 875
Name- Revd. Henry Green (Elder)
Date of Application- Jan.19 , 1869
Remarks- See descriptive list for No. 425. This deposit is made for a/c of the church and pay of the different preachers of this division.
Signature- yes

Account Number- 876
Name- Revd. Anthony Ross (Elder)
Date of Application- Jan. 19, 1869
Remarks- See descriptive list for No. 425. This deposit is made for a/c of the church and pay of the different preachers of this division.
Signature- yes

Account Number- 877
Name- Revd. James M. Vance
Date of Application- Jan. 19, 1869
Father or Mother? Married?- Mathilda Vance
Name of Children- James M. & Charles W.
Place of Birth- Nashville Tenn
Residence- 324 Custom House St.
Remarks- Dist. of Shreveport- Deposit made for the same purpose as Rev. Green & Ross.
Signature- yes

Account Number- 878
Name- Rev. Emperor Williams
Date of Application- Jan. 19, 1869
Father or Mother? Married?- Diana
Name of Children- Francis William
Place of Birth- Nashville Tenn
Residence- corner Magazine & Lyon
Occupation- Preacher
Remarks- Deposit for same purpose as ever.
Signature- yes

Account Number- 879
Name- Thomas County
Date of Application- Jan. 20, 1869
Father or Mother? Married?- Celine County
Name of Children- Lucy, George & Emma
Regiment and Company- Co. D 70th U.S.C.
Place of Birth- Maryland
Residence- Algiers
Remarks- for cert. deposit No. 20
Signature- yes

Account Number- 880
Name- Mary Williams
Date of Application- Jan. 20, 1869
Height and Complexion- Light about 24 yrs.

Father or Mother? Married?- Moore A. Williams
Name of Children- Anna Eliza & Mathilda
Place of Birth- Wilkinson Co. Miss
Residence- Washington St. between Clara & Magnolia
Occupation- Cook
Remarks- The depositor is the sister of the late Harriet Marshall depositor No. 593- Anna Eliza is blind.
Signature- x

Account Number- 881
Name- William Scruggs
Date of Application- Jan. 20, 1869
Height and Complexion- Black 24 yrs. old
Father or Mother? Married?- single
Name of Children- none
Regiment and Company- Teamster U.S.A.
Place of Birth- Franklin Tenn
Residence- St. Louis Mo on 10th St. between Walnut & Clark Ave.
Occupation- Steam boating
Remarks- Father Alfred Scruggs- mother- Lishy- sister Harriet- brother Ned all in Franklin Tenn
Signature- x

Account Number- 882
Name- Revd. James Allen
Date of Application- Jan. 20, 1869
Height and Complexion- Black 51 years old
Father or Mother? Married?- widow
Name of Children- Mrs. S. Johnson
Place of Birth- Buckingham Co. Va
Residence- 118 Custom House
Occupation- Preacher- Missionary
Remarks- In case of death I want all deposits to be given to my daughter Mrs. S. Johnson
Signature- yes

Account Number- 883
Name- Anatole L. Boree
Date of Application- Jan. 21, 1869
Remarks- See descriptive list No. 408
Signature- yes

Account Number- 884
Name- Joseph Craig
Date of Application- Jan. 21, 1869
Height and Complexion- Black
Father or Mother? Married?- Mary Jane
Name of Children- Mary Elizabeth 6 & Emma 1yr. 8 mo.
Regiment and Company- Co. A 74th U.S.C.T.
Place of Birth- Washington DC
Residence- 228 Freret St. between Julia & Cypress
Occupation- Policeman No. 68
Remarks- Been in N O 18 years- father James Craig- mother Mary Elizabeth- brother Henry Craig all in Washington DC- wife can draw- Wife born in N O, Black 36 years old, Occupation- washing, ironing & cooking- children Mary Elizabeth & Emma Jane- mother Elizabeth Walker- father not known- no brothers or sisters. June 15 1870 Mr. Craig has this day signed his name having learned to write since he made the first deposit.
Signature- x & yes

Account Number- 885
Name- James Sheehan
Date of Application- Jan. 22, 1869
Height and Complexion- White 23 yrs. old
Father or Mother? Married?- single
Name of Children- None
Regiment and Company- late Co. D 5th Calvary
Place of Birth- Clare Co Ireland
Residence- corner Girod & Old Levee
Occupation- Laborer
Remarks- Father James Sheehan died in Ireland 15 or 16 yrs. ago- mother Briget Daly died 10 yrs. ago in NY- no relatives living- brothers John, Michael & Patrick all dead- sisters Margaret, Kate & Annie all dead.
Signature- yes

Account Number- 886
Name- Edward Johnson
Date of Application- Jan. 22, 1869
Height and Complexion- Black
Father or Mother? Married?- Jane Bailey

Name of Children- none
Regiment and Company- Co. F 92nd U.S.C.T. Private
Place of Birth- Clinton La
Residence- Donaldsonville La
Occupation- Farming at Charles Cox Plantation
Remarks- Mother Esther Porter lives with him (later entry) mother Esther Moore- father Albert Johnson- mother living at Mr. Ben Tiro-
Signature- x

Account Number- 887
Name- James H. Smith
Date of Application- Jan. 22, 1869
Height and Complexion- Brown 26 yrs. old
Father or Mother? Married?- Frances Smith
Name of Children- none
Regiment and Company- on the Dacotah U.S.N.
Place of Birth- Norfolk Va
Residence- St. Anthony between Villere & Robertson
Occupation- Coal & Wood Vendor
Remarks- Mother Louisa Smith- father James H. Smith.
Signature- yes

Account Number- 888
Name- Betsy Sutton
Date of Application- Jan. 23, 1869
Height and Complexion- Yellow 44 yrs. old
Father or Mother? Married?- Duke Powell
Name of Children- none
Place of Birth- Eastern Shore Md
Residence- Baronne St. between Julia & Girod
Occupation- Washing & Ironing
Remarks- Henry Wilson is the only kin she has here- he is the son of her sister Sally Shields- mother Betsy Sutton- father was a white man called Capt. Anthony- she is married to Duke Powell a mulatto and has not seen him for six years and does not know where he is.
Signature- x

Account Number- 889
Name- M.C. Cole treasurer La Annual
Date of Application- Jan. 25, 1869
Height and Complexion- White
Father or Mother? Married?- Julia B. Cole
Place of Birth- Utica NY
Residence- 203 Camp St.
Occupation- Editor & Minister
Remarks- This money is deposited as treasurer of Louisiana Annual Conference M.E. Church
Signature- yes

Account Number- 890
Name- Nancy Richardson
Date of Application- Jan. 25, 1869
Height and Complexion- Black age 74(?)
Father or Mother? Married?- widow of John Richardson of 74th(?) U.S.C.T.
Place of Birth- Chesterfield Co. Va
Residence- corner Hospital & Dauphine St.
Occupation- too old for any occupation
Remarks- Father Moses- mother Miami- I left them both in Va- I came to N O at the time of the first cholera- have no relation living known to her-Malinda (my sister) was sold from Va before I left- never could find her- Note a man by the name of Joseph Thomas came in with her.
Signature- x

Account Number- 891
Name- Prosper Berard
Date of Application- Jan. 25, 1869
Father or Mother? Married?- Charlotte
Name of Children- Ernestine, Celina, Emile & Louise
Regiment and Company- Co. F Private 78th U.S.C.T.
Place of Birth- St. Martinville La
Residence- New St. Bernard St.
Occupation- Carpenter
Remarks- Father dead- mother named Zelphire lives with him- one brother Edward-two sisters Rose & Hortense
Signature- x

Account Number- 892

Name- Malvina Perret
Date of Application- Jan. 25, 1869
Height and Complexion- Black
Father or Mother? Married?- Father William Preston
Name of Children- Mariann
Place of Birth- Africa
Residence- Laurel St. between Lyon & Bordeaus St. City of Jefferson
Remarks- This money is deposited by Mrs. Isabella Preston for her grandchild Malvina Perret- not to be drawn till she is of age- She will be 15 years old on the 1st day of March next.
Signature- x

Account Number- 893
Name- Thomas Warrenton Wickham
Date of Application- Jan. 26, 1869
Height and Complexion- Light
Father or Mother? Married?- single
Name of Children- none
Regiment and Company- Sergt. Co. A 39th U.S. Infantry
Place of Birth- Henrico Co. Va
Residence- in Garrison at Ship Island
Occupation- Soldier
Remarks- Mother Isabella Kinsley (?) in Henrico Co. Va- father William C. Wickham in Hanover Co. Va- brother Charles died in Hanover Co. when Thomas was young.
Signature- yes

Account Number- 894
Name- Alexis Rovira
Date of Application- Jan. 26, 1869
Height and Complexion- Yellow
Father or Mother? Married?- Father John- mother Eliza Gardner- single
Name of Children- none
Regiment and Company- Co. H 74th U.S.C.T.
Place of Birth- New Orleans
Residence- 182 St. Philip
Occupation- Barber
Remarks- Father in Europe- mother died in 1843 in N O- brothers Adolphus died in N O Augustus was drowned June 13, 1868 between Baton Rouge & Bayou Sara

Signature- yes

Account Number- 895
Name- Mrs. Elizabeth Nash
Date of Application- Jan. 26, 1869
Father or Mother? Married?- widow
Place of Birth- Culpepper Co. Va
Residence- Jackson St. corner Coliseum
Occupation- Washer woman
Remarks- Left relatives in Va some 10 years ago- This first deposit was made by Mr. A.J. Davis

Account Number- 896
Name- Warren County
Date of Application- Jan. 27, 1869
Height and Complexion- Black 28 yrs. old
Father or Mother? Married?- Melvina
Name of Children- Sam County about 11 years old
Regiment and Company- Co. D 70th U.S.C.T.
Place of Birth- Alexandria La
Residence- Algiers corner Madison & Market
Occupation- Steam boating
Remarks- He does not know where his son is- has not heard of him for the last 3 years.
Signature- x

Account Number- 897
Name- Albert Wilson
Date of Application- Jan.27 , 1869
Height and Complexion- Black 25 yrs. old
Father or Mother? Married?- Father George- mother Jule- single
Name of Children- none
Regiment and Company- Co. G Private 48th U.S.C.T.
Place of Birth- Bolivar Co. Miss
Residence- Marine Hospital Poydras St. between Dorgenois & Rocheblave
Occupation- Laborer
Remarks- Went to Louisville Ky there 9 yrs. then back to Bolivar- he lost his left leg at the storming of Ft. Blakely Ala-has been in N O since he was wounded-father died in Bolivar when he was a little child-

mother died about 10 yrs. ago in same place- brother Andrew was shot when Albert was wounded- sisters Maria & Minerva dead- Evelina Kyder his half sister lives in Bolivar Co. Miss- he has not seen sister for 8 yrs.- no other relatives.
Signature- x

Account Number- 898
Name- Frederic Epps
Date of Application- Jan. 29, 1869
Height and Complexion- Black
Father or Mother? Married?- Lou Robertson she died about 3 years ago in Ouachita Parish
Place of Birth- Petersburg and raised there until 14 yrs. of age
Residence- 75 Orange St. between St. Thomas & Chippewa
Occupation- Laborer- works on the Levee unloading vessels
Remarks- Father Phil resided in Petersburg- left him 15 yrs. ago- don't know if he is dead or alive- mother Philis left her at the same time don't know if she is living- brothers Robert, William Henry, John & Dave are dead- there were 6 brothers & no sisters he is the only one living.
Signature- x

Account Number- 899
Name- Yorick H. Campbell
Date of Application- Jan. 29, 1869
Height and Complexion- Yellow 25
Father or Mother? Married?- single
Place of Birth- New Orleans
Residence- 309 2nd St. between St. Charles & Carondelet
Occupation- Boss Drayman
Remarks- Henry Campbell his father died July 24, 1853 in N O- mother Prescilla Campbell lives with him- he was raised in this city- 1 sister Mary Jane Graves- 1 brother William died very young.
Signature- yes

Account Number- 900
Name- Elizabeth Yarrington
Date of Application- Jan. 30, 1869
Height and Complexion- White 10 yrs. old
Father or Mother? Married?- Father Col. Yarrington- mother Julia
Place of Birth- New Orleans
Residence- 212 Gravier St.
Occupation- Going to Mr. Williams school on Gravier St.
Remarks- She is The only child
Signature- yes

Account Number- 901
Name- Anthony Bingman
Date of Application- Feb. 1, 1869
Height and Complexion- Black 26 yrs. old
Father or Mother? Married?- Ellen Jones
Name of Children- Mary Bingman
Regiment and Company- Co. D 70th U.S.C.T.
Place of Birth- Alexandria Rapides Parish
Residence- corner Chartres & Poland Sts.
Occupation- Laborer
Remarks- Father John Bingman was living in Rapides Parish before the war he died 5 yrs. ago whilst in the army- mother Cynthia died in Rapides Parish about 20 yrs. ago- have no relations living except one aunt Maria his mother's sister living in Rapides Parish
Signature- x

Account Number- 902
Name- Benjamin Brown
Date of Application- Feb. 1, 1869
Height and Complexion- Black
Father or Mother? Married?- Mary Geal
Name of Children- none
Place of Birth- Montgomery Ala
Residence- 462 Josephine St. between Laurent & Basin Sts.
Occupation- Carpenter
Remarks- Father Benjamin Brown- mother Barby- he was told this by parties who know as they left when he was about 4- he doesn't know if they are living and has no other relatives living.
Signature- yes

Account Number- 903
Name- Newman Taylor
Date of Application- Feb. 2, 1869
Height and Complexion- Black
Father or Mother? Married?- single
Name of Children- none
Place of Birth- Bowling Green Co. Ky
Residence- corner Roman & Gasquet St.
Occupation- Dining Room Servant
Remarks- Father Vincent Taylor died about 8 months ago- mother Jenny Taylor died about 6 yrs. ago- 4 sisters living Esther, Lucy. Henrietta & Canilla all except Canilla live in the city- 2 brothers Jordan & Henry- Henry lives down the coast.
Signature- x

Account Number- 904
Name- John White
Date of Application- Feb.2 , 1869
Height and Complexion- Black 55 yrs. old
Father or Mother? Married?- Phonetta White
Name of Children- Sarah about 24 & Adeline about 20
Place of Birth- at Havre de Grace about 6 miles Baltimore
Residence- Greenville Jefferson Parish little above the Hospital U.S.
Occupation- Laborer- gathering wood in the river
Remarks- He came to this city in 1844 from Baltimore Md
Signature- x

Account Number- 905
Name- Harry A. Oliver
Date of Application- Feb. 2, 1869
Height and Complexion- White
Father or Mother? Married?- Harriet A. Oliver
Name of Children- George Calvin Oliver
Place of Birth- North Carolina
Residence- 180 Erato St.
Occupation- "Gentleman"
Signature- yes

Account Number- 906
Name- Mrs. Margaret Becker
Date of Application- Feb. 2, 1869
Height and Complexion- White
Father or Mother? Married?- John P. Becker
Name of Children- none
Place of Birth- Germany
Residence- 377 Magazine
Occupation- Recorder 1st Dist.
Remarks- This deposit made by Recorder Becker.
Signature- John P. Becker

Account Number- 907
Name- Louis Charles Rondanez Jr.
Date of Application- Feb. 3, 1869
Height and Complexion- White 4 yrs. old
Place of Birth- New Orleans
Residence- 167 Custom House St.
Occupation- none
Remarks- This deposit was made by his father Dr. L.C. Rondanez subject to withdrawal by himself or order.
Signature- L. Rondanez

Account Number- 908
Name- James Boyd
Date of Application- Feb. 5, 1869
Height and Complexion- Black 38 yrs. old
Father or Mother? Married?- Father James- mother Nancy- stepfather- Homer Williams- single
Name of Children- none
Place of Birth- Louisville Ky
Residence- 159 Perdido St. (later entry) Louisville
Occupation- Porter on Steamboat Governor Allen
Remarks- Mother in Cloverport Ky- father died in St. Louis Mo 26 yrs. ago- brothers John & William - sisters Margaret , Jenny, Susan & Mary all in Cloverport- brother Kiah dead- This deposit made by Mrs. Georgia Riley for his a/c.

Account Number- 909
Name- Rosa Franklin
Date of Application- Feb. 6, 1869
Height and Complexion- Black 19 yrs. old
Father or Mother? Married?- single

Place of Birth- Mobile Ala
Residence- Franklin St. between Custom House & Canal
Occupation- Washer woman
Remarks- Transferred from Mobile Branch No. 2070- father dead- mother Ann Smith of Mobile- brothers Philip Johnson & Frank Joseph in Mobile- sister Eliza Franklin- W.W.D. Turner atty. for collecting $20. to be paid her on the 1st of June at the Mobile Branch.

Account Number- 910
Name- Elizabeth Shields
Date of Application- Feb. 6, 1869
Height and Complexion- Light 14 yrs. old
Place of Birth- Adams Co. Miss at Dr. W.N. Mercer's Plantation
Residence- Canal St. between Baronne & Carondelet
Occupation- House Servant
Remarks- Mother Hannah Taylor- father Wilmer Shields-sister Martha Shields- no brothers all living at Dr. Mercer's residence.
Signature- yes

Account Number- 911
Name- Mary Turner
Date of Application- Feb. 6, 1869
Height and Complexion- Black 13 yrs. old
Place of Birth- New Orleans La
Residence- Johnson St. between Canal & Gasquet
Occupation- House Servant
Remarks- Mother Lucy Ann Washington- father Theopile Turner died about 10 yrs. ago-brothers Paul & James Turner- sister Maria Washington all living together
Signature- yes

Account Number- 912
Name- Mary Lockwood
Date of Application- Feb. 8, 1869
Height and Complexion- Black 30 yrs. old
Father or Mother? Married?- William J. Lockwook

Name of Children- Victorine Ferguson 16 yrs. old
Place of Birth- Washington DC
Residence- 145 1/2 Perdido St. (May 30, 1870) resides now at 291 Poydras St.
Occupation- Yellow Fever Nurse
Remarks- Mother Emily Johnson is living in Charles Co. Md- father William Short died about 25 yrs. ago in Nangimoy Charles Co. Md- he belonged to Cecilia Dicey- daughter can draw- born & raised in N O description- yellow, short & fat.
Signature- x

Account Number- 913
Date of Application- Feb. 8, 1869
Remarks- See No. 899

Account Number- 914
Name- Eliza Pitman
Date of Application- Feb. 9, 1869
Height and Complexion- Yellow
Father or Mother? Married?- Albert Pitman
Name of Children- Zelie 20 & Corinne 13
Place of Birth- New Orleans
Residence- Gravier St. near Bolivar
Occupation- Midwife
Remarks- Father William Green died when she was a child- mother Dolly died in 1862 in this city- brother John in this city- the first deposit was made for her by Mr. Jacob Cheek- Mrs. Pitman desires that whenever Mr. Jacob Cheek should come with her book, he should be given what amount her asks of her deposits.
Signature- x

Account Number- 915
Name- Edmund Jones
Date of Application- Feb. 9, 1869
Height and Complexion- Black 44 yrs. old
Father or Mother? Married?- Lisa Jones
Name of Children- none
Regiment and Company- Co. E 97th U.S.C.T.
Place of Birth- Carolina Co. Va
Residence- Bayou Lafourche Assumption Parish
Occupation- Farming

Remarks- Edmund Jones was wounded in the leg at Pollard In Florida- Father Rueben Jones died about 40 yrs. ago- mother Meriky Jones does not know where she is or if she is living- brother Warren Jones when last heard from was in N O.
Signature- x

Account Number- 916
Name- Aaron Brazier
Date of Application- Feb. 9, 1869
Height and Complexion- Black 30 yrs. old
Father or Mother? Married?- single
Name of Children- none
Place of Birth- Hope's Plantation St. John the Baptist Parish
Residence- Marmillion's Plantation St. John the Baptist Parish (Sept. 5, 1870) Aaron has moved to Mr. Marmillion's brother's place about two miles from his former place.
Occupation- Farming
Remarks- Mother Mary Thomas resides with him- father Amos Brazier died about 20 yrs. ago- brother Sydned Thomas is also on the same plantation.
Signature- x

Account Number- 917
Name- Lutheran Benevolent Society No.2
Date of Application- Feb. 9, 1869
Remarks- Account opened by Rev. Eugene P. Royal, the money can only be drawn by Mr. Royal personally or by written order signed by President, secretary, & treasurer.
President- Eugene P. Royal
Secretary- Jacob Smith
Treasurer- Henderson Duncan
Record for Eugene P. Royal No. 124 Jan. 24, 1870- the following parties were this day named by Rev. E.P. Royal as the trustees- all checks must be signed by three regular officers and at least three trustees: Ralph Burrow, Dede Bienaime, William Andrew & Philip Peter
Signature- yes

Account Number- 918
Name- Isaac Young
Date of Application- Feb. 10, 1869
Height and Complexion- Black 27 yrs. old
Father or Mother? Married?- single
Name of Children- none
Regiment and Company- Wagoner Co. H 39th U.S. infantry
Place of Birth- Scott Co. Ky
Residence- Ship Island Miss
Occupation- Soldier at Garrison Ship Island
Remark- Selvy his mother, his father Edward, & brother William Young all live together in Scott Co. Ky-
Signature- yes

Account Number- 919
Name- Ausey Shorter
Date of Application- Feb. 11, 1869
Height and Complexion- Black about 50
Father or Mother? Married?- Father Charles- mother Rachel- wife Betsy County
Name of Children- Maria 7, Ausey 4 & Ned 2
Regiment and Company- Co. D 70th U.S.C.T.
Place of Birth- Eastern Shore Md
Residence- on Dr. Clark's place above Alexandria
Occupation- Farmer
Remarks- Came here when a sucking baby- at Dr. Clark's place about 5 miles above Alexandria- children Thomas, Charles, & Eureline are dead- father died when cholera 1st came about in La- mother lives on
Bayou La Mary about 15 miles below Alexandria- brothers Charles, Sawny & George all dead- sisters Anny, Emiline & Kizzy all dead.
Signature- x

Account Number- 920
Name- Frederick County
Date of Application- Feb. 11, 1869
Height and Complexion- Black about 40
Father or Mother? Married?- Father Harry- mother Netty- wife Maria

Name of Children- Thomas dead
Regiment and Company- Co. D 70th U.S.C.T.
Place of Birth- Eastern Shore Md
Residence- Roger Roberts place about 15 miles below Alexandria
Occupation- Farmer
Remarks- Came from Md when about 12 yrs. old to Alexandria at Dr. Maddox place- father on Dr. Clark's place- mother died on Dr. Maddox place about 15 yrs. ago- brothers; Warren & Thomas on boats in Miss.- Jacob dead- Ned dead- Henry Orbin in Maryland- sisters Betsy wife of Ausey Shorter (No. 919) & Julia dead.
Signature- x

Account Number- 921
Name- Augustus & Patience Livingston
Date of Application- Feb. 11, 1869
Height and Complexion- Dark Brown
Father or Mother? Married?- Father William- mother Betsy Watson- wife Patience
Name of Children- Frederick 26
Regiment and Company- Co. E 70th U.S.C.T.
Place of Birth- Norfolk Va
Residence- Rapides Parish (in town)
Occupation- Painter (tailor by trade)
Remarks- Father died at Norfolk was killed in duel when Augustus was 12- mother died there 12 yrs. before he left- brother Richard Watson in Norfolk- sister Emily Ann dead- left Va when 22 yrs. old came to N O was here a month then sold to Parish Rapides on Bayou Robert about 5 miles from Alexandria- See record for Patience below.
Signature- x

Account Number- 921
Name- Patience Livingston
Date of Application- Feb. 11, 1869
Height and Complexion- Black about 55
Father or Mother? Married?- Father Ishmael- mother Patience- husband Augustus Name of Children- (see above)
Place of Birth- Camden NC
Remarks- Came to N O when a young girl- father died in NC about 30 yrs. ago- mother died there about 35 yrs. ago- brothers Tom, Jesse & March all dead- sisters Betsy & Alesf were left in NC.
Signature- x

Account Number- 922
Name- Claiborne McCabe
Date of Application- Feb. 11, 1869
Plantation- Always lived on same place.
Height and Complexion- Black 38
Father or Mother? Married?- Father Ned- mother Maria- wife Caroline
Name of Children- Lucy 8, Milton 13, Sam 12, Mary 6 months & George 2
Regiment and Company- Co. D 70th U.S.C.T.
Place of Birth- Bayou "Courtney" 22 miles from Alexandria
Residence- Joe Manning's Place
Occupation- Farming
Remarks- Children Aleck, Seymour & Sally all dead- father & mother on place with him- brothers Jim & Britt both dead- sisters Fanny, Louisa & Lusanna all on same place with him-Fanny's husband Sam Peek dead- Louisa is wife of Bill Neal.
Signature- x

Account Number- 923
Name- William Brooks
Date of Application- Feb. 11, 1869
Height and Complexion- Black about 20
Father or Mother? Married?- Father Dennis- mother Hannah- wife Henrietta
Name of Children- Frank 1 yr..
Regiment and Company- Co. E 70 th U.S.C.T.
Place of Birth- Spriggs plantation on Red River
Residence- 83 Congress St.
Occupation- Laborer
Remarks- Came out of Army here- been here 3 yrs. - Child 2 days old dead- father lives up Red River- mother died while he was in Army- brothers Jerry, Dennis & David all in city- sister Mary Ann in city.
Signature- x

Account Number- 924

Name- Peter Bogan
Date of Application- Feb. 11, 1869
Height and Complexion- Black 25 "rings on fingers"
Father or Mother? Married?- Father Peter- mother Judy- wife Rosa
Name of Children- 2 babies dead
Regiment and Company- Co. D 70th U.S.C.T.
Place of Birth- Williamsburg Va
Residence- Algiers
Occupation- Hostler
Remarks- Came from Va when 14 yrs. old to N O was in city 11 mos. then to Rapides Parish- father dead never saw him- mother in Va- bother Henry sold out here 7 yrs. before Peter and they met for the first time year before last on Levee- Henry is in Algiers-James, Oliver & Simon(?) all in Va- sisters Caroline, Ann Eliza, Sally, & Minervy all in Va- brother John dead.
Signature- x

Account Number- 925
Name- James B. Berry
Date of Application- Feb. 12, 1869
Height and Complexion- 73 yrs. old
Father or Mother? Married?- widower- wife's name Appleby
Name of Children- adopted Ann Maria Francis Bond
Place of Birth- Baltimore Md
Residence- 482 St. Ann
Occupation- Barber
Remarks- Sisters- Elizabeth, Emilia & Martha Ann Berry all in Baltimore.
Signature- yes

Account Number- 926
Name- Daniel Moore
Date of Application- Feb. 12, 1869
Height and Complexion- Black 55 yrs. old
Father or Mother? Married?- single- he would not have his wife's name put down
Name of Children- Peter 4 months old
Place of Birth- North Carolina
Residence- Elmira St.
Occupation- Wood Chopper
Remarks- About 50 yrs. ago he left his mother Darkess, his father Primus, & his sisters Martha & Lucy all belonging to Mr. Dirden in NC- he came to La with Thomas Overton Moore.
Signature- x

Account Number- 927
Name- George Spruel
Date of Application- Feb. 13, 1869
Height and Complexion- Brown 45
Father or Mother? Married?- Father David- mother Rachel- wife Eliza
Place of Birth- Roanoke River Washington Co. NC
Residence- Mason St. near corner Greatman or Dauphine St. will move to Prieur St. between St.Bernard & St. Antoine
Occupation- Cooper works for Mr. Haman
Remarks- Left North Carolina when 35 yrs. old- came to N O then went to St. Bernard Parish there 6 yrs. Children Daphny, Bannister, Mary Jane & Louisa all dead- father died in Terrell Co. 16 yrs. ago- mother in NC- brothers David & Bannister both in NC- sisters Mary wife of Maxwell Beasley, Caroline wife of Silas Mann, Eliza wife of Jas Whidby all in NC- brother Ephraim dead.
Signature- x

Account Number- 927
Name- Eliza Spruel wife of George
Father or Mother? Married?- Father Hautess- mother Louisa- husband George
Name of Children- Daphny by George (Banister, Mary Jane & Louisa) by Charles
Place of Birth- Charleston SC raised in La
Remarks- Brother Peter Fische

Account Number- 928
Name- Elias Owens
Date of Application- Feb. 13, 1869
Height and Complexion- 48 Dark Brown
Father or Mother? Married?- Father Archy- mother Scylla- wife Lucy
Regiment and Company- Co. F 78th U.S.C.T.

Place of Birth- Flemingsburg Ky
Residence- 131 Seventh St.
Occupation- Brush maker works for Mr. Kilman
Remarks- Left Ky on Aug. 17, 1855 came to Baton Rouche- came here in 1863- children Amanda, Elias, Albert, Charles & Eliza Ann all dead- Father died in Ky 1838- mother died there in 1853- brother George in Frankfort Ky- sister Martha in Natchez Miss.- brothers John & Alfred- sisters Amanda & Sarah all dead
Signature- x

Account Number- 929
Name- Robert Jones
Date of Application- Feb. 13, 1869
Height and Complexion- Black 29
Father or Mother? Married?- Father Robert- mother Lorena- wife Louisa
Name of Children- Bervick 5
Regiment and Company- Co. F 78th U.S.C.T.
Place of Birth- Bayou Sara
Residence- Terrebonne Station La
Occupation- Farming works for G.W.Woodruff
Remarks- Left Bayou Sara 15 years ago went to Bayou Black- then into Army- child Anthony dead- Father died at Bayou Black 18 years ago- mother died same place 7 years ago- brothers Ephraim at Terrebonne Station & Adam Georgia at Lufwish Crossing- sisters Edmonia wife of Oguch Baptiste at Terrebonne Station, Margaret wife of William Stickman at Bayou Black & Nadey at Bayou Black- sisters Courtney Jones, Silvy, Minerva, Malvina & Anna all dead.
Signature- yes

Account Number- 930
Name- John Henderson
Date of Application- Feb. 13, 1869
Father or Mother? Married?- Jane Henderson
Name of Children- Albert Henderson 2 yrs. old March 2, 1869
Regiment and Company- Sergt. Co. B 10th Heavy Artillery

Place of Birth- Columbus Va
Residence- Howard St. between Poydras & Lafayette
Occupation- Laborer at Cotton Presser
Remarks- Left Columbus Va when he was about 6 yrs. old- mother Tilda Henderson lives with him- father Archy Henderson died when he was about 7- brother Augustus Henderson.
Signature- yes

Account Number- 931
Name- Theodule Piquery
Date of Application- Feb. 15, 1869
Height and Complexion- 27 Brown
Father or Mother? Married?- Father Theodore- mother Nancy- wife Francis Adele
Name of Children- Emma 15 months
Regiment and Company- Co. A 78th U.S.C.T.
Place of Birth- Franklin La
Residence- corner Conti & Burgundy
Occupation- Painter
Remarks- Came to N O 1862- father died here 12 yrs. ago- mother died 6 months after father- brother Charly Nancy Co. I 39th- brothers dead- mother had 12 children- Theodule youngest- sister Cecilia wife of Iule Caliste in city- Josephine dead & other babies dead.
Signature- x

Account Number- 932
Name- John Messiah
Date of Application- Feb. 15, 1869
Height and Complexion- 52 Dark Brown
Father or Mother? Married?- Father John- mother Virginia- wife Virginia
Name of Children- Leonore 10 yesterday, George 8, Virginia 4 & Anna 3
Place of Birth- Richmond Va
Residence- 141 St. Charles St.
Occupation- Drayman
Remarks- Left Va 20 yrs. ago came to N O- father died in Richmond about 25 yrs. ago- mother died about 3 or 4 months before father- child John dead- brother George Quickly dead.
Signature- yes

Account Number- 933
Name- William Alexander Baron
Date of Application- Feb. 15, 1869
Height and Complexion- 29 Brown
Father or Mother? Married?- Father Peter- mother Prudence
Regiment and Company- Co. B 74th U.S.C.T.
Place of Birth- New York City
Residence- 10 Rampart St. below Canal
Occupation- Tailor
Remarks- Was taken to West Indies when 2 yrs. old- was there 2 years then came here- went to NY in 1864- father died in NY when William was 17 months old- mother with William.
Signature- yes

Account Number- 934
Name- Sam L. Harris
Date of Application- Feb. 15, 1869
Height and Complexion- White 34
Father or Mother? Married?- Alice Wilde
Place of Birth- Boston Mass
Residence- Beaufort SC
Occupation- General Inspector F.S. & T. Co.
Signature- yes

Account Number- 935
Name- Amanda Jones
Date of Application- Feb. 15, 1869
Height and Complexion- 25 Brown
Father or Mother? Married?- Father Frank Roberts- mother Winnie- husband Archy Jones
Name of Children- Elizabeth 6 & Margaret 10 months on the 17th
Place of Birth- Amelia Co. Va
Residence- 10 Adele St.
Occupation- husband runs on Steamboat "Vicksburg"
Remarks- Left Va when 6 or 7 yrs. old came to Tereington Mo stopped two years then to N O- children Frank, Winny, Amy & others no named dead- father died here when Amanda was a child over 20 yrs. ago- mother with daughter- brother Dick left here in the war- John dead- sisters; Berthea sold away from Va- Margaret wife of Herod Clay in N O- Elizabeth wife of Sam Bland in Vicksburg- Virginia & Emily both dead.
Signature- x

Account Number- 936
Name- Franklin Petaway
Date of Application- Feb. 15, 1869
Height and Complexion- Black 29
Father or Mother? Married?- Father Frank Spicer- mother Harriet Petaway- wife Mary Ann
Regiment and Company- Co. F 70th U.S.C.T.
Place of Birth- Southampton Va
Residence- Derbigny between Julia & Cypress
Occupation- in Medical Purveyors Dept.
Remarks- Sold out here when a baby to Alexandria- made N O home since came out of Army- father dead so his mother said- mother died in Alexandria when he was 15 or 16- brother Douglas drowned in Red River 12 miles below Alexandria.
Signature-yes

Account Number- 937
Name- Benjamin Tompkins
Date of Application- Feb. 15, 1869
Height and Complexion- Black 40 last Christmas
Father or Mother? Married?- Father Soloman- mother Hannah- wife Virginia
Name of Children- Soloman 16 months
Regiment and Company- Co. F 97th U.S.C.T.
Place of Birth- Matthews Co. Va
Residence- Poland between Royal & Dauphin
Occupation- Longshoreman
Remarks- Left Va in 1859 was in Ascension from 1859 -1862 then N O- children- Benjamin dead- father drowned in Chesapeake Bay Hampton Road 25 yrs. ago- mother died in Va about 30 yrs. ago- brother- Soloman in Va- Kit dead- sisters Harriet & Sally in Va.
Signature- x

Account Number- 938
Name- Christopher Stump
Date of Application- Feb. 15, 1869

Height and Complexion- Black 38
Father or Mother? Married?- Father
Sam- mother Minervy Childrars- wife
Emeline
Place of Birth- Nashville Tenn
Residence- 8th between Dryades & St.
Denis
Occupation- Sampler & Weigher
Remarks- Left Tenn in 1857 & came to N
O- father died out here- he was sold
away from Nashville when Christopher
was a small boy- mother died in Nashville
when he was small- brother David died in
Nashville & sister Jane died same place.
Signature- x

Account Number- 939
Name- Albert Parker
Date of Application- Feb. 15, 1869
Height and Complexion- 23 Dark Brown
Father or Mother? Married?- Father
Albert- mother Julia- single
Place of Birth- New Orleans
Residence- 168 Melpomene St.
Occupation- Jobber
Remarks- Father died year ago Dec.
20th- mother lives with him- brothers
James & Richard in N O- Henry &
Lorenzo both in Navy- Robert dead-
Henry is on the Tallahassee.
Signature- yes

Account Number- 940
Name- Duncan Macgibbon
Date of Application- Feb. 15, 1869
Height and Complexion- White 12
Father or Mother? Married?- Father Dr.
Duncan- mother Jane
Place of Birth- Ooaca Miss
Residence- 404 Baronne St.
Remarks- Father died 10th last April-
brothers John & James dead- sister Katy
dead.
Signature-yes

Account Number- 941
Name- Alfred Parker
Date of Application- Feb.15, 1869
Height and Complexion- Brown 28
Father or Mother? Married?- Father
Elijah- mother Charity- wife Lucy

Name of Children- Alfred 1 yr. & Mary
dead
Regiment and Company- Co. B 10th
Heavy Artillery U.S.C.T.
Place of Birth- Franklin Co. NC
Residence- corner Camp & Harmony
Occupation- Cooper working with
Bricklayer
Remarks- Came here when 7 yrs. old-
father died here 1 yr.. ago- mother died
here about 2 months before father-
brothers Philip Hunter, Adolph Mallen &
Edward Mallen all in city, Glasgow dead-
sisters Martha wife of Robert Brown,
Clementine & Josephine all in city-
Signature- x

Account Number- 942
Name- Aaron McKay
Date of Application- Feb. 16, 1869
Height and Complexion- Black 25
Father or Mother? Married?- Father
Joseph Green- mother Riddy- wife Nancy
Name of Children- Margaret 16 & Martha
12
Regiment and Company- Co. A 74th
U.S.C.T.
Place of Birth- Nashville Tenn
Residence- St. Bernard between
Johnson & Pieur Sts.
Occupation- Laborer
Remarks- Came to Canton Miss when
about 11 yrs. of age- came here since
war- parents in Williamson Co. Tenn-
brothers; Wellington in N O, Peter in
Miss, Isam in Nashville Tenn & Joseph
with father- sisters; Lorena in N O- Miney
wife of John Pawny in Tenn, Sally in
Memphis & Penny with mother, Dorthulia
& Christina both dead.
Signature- yes

Account Number- 943
Name- Charles Gore
Date of Application- Feb. 16, 1869
Height and Complexion- Dark Brown
says about 24 is probably older
Father or Mother? Married?- Father
Geuin probably Guillamen- mother Phillis-
wife Elizabeth
Name of Children- Joseph 2 yrs. old in

Jan 1872
Regiment and Company- Co. E 70th U.S.C.T.
Place of Birth- Eppyville Parish
Residence- Derbigny St. between St. Louis & Toulouse
Occupation- Mortar Carrier
Remarks- Came to N O since war- buried 3 children not named- father died here when Charles was a small child- mother died in Eppyville Parish when he was a child she died before father- sisters Charlotte & Phillis both dead- wife can draw with book.
Signature- x

Account Number- 944
Name- Bennett Dunford
Date of Application- Feb. 16, 1869
Height and Complexion- Brown 39
Father or Mother? Married?- Father Joseph- mother Clara
Regiment and Company- Co. B 74th U.S.C.T.
Place of Birth- Pensacola Fla
Residence- Claiborne between Ursulines & St. Philips
Occupation- Bricklayer "Kettle -setter"
Remarks- Came here 20 yrs. ago- wife Emily dead- father died in Plaquemines Parish in the war or "just in the beginning"- mother died in Pensacola when he was 3 yrs. old- brothers; Joseph & Breno dead & Manassas went to England- sisters; Cedelze, Therese & Maricria all dead- cousin Milty Nicolls wife of Evarico Grouex lives same place as Bennett.
Signature- x

Account Number- 945
Name- Green Webster
Date of Application- Feb. 16, 1869
Height and Complexion- Black 30
Father or Mother? Married?- Father Jesse- mother Sarah
Regiment and Company- Co. D 70th U.S.C.T.
Place of Birth- Alexandria La
Residence- Patterson St. Algiers
Occupation- Laborer
Remarks- Came here when mustered out- father died in Alexandria about 12 yrs. before the war- mother died in Thibodeaux while he was in the service- brothers; Alfred & Jesse in Algiers, Dan, Demps, William, & Jesse all dead- sisters; Louisa sold to Texas & Lucy dead.
Signature- x

Account Number- 946
Name- Cooley Henderson
Date of Application- Feb. 16, 1869
Height and Complexion- Black 25
Father or Mother? Married?- Father Bill Wilson- mother Margaret- stepfather Gabriel Riley- wife Mary
Name of Children- Sophy 1
Regiment and Company- Co. E 70th U.S.C.T.
Place of Birth- Lake Concauly
Residence- 106 Toulouse St. Mar. 12 on Le Bais Plantation
Occupation- Laborer
Remarks- Raised on Bayou Corta- stopped here when mustered out- father died on the lake before Cooley can recollect- mother lives with him- brother Lewis Foster at home- sister dead not named.
Signature- x

Account Number- 947
Name- John Johnson
Date of Application- Feb. 16, 1869
Height and Complexion- Brown 25
Father or Mother? Married?- Father James- mother Nancy- wife Louisa
Name of Children- Louisa
Regiment and Company- Co. B 78th U.S.C.T.
Place of Birth- Donaldsonville
Residence- 569 Dryades St. Aug. 31, 1869 lives now St. Denis near corner 4th
Occupation- Laborer
Remarks- Came here about 10 yrs. before the war- father in Donaldsonville- mother same place as John- sister Crelia Ann dead- mother was sold away from her daughters before John was born.
Signature- x

Account Number- 948
Name- Oscar Pilman
Date of Application- Feb.17 , 1869
Height and Complexion- Light 24
Father or Mother? Married?- Father Charles- mother Zinette- wife Elizabeth
Name of Children- Joanna 3
Regiment and Company- Co. D 6th La. U.S.C.T.
Place of Birth- Algiers La
Residence- Patterson St.
Occupation- Pilot
Remarks- Father in N O- mother in Algiers- child Mary dead- brother Jules Dupare in Algiers & Joseph dead- (states that he deposits the money for a lady but does not wish to give her name- this memorandum will have no effect in case of his death but is simply put down as a fact for identification)
Signature- yes

Account Number- 949
Name- William Martin
Date of Application- Feb. 17, 1869
Height and Complexion- Brown 60
Father or Mother? Married?- Father Martin- mother Phillis- wife Jane
Name of Children- Corey Ann 10
Place of Birth- Attakapas Co.
Residence- corner Broad & Poydras
Occupation- Cotton Sampler & Weigher
Remarks- In N O about 30 yrs.- father died in St. Martinsville about 35 yrs. ago- mother died there about 3 yrs. after father- brothers; Jance in N O- Lazeine & Washington both dead- sisters; Viny in N O, Salis in Attakapas & Mary dead.
Signature- x

Account Number- 950
Name- Lewis Taylor
Date of Application- Feb. , 1869
Height and Complexion- Black 27
Father or Mother? Married?- Father William- mother Josephine- wife Lavinia
Regiment and Company- Co. H 74th U.S.C.T.
Place of Birth- on Red River
Residence- corner Roman & Lafayette
Occupation- Farmer
Remarks- Raised at Bayou Sara- child William dead- father died at Bayou Sara before Lewis can remember- mother died in St. John Baptiste Parish when he was in the service- brother Charles dead- sister Lydy Ann in N O & Milly dead
Signature- x

Account Number- 951
Name- Francis Sophronia Dunn
Date of Application- Feb. 17, 1869
Height and Complexion- Brown 33
Father or Mother? Married?- Father Thomas- mother Rosella- husband Joseph
Place of Birth- Decatur Ga
Residence- 132 Perdido
Occupation- of husband- Warehouse man
Remarks- Came here from Decatur & has been here 14 yrs.- money from 5ct Laring's (?) Bank Boston Mass- father in Decatur- mother died in Decatur 3 months ago- brother Felix in Little Rock Ak- sister Caroline wife of Joseph Green in Atlanta Ga- sister Calistia dead.
Signature- x

Account Number- 952
Name- Prudence Baron
Date of Application- Feb. , 1869
Height and Complexion- Brown 48
Father or Mother? Married?- Father Nicholas Vors- mother Netty Butler- husband Peter
Name of Children- William Alexander 29 (see record 933)
Place of Birth- Washington DC
Residence- 10 Rampart St.
Occupation- keeps Lodging Rooms
Remarks- Came from Washington in 1832- remained here 2 yrs. then to NY then to West Indies then here in 1843- husband died in NY when William her son was 17 months old- father died before she can remember- mother died about 6 months before William was born- brothers; Charles heard of him 12 or 15 yrs. ago in East Indies, William & John both dead- sister Mary Ann wife of Nathaniel Dunlop (with Mrs. Baron) &

Priscilla dead.
Signature- yes

Account Number- 953
Name- Frank McKinney
Date of Application- Feb. 18, 1869
Height and Complexion- Brown born Oct. 11, 1842
Father or Mother? Married?- Father Tom- mother Ann- wife Agnes
Name of Children- Julia Ann 1 yr.. 4 mos. (later entry) Horatio McKinney 2 mos. on Sept. 27, 1869
Regiment and Company- Co. E 90th(?) U.S.C.T.
Place of Birth- Rapides Parish 8 miles from Alexandria in Red River
Residence- 489 Poydras St.
Occupation- Meat Store corner Magazine & Lafayette
Remarks- Went to Natchez in 1864- came here in Mar. 1866- heard his father went to NC when he was at Natchez Miss- mother died in Rapides Parish when he was about 14 yrs. old- child Henry Franklin dead- brothers; Patrick Rixon 9 miles above Vicksburg & John Baptiste Dyson dead- sisters; Lucy wife of Peter Perry in Jefferson City, Sophy wife of John Walker on Bayou Black on "Alphonse" place & Angeline dead.
Signature- yes

Account Number- 954
Name- Ananias Hall
Date of Application- Feb. 18, 1869
Height and Complexion- Black 23
Father or Mother? Married?- Father Adam- mother Sarah- wife Effie Ann
Regiment and Company- Co. E 70th U.S.C.T.
Place of Birth- Alexandria Rapides Parish
Residence- 5 miles from Alexandria
Occupation- Farming
Remarks- Has not seen wife since he was a soldier- Ananias lives with his father- mother died when he was a baby- brothers; Edward More in N O, Hanover Hall, Thomas, Adam & Ben all at home, Philip dead- sisters; Maria wife of Beverly Thompson on Red River where Ananias was born, Irena & Mimy dead.
Signature- x

Account Number- 955
Name- John De Gar
Date of Application- Feb. 19, 1869
Height and Complexion- Black 28
Father or Mother? Married?- Father Bob- mother Sally- step father Sam McTire- wife Hester
Regiment and Company- Co. B 80th U.S.C.T.
Place of Birth- Assumption Parish
Residence- Back Brick yard in Carrollton
Occupation- Planting
Remarks- Been in Carrollton about a year & a half- father died in Assumption Parish when he was 8 or 9- mother died same place about 4 1/2 yrs. ago- brothers; Sam Veel in Bayou Lafourche, Antoine near Donaldson, Frank & Narcisse both dead- sisters; Ligibeth McTire in Baton Rouche, Ella Zeel, Francois & Eglantine all dead- step father lives in Algiers.
Signature- x

Account Number- 956
Name- Henry Allen
Date of Application- Feb. 19, 1869
Height and Complexion- Dark Brown 23
Father or Mother? Married?- Father Richard Rucker- mother Ann- wife Celestine
Name of Children- Annie 5
Regiment and Company- Co. G 96th U.S.C.T.
Place of Birth- Hartfordville KY
Residence- next to Brick yard in Carrollton
Occupation- Laborer
Remarks- Left Hartfordville 8 years before the Yankees came here- father & mother in Hartfordville- brothers; Horace & James Thomas in Hartfordville, D. Wilton & Isaac dead- sisters Clementine & Ann Maria both in Ky.
Signature- x

Account Number- 957
Name- William Obar

Date of Application- Feb. 20, 1869
Height and Complexion- Black 24
Father or Mother? Married?- Mother Katrine- wife Frances Elizabeth
Name of Children- Thomas William 3 mos.
Regiment and Company- Co. E 78th U.S.C.T.
Place of Birth- Thibodeauxville Bayou Lafourche
Residence- Greensville Jefferson Parish
Occupation- Laborer
Remarks- Stopped here when mustered out- never knew his father- mother died in Thibodeauxville about 15 yrs. ago- brothers; Gus in Attakapas Bayou Teche & Joe dead- sisters; DeMatile at Attakapas, Odelia & Eliza at Thibodeauxville- children Joseph William (two same name dead)
Signature- x

Account Number- 958
Name- Robert Thomas Henderson
Date of Application- Feb.22 , 1869
Height and Complexion- Black 28
Father or Mother? Married?- Father William- mother Nancy
Regiment and Company- Co. H 74th U.S.C.T.
Place of Birth- near Lexington Ky
Residence- Washington St. between Dryades & Bacchus
Occupation- Tailor works for Oldendorf 188 Rampart
Remarks- Went to Greensboro Ga when about 8 yrs. old & left there last part 1859- parents in Ky- heard about 2 yrs. ago that his parents & sister were living- sister Mary in Ky- before was on Dr. Stone's place about 100 miles up river in Ipperaville Parish.
Signature- yes

Account Number- 959
Name- Lumas Hoyt Pease
Date of Application- Feb. 23, 1869
Height and Complexion- White 45
Place of Birth- Winsted Conn
Residence- 148 Julia St.
Occupation- Chaplain "Am. Seamen's Friend Society"
Signature- yes

Account Number- 960
Name- C.S. Sauvinet Special Agent in Trust for Jennie Justice
Date of Application- Feb. 23, 1869
Height and Complexion- about 20
Father or Mother? Married?- Father Simon- mother Kitty
Place of Birth- Alexandria
Residence- Alexandria at home
Occupation- working for father
Remarks- Description given by her half brother Ben Spry- mother died last summer- she had only one child by Simon- she had three children by former husband Sam Spry- Benjamin Spry in city at Gumbele (?) Hotel- Lew Brown (died about 3 mos. after mustered out) & Eliza Ann widow of Bob Hinson in Alexandria- sisters dead Sophy & Louisa & 2 babies all small children.

Account Number- 961
Name- Mitchell Hopes
Date of Application- Feb. 23, 1869
Height and Complexion- Black about 59
Father or Mother? Married?- Father Baoler- mother Mony- wife Silvy
Name of Children- Charles & Alexander left near Vicksburg 35 yrs. ago
Place of Birth- Orange Co. Va
Residence- 322 Melpomene St.
Occupation- Cotton
Remarks- Left Va when between 12 & 13 years of age- went to Saline Co. Mo there til 21 then to La has been here 35 yrs.- parents in Va has not heard from them since he was 14- brothers Simon, Rueben & James all in Va- sisters Tabby in St. Louis, Hannah in Saline Co. Mo- 2 little sisters in Va he can't remember their names.
Signature- yes

Account Number- 962
Name- Charles Cray
Date of Application- Feb. 24, 1869
Height and Complexion- about 60 Dark Brown
Father or Mother? Married?- Father

127

Isaac- mother Maria- Wife Fanny
Name of Children- Daniel 22, Henderson 16 & Harriet 29 wife of Alfred Thoroughgood
Place of Birth- Talbot Co. Md- 5 miles of Easton
Residence- 121 Galvez St.
Occupation- Coffee Inspector
Remarks- Left Md when 11 or 12 been in N O and Miss ever since- father in Md- mother died in Md before Charles left- children Charles & others dead- brother (only one) dead- sister Rachel came away from Md when he did and was sold away in N O- Eliza & Cely in N O- Lucy came out same time as other, don't know where she is- Eliza is the widow of Nelson- Cely is the widow of Benton.
Signature- x

Account Number- 963
Name- Elnora M. Ryder
Date of Application- Feb. 24, 1869
Height and Complexion- White 21 yrs. old
Father or Mother? Married?- single
Name of Children- none
Place of Birth- New York City
Residence- 516 Magazine St.
Occupation- none
Remarks- Mother's name Elnora D. Ryder resides in New York City- father Charles F. Ryder died 17 yrs. ago- sisters; Emma Ryder Solanes lives at 516 Magazine St. & Isabella Ryder wife of Mr. John Delaney in NY.
Signature- yes

Account Number- 964
Name- Jackson Nance
Date of Application- Feb. 24, 1869
Height and Complexion- Black 32
Father or Mother? Married?- Father Stephen- mother Sarah- wife Isabella
Name of Children- Maria 8 & Dave 9
Regiment and Company- Co. A 48th U.S.C.T.
Place of Birth- Richmond Co. NC
Residence- St. Louis Mo has been living there 2 yrs.
Occupation- Steam boating

Remarks- Left NC 18 yrs. ago went to Muscogee Co.- to Columbus Ga was there 7 or 8 yrs. then came here- father in NC- mother was sold away when he was a child- children & wife in Columbus Ga- brothers; Lazarus, Henry, & Berry all in NC- sister Jane was taken with mother.
Signature- x

Account Number- 965
Name- Troy Parker
Date of Application- Feb. 26, 1869
Height and Complexion- Black 28
Father or Mother? Married?- Father Harry- mother Mary- wife Margaret King
Regiment and Company- Co. I 50th U.S.C.T.
Place of Birth- Alexandria La
Residence- Howard between Gravier & Perdido
Occupation- works at Sawmill on St. Joseph St.
Remarks- Been in NO going on 4 yrs.- Pheobe was his wife- she has left him and has another husband- Father died here about 5 yrs. ago- mother died in Rapides Parish- sisters Delphy in Rapides, Delia in N O & Lucy dead- brother Jefferson dead.
Signature- x

Account Number- 966
Name- Vicksburg Branch
Date of Application- Feb. 23, 1869
Remarks- Benj. A. Lee cashier

Account Number- 967
Name- Society of St. John the Baptist
Date of Application- Feb. 26, 1869
President- Frank Molemasse
Vice- Robert Butler
Treasurer- William Cooper our depositor #7 (later crossed out)
Secretary- Xavier Bossiere (later crossed out)
Remarks- The officers of that society will leave Their signatures or record in a few days. A. Pailles (later crossed out) Jan. 72
President- William Richard
Vice- Jean Edmond

Treasurer- Wm. Cooper our depositor
Secretary- Jno. Peter
Wm. Cooper will draw

Account Number- 968
Name- Nelson Wilson
Date of Application- Feb. 27, 1869
Height and Complexion- Dark Brown 24
Father or Mother? Married?- Father George- mother Aneke- wife Charlotte
Regiment and Company- Co. B 75th U.S.C.T.
Place of Birth- Terrebonne Parish
Residence- corner Fulton & St. James Sts. May 25, 1870 resides now 574 St. Thomas St.
Occupation- Policeman
Remarks- Been in the city since 1865- father died in Terrebonne Parish July 23, 1865- mother died there about 12 years ago- brothers; Abram Kirby & Lewis Mangel in Terrebonne Parish, Anderson Wilson last seen up the river he went into the Army & Roberson dead- sisters; Harriet, Fanny Mangel, Silvy wife of Wm. Body & Phene wife of Sam Denny all in Terrebonne- Nancy wife of James Citizen in Donaldsonville, Winny dead.
Signature- x

Account Number- 969
Name- Franklin Petaway
Date of Application- Feb. 27, 1869
Remarks- See record #936

Account Number- 970
Name- Henry Clay
Date of Application- Feb. 27, 1869
Height and Complexion- Black 47
Father or Mother? Married?- Father Harry- mother Aggy- wife Lucinda
Name of Children- adopted child Georgiana 15
Place of Birth- Richmond Va
Residence- 129 Franklin St.
Occupation- Confectionery Store 131 Perdido
Remarks- Left Va before he was one year old- went to Ky was there 2 or 3 years- then to Mo there til he was 9 yrs. old- then La Rapides Parish came to N O in Oct. 1842- Father died in Indiana before he was a year old- mother died in Parish of St. Landry about 12 yrs. ago- brothers Benjamin & George Washington both dead, Harrison in Mo- sisters Maria in Mo & Ellen dead
Signature- yes

Account Number- 971
Name- William & Dicy Henry
Date of Application- Feb. 27, 1869
Remarks- Account opened by William Henry- money can be drawn by either see records following.

Account Number- 971
Name- William Henry
Date of Application- Feb. 27, 1869
Height and Complexion- Black 48
Father or Mother? Married?- Father Billy Buck- mother Catherine Henry- wife Dicy Alexander
Place of Birth- Richmond Va
Residence- 477 Hercules St. June 12, 1869 moved to Melpomene St. between Franklin & White
Occupation- Cotton Weigher & Sampler
Remarks- Left Va 22 or 23 yrs. ago- came to Natchez there 13 months- then to Pickneyville there 11 months- then came here- father died in Richmond about 14 yrs. ago- mother died in King William Co. 40 miles from Richmond one year before his father- children John Henry & daughter left in Richmond- brother Augustus in Richmond- sisters Louisa Hill, Peggy & Catherine with mother below Richmond, Patsy dead- wife can draw.
Signature- x

Account Number- 972
Name- Philip Jason Frederick Woods
Date of Application- Feb. 27, 1869
Height and Complexion- Black 50 years
Father or Mother? Married?- Father Frank- mother Rachel- wife Ellen
Place of Birth- New Orleans
Residence- 261 St. Mary's
Occupation- Works in Cotton
Remarks- Wm. Henry a/c 971 with Mr.

Woods- father died here when Philip was small- mother died here when Philip was about 9 before death of his father- Philip was brought up by Mr. Jason- brother Joseph in N O & Benjamin left N O some years ago- sister Ann lives above Jefferson- parents came from Maryland.
Signature- yes

Account Number- 973
Name- Elijah Anderson
Date of Application- Feb. 27, 1869
Height and Complexion- Black
Father or Mother? Married?- Father Elijah Towns- mother Mary- wife Nancy
Regiment and Company- Co. A 78th U.S.C.T.
Place of Birth- 20 miles from Montgomery Ala
Residence- Broad St. below Claiborne
Occupation- Rolls Coll at Peterson's Coal Yard at Mint
Remarks- Left Ala when Pensacola Fla. surrendered & went to Pensacola- one year there- then N O to the Army- he was 23 when he came from Montgomery- calls his mother "Little Mary"- he's not seen his father since he was small boy- father sold away- mother in Ala where he came from- had child in Ala Elijah Anderson also Ausy (dead)- brothers; Frank, Lewis, Tom & Jack all in Ala- sisters; Lucinda wife of Charles Foster & Sicily all in Ala in same place where he was brought up about 20 miles from Montgomery.
Signature- x

Account Number- 974
Name- Samuel Smith
Date of Application- Mar. 1, 1869
Height and Complexion- Dark Brown 15 yrs. 2 months
Father or Mother? Married?- Mother Ellen Smith- step father Daniel Brown
Place of Birth- Jackson Miss
Residence- 252 Julia St. U.S. Bakery
Occupation- works in Bakery
Remarks- Left Jackson before he could remember came to La to Bayou Mason to Milliken's Bend to Natchez then to N O- mother at Hutchins landing- brothers Ely Smith at Milliken Bend, Amos dead- sister Carolina dead.
Signature- yes

Account Number- 975
Name- Auguste Baptiste
Date of Application- Mar. 1, 1869
Height and Complexion- Brown 26
Father or Mother? Married?- Father Auguste- mother Victorine- wife Priscilla Davis
Name of Children- Augustine 1 1/2
Regiment and Company- Co. A 7th U.S.C.T.
Place of Birth- New Orleans
Residence- Orleans between Galvez & Johnson
Occupation- Carpenter
Remarks- Child Oscar Charles dead- father died when Auguste was young- mother in city.
Signature- x

Account Number- 976
Name- Charles & Eliza Parker
Date of Application- Mar. 1, 1869
Remarks- Money can be drawn by either- see record # 230

Account Number- 977
Name- William Raymond Page
Date of Application- Mar. 1, 1869
Height and Complexion- White 27 June 1968
Father or Mother? Married?- Father Joseph- mother Mary Ann
Place of Birth- New Orleans
Residence- corner St. Charles & Poydras
Occupation- Printer
Remarks- Has lived in California, France & Pittsburgh Penn- parents reside in Pittsburgh.
Signature- yes

Account Number- 978
Name- Sixth St. Relief Society
Date of Application- Mar. 2, 1869
Remarks-
James Briller- President
Wm. Hall- Vice Pres.

Elisha Hopkins- Secretary
Money can only be drawn on the order of the three officers.
Jan. 17, 1870
Cavallier J. Thomas- Sec.
Francis Johnson- Chairman
July 13, 1871
Pres.- James Briller
Vice Pr.- F. Johnson
Sec.- C.J. Thomas
Money to be drawn by the above.
See records James Briller, Wm. Hall & Elisha Hopkins.

Account Number- 978
Name- James Briller
Date of Application- Mar. 2, 1869
Height and Complexion- Black 27
Father or Mother? Married?- Father Charles- mother Silvy
Place of Birth- Nackatoch La
Residence- corner Poeyfarre & Magazine
Occupation- Cook
Remarks- Living here 2 yrs. the 4th day March- father left Nackatoch when the place was taken- mother died there about 26 yrs. ago- brother John Pleasant in N O- sister Judy dead.
Signature- yes

Account Number- 978
Name- William Hall
Date of Application- Mar. 2, 1869
Height and Complexion- Brown 21 Oct. 17, 1868
Father or Mother? Married?- Father Robert- mother Bridget
Place of Birth- Attakapas La
Residence- corner 4th & St. Dennis with parents
Occupation- School Teacher
Remarks- Came here in 1864- brothers; Robert in city & John dead- sisters; Margaret & Charity in city- 4 children his brothers & sisters dead.
Signature- yes

Account Number- 978
Name- Elisha Hopkins
Date of Application- Mar. 2, 1869
Height and Complexion- Black 24 Mar. 16, 1868
Father or Mother? Married?- Father Annison- mother Elsie Morton- step father George Morton
Regiment and Company- Co. A 4th Cavalry
Place of Birth- Lafourche Parish La
Residence- St. Denis between 1st & 2nd
Occupation- "Studying Divinity" at First Church
Remarks- Came here in 1862- father died in Lafourche Parish when he was small- mother died there in 1867- step father died there in 1856- brothers Wyatt Morton in N O, James & Wesley Hopkins dead- sisters; Louisa Hopkins & Matilda Morton & others all dead.
Signature- yes

Account Number- 979
Name- Armand Populus
Date of Application- Mar. 2, 1869
Height and Complexion- Light Brown 29
Father or Mother? Married?- Father Henri- mother Josephine Sherman- wife Rosa Williams
Name of Children- Henry Populus
Regiment and Company- 1st then 74th Co. A or D U.S.C.T.
Place of Birth- New Orleans
Residence- 309 St. Ann St.
Occupation- Bricklayer
Remarks- Came from Mexico about 9 yrs. ago went there when about 8 mos. old- father in Mexico- mother died in Mexico since the war- brothers; Henri & Artoulou- sisters; Maria, Theodora, Florentia, Jorquena & Annica all live in Tampico Mexico.
Signature- yes

Account Number- 980
Name- Louis Bass
Date of Application- Mar. 2, 1869
Height and Complexion- White 16
Father or Mother? Married?- Father John M.- mother Adelada
Place of Birth- New Orleans
Residence- 110 Bienville St.
Occupation- last worked at John Gauche

corner Camp & Poydras
Remarks- Brother Arthur 14.
Signature- yes

Account Number- 981
Name- Jacques Questy
Date of Application- Mar. 2, 1869
Height and Complexion- Brown 50
Father or Mother? Married?- Father John- mother Annette- single
Name of Children- Jacob 24 & Joseph 22
Place of Birth- New Orleans
Residence- St. John Baptist between St. Bernard & Annette
Occupation- School Teacher
Remarks- Parents dead- children living in city.
Signature- yes

Account Number- 982
Name- Peter Raymond
Date of Application- Mar. 3, 1869
Height and Complexion- Light Brown 39
Father or Mother? Married?- Father Peter- mother Harriet- wife Clotide
Name of Children- Peter 15, Fred 5, Robert 4, Reta 3, Ermina 15 mos. & Phillisene 6
Place of Birth- New Orleans
Residence- 228 St. Louis St.
Occupation- Carpenter
Remarks- Father died in city 10 yrs. ago- mother in city- brother Edward Johnson in county 2 miles from Carrollton- sisters; Selina Shurbare, Coralene & Alphonsine all with mother.
Signature- yes

Account Number- 983
Name- Crawford Simson
Date of Application- Mar. 3, 1869
Height and Complexion- Black 35   Aug. 1, 1868
Father or Mother? Married?- Father Julius- mother Seny
Regiment and Company- Co. K 74th U.S.C.T.
Place of Birth- Rappahanock Co. Va
Residence- Marine Hospital (patient)
Occupation- Sailor
Remarks- When about 6 went to Brown Co. Mo near Columbia there til 1859 then came here- don't remember father- mother in Columbia, Mo (Brown Co.)- brother Henry- sister Ann both with mother.
Signature- yes

Account Number- 984
Name- Josephine Dent
Date of Application- Mar. 3, 1869
Height and Complexion- Black 23
Father or Mother? Married?- Father William Lameston- mother Mary Reed- husband Alfred
Place of Birth- Plaquemines Parish down coast
Residence- P. St. between Royal & Bourbon
Occupation- Washing & Sewing
Remarks- Came to city 5 yrs. ago- husband died here a year ago- father down coast- mother died with her daughter on last Mardi Gras- children Louis & Arre both dead- brothers 3 all dead can't remember names- sisters Jane, Caroline & Celestine all dead- cousin Francis Lewis lives with her.
Signature- x

Account Number- 985
Name- James Henry Parker
Date of Application- Mar. 3, 1869
Height and Complexion- Brown 25
Father or Mother? Married?- Father Albert- mother Julia
Regiment and Company- Co. K 74th U.S.C.T.
Place of Birth- New Orleans
Residence- Melpomene between St. Charles & Appollo
Occupation- Porter No. 82 Gravier
Remarks- Father died her Dec. 20, 1868- mother lives with him- brothers; Albert 24 & Richard in city, Lorenzo in Navy Hospital at Washington, Henry on Steamer Tallapoosa, Robert dead.
Signature- yes

Account Number- 986
Name- William Fisher
Date of Application- Mar. 3, 1869

132

Height and Complexion- Black 26
Father or Mother? Married?- Father
Thomas- mother Peggy- wife Ony
Regiment and Company- Co. F 74th
U.S.C.T.
Place of Birth- Richmond Va
Residence- corner Gaienne & Constant
Sts.
Occupation- Steam boating
Remarks- Left Richmond 3 yrs. before
war & came to N O- he lost use of left eye
mortar got into it in Va- children dead
Thomas & Duncan Jones all can
remember- father died in Vicksburg
about 4 yrs. ago- mother in Vicksburg-
brothers Andrew & Soloman in
Vicksburg- sisters; Margaret wife of
Gilbert Middleton, Nancy & Nicissy all in
Vicksburg, Ermin wife of Allen Douglas in
Monroe.
Signature- x

Account Number- 987
Name- James Douglas
Date of Application- Mar. 3, 1869
Height and Complexion- Black 34
Father or Mother? Married?- Father
Nathen Brill- mother Dinah- wife Lucy
Pryor
Name of Children- Lucy 5 mos.
Regiment and Company- Co. A 80th
U.S.C.T.
Place of Birth- Southampton Va
Residence- Burdock St. Carrollton
Occupation- Laborer
Remarks- Came to False River Pointe
Coupee Parish La about 3 yrs. before
war- been in Carrollton since mustered
out- never saw his father died before he
was born- mother died in Va 5 or 6 yrs.
before he left- brother Dempsey sold out
here about 4 yrs. before James- sister
Huldy dead.
Signature- yes

Account Number- 988
Name- Edward Reed
Date of Application- Mar. 3, 1869
Height and Complexion- Black 36 next
July
Father or Mother? Married?- Father
William- mother Silvy- wife Ann
Name of Children- Martha Ann 5 mos.
March 7th
Regiment and Company- Co. D 80th
U.S.C.T.
Place of Birth- Jackson Miss
Residence- Quenett's place between
Fort Bank & Carrollton Ferry
Occupation- working on farm
Remarks- Left Jackson Miss when 12
yrs. old & came to Jackson La- father
died in Miss long before rebellion- mother
died in Baton Rouge about 5 yrs. ago-
children dead; Edward, Howard, Richard,
Lizzie & one more boy- sister Page on
Bayou Lafourche- had not heard from her
for 8 yrs. till last monday- mother had 9
children only two living.
Signature- x

Account Number- 989
Name- Joshua William
Date of Application- Mar. 4, 1869
Height and Complexion- Brown 32
Father or Mother? Married?- Father
William Wagner- mother Mary- wife Clara
Name of Children- adopted child
Alphonse 6 yrs. July 4, 1869
Regiment and Company- Co. F 73rd
U.S.C.T.
Place of Birth- New Orleans
Residence- Roman between St. Bernard
& Orleans
Occupation- Porter with A. Brousseau &
Co. 19 Chartres St.
Remarks- Father died when he was small
boy- "sucking baby"- mother was sold
away when he was about 8 yrs. of age-
suppose she was sold to Mississippi-
wife can draw.
Signature- yes

Account Number- 990
Name- Rufus King Howell
Date of Application- Mar. 4, 1869
Height and Complexion- White 9
Father or Mother? Married?- Father
Rufus King- mother Eliza
Place of Birth- New Orleans
Residence- 8 Euterpe
Remarks- Step brother John 24- sisters;

133

Minnie 7, May 6, Clara 2 & Ellen 6 mos.
Signature- yes

Account Number- 991
Name- Minnie Howell
Date of Application- Mar. 4, 1869
Height and Complexion- White 7
Remarks- See record 990

Account Number- 992
Name- May Howell
Date of Application- Mar. 4, 1869
Height and Complexion- White 6
Remarks- See record 990

Account Number- 993
Name- Partheana Mason
Date of Application- Mar. 4, 1869
Height and Complexion- Very Light 25
Father or Mother? Married?- Father Joseph- mother Jane
Place of Birth- Madison Co. Ky
Residence- at Judge Howell's 8 Euterpe St.
Occupation- Servant
Remarks- Left Ky when very small and came to Natchez- came here just before close of war- has not heard from parents since she left- brothers; Roy & Granville in Ky- Henry dead- sisters; Adaline & Rose Ann both left in Ky.
Signature- yes

Account Number- 994
Name- Robert Robertson
Date of Application- Mar. 4, 1869
Height and Complexion- Dark Brown 25
Father or Mother? Married?- Father Phil- mother Sisily- wife Polly
Regiment and Company- Co. I 97th U.S.C.T.
Place of Birth- Richmond Va
Residence- Kinnersville 10 miles from New Orleans
Occupation- working in Levee
Remarks- Left Va 3 yrs. before war & came here- father died in Richmond Va when he was small- mother in Va- brothers Tom & Jacob in Richmond- sister Lizzie dead.
Signature- yes

Account Number- 995
Name- Charles Ennis
Date of Application- Mar. 4, 1869
Height and Complexion- Black 35
Father or Mother? Married?- Father Charles- mother Cornelia- step father William Steward- wife Permelia
Regiment and Company- Co. F 70th U.S.C.T.
Place of Birth- Rapides Parish
Residence- Rousseau St. between Philip & Lyssno
Occupation- Wheeling Coal
Remarks- Came to city 3 yrs. ago- was called Jones Ennis in regiment- Father died in Army 4 yrs. ago- mother in city- buried 2 children not named- brothers; Isaac in Alexandria, Edmund in Arkansas, Alford dead- sisters; Silvy wife of Joe Stoney in city, Versy wife of Henry Vichy in city, Mary widow of Sandy Williams in city.
Signature- x

Account Number- 996
Name- Washington Green
Date of Application- Mar. 4, 1869
Height and Complexion- Black
Father or Mother? Married?- Father Jacob- mother Maria- wife Mary Jane
Name of Children- Henry 11 & Washington 9
Regiment and Company- Co. F 70th U.S.C.T.
Place of Birth- up Red River At Porteage
Residence- Rousseau St. Near Philip St.
Occupation- Rolling Coal
Remarks- Lived in city about 3 yrs.- children Maria, Dan & Aaron dead- father in Alexandria- mother down the coast at Leary's place- brother George Henry in city- sisters; Loretta wife of August down coast- her husband in Attakapas, Susan dead.
Signature- x

Account Number- 997
Name- Jordan Hayes
Date of Application- Mar. 5, 1869
Height and Complexion- Dark Brown 25

Father or Mother? Married?- Father Jordan- mother Mahala- wife Ann Place of Birth- Wilkinson Co. Miss Residence- At. Ann between Johnson & Galvez
Occupation- works at A. Brousseau & Co. 19 Chartres St.
Remarks- Left Miss when about 2 yrs. old & came to Attakapas La- father went in Army hasn't heard from him- mother died 12 yrs. before war in Attakapas- brothers; Rufus & Isaac in city, Heiram, Texas and others all dead- sisters Dorcas wife of William Robinson at Bayou Dedelino (go by Algiers canal), Louisa dead.
Signature- x

Account Number- 998
Name- James Ransom
Date of Application- Mar. 6, 1869
Height and Complexion- Black 49
Father or Mother? Married?- Father James- mother Hannah- wife Sarah
Place of Birth- Matthias Co. Va
Residence-206 Jaskett St.
Occupation- Bricklayer
Remarks- Left Va when about 8 yrs. of age & came here- child Charlotte 21 widow of Louis (illegitimate daughter)- father & mother in VA- has not heard from them for 41 yrs.- brother Richard in Va- sisters Betsy & Polly in Va- wife can draw.
Signature- x

Account Number- 999
Name- Lutheran Benevolent Society
Date of Application- Mar. 6, 1869
Remarks-
Pres.- Rev. E.P. Royal depositor No. 124
Sec.- Fletcher T. Chinn
Treas.- Peter Ricks
Collector- George Williams
Money can only be drawn by written order signed by all officers.
Trustees can draw
Geo. Williams- Director
Jules Ogilvie- Sec.
Jacob Cheeks- Treas.
July 7, 1870

Newly elected board
William Butler - Director
George Williams- Treasurer
Leonard Cambridge- Trustee
Nov. 10, 1873
William Butler is no longer associated with group
New Officers
Geo. Williams- Director
Jules E. Ogilvie- Sec.
Jacob Cheeks- Treas.
Committee Appointed
George A. Washington- Chairman
David Cosby
Leonard Cambridge

Account Number- 999
Name- Fletcher T. Chinn
Date of Application- Mar. 6, 1869
Height and Complexion- Black 21
Father or Mother? Married?- Father Scott- mother Writhe- wife Martha
Place of Birth- Nashville Tenn
Residence- 277 St. Louis St.
Occupation- School Teacher
Remarks- Been here about 19 yrs.- parents in city- brothers; Walter & Charles in city, Isaac dead- sister Victoria wife of Charles Steverson in city, Sarah in Washita or Vicksburg, Caroline wife of Jack Elder in St. James Parish, Roxanne & Milly Franklin both dead
Signature- yes

Account Number- 999
Name- George Williams
Date of Application- Mar. 6, 1869
Height and Complexion- Dark Brown 32
Father or Mother? Married?- Father Noel- mother Leah- wife Celestine
Regiment and Company- 7th & 10th U.S.C.T.
Place of Birth- New Orleans
Residence- 66 Liberty St.
Occupation- Laborer
Remarks- Father died in city 17 yrs. ago- mother at 64 Liberty St.- children one not named dead- brothers all dead never heard names- sister Cecile dead.
Signature- yes

Account Number- 1000
Name- John Wallace Hutchinson
Date of Application- Mar. 6, 1869
Height and Complexion- Brown 32
Father or Mother? Married?- Father William- mother Henrietta- wife Harriet
Name of Children- George 6, Charley 4 & Arthur 1
Place of Birth- Covington St. Tammany Parish
Residence- 3 Prieur St.
Occupation- Brick Mason
Remarks- Is a member of the Legislature- father died across the lake- mother lives over there- brothers; George & William in City- sisters: Elizabeth wife of F.C. Antoine, Henrietta wife of Jas. H. Ingraham both in city & Mary Jane all in city, Cornelia across the lake.
Signature- yes

Account Number- 1001
Name- Sidney Aldron & Mary Franklin
Date of Application- Mar. 6, 1869
Sidney 's Information
Height and Complexion- Black 21
Father or Mother? Married?- Father Charles- mother Malise
Place of Birth- Natchez Miss
Residence- 18 Liberty St.
Occupation- Steam boating (later entry) Shoemaker
Remarks- Sidney went to Cincinnati Ohio in 1849- came here in 1863- father on steamer "Leo" mother in city-money to be drawn by either.
Signature- yes
Mary's Information
Height and Complexion- Light Brown
Father or Mother? Married?- Father Ben- mother Rachel
Place of Birth- New Orleans
Residence- Girod between Rampart & Basin with mother Sept. 8, 1870 lives now corner Bienville & Galvez
Occupation- Servant in House
Remarks- Father died when she was a small child- mother in city- sisters Lucy in city & Flaggy dead.
Signature- x

Account Number- 1002
Name- Andrew Hunter
Date of Application- Mar. 6, 1869
Height and Complexion- Black 45
Father or Mother? Married?- Father Doctor- mother Leah- wife Margaret
Name of Children- Ellen 15, James & Robert (both dead)
Regiment and Company- Co. E 70th U.S.C.T.
Place of Birth- Sumner Co. Middle Tenn.
Residence- 373 St. Andrew St.
Occupation- Steam boating
Remarks- Left Tenn about 3 yrs. before Mexican War & went to Texas-came here from Memphis in 1859- children John, William & Patsy in Alabama somewhere, born in slavery time, Illegitimate- father in Houston Texas, supposes he is dead he would be 100 yrs. old- mother died in Houston about 23 yrs. ago- brother John in Eeberville Parish- sisters; Martha wife of Burril Robinson & Mary both in Eeberville Parish- lost end if thumb & forefinger of right hand when he was about 15 in a straw cutter.
Signature- x

Account Number- 1003
Name- George W. Price
Date of Application- Mar. 6, 1869
Height and Complexion- Brown 22
Father or Mother? Married?- Father Joseph- mother Lavinia
Regiment and Company- Co. C 39th U.S.C.T.
Place of Birth- Nashua NH
Residence- Nashua NH
Occupation- Soldier
Remarks- Came here last May as a soldier- parents in Nashua NH- brothers; Joseph, Thaddeus & Jimmy- sister Mary Alice- all at home- brothers George Washington & Oranys both dead.
Signature- yes

Account Number- 1004
Name- Daniel Barnett
Date of Application- Mar. 8, 1869
Height and Complexion- Black 47

Father or Mother? Married?- Father Durby- mother Nancy- wife Eliza Place of Birth- Green Co. Ky Residence- corner St. Louis & Dorgenois Occupation- Baggan Wagon Remarks- Left Ky about 20 years ago & came to the coast above mouth of Red River- been in city 5 yrs.- father died in Ky about 15 yrs. ago- mother in Green Co. Ky- brother Joe in Ky- sisters Jenny wife of Robinson Ray & Fanny both in Green Co.- brothers Jep, George Washington & Daniel Jefferson all dead- sister Lucy dead.
Signature- yes

Account Number- 1005
Name- George Washington
Date of Application- Mar. 8, 1869
Height and Complexion- Brown 26
Father or Mother? Married?- Father William- mother Martha- wife Josephine
Name of Children- Charles 6 mos.
Regiment and Company- Co. H 74th U.S.C.T.
Place of Birth- New Orleans
Residence- Assumption Parish
Occupation- Store Keeper
Remarks- Parents at 81 Gasquet St.- buried one child not named- half brothers; Mons Osborne & Alexander Armistead in city- brother Willis Washington dead- sister Matilda in city.
Signature- yes

Account Number- 1006
Name- Lucy Carter
Date of Application- Mar. 8, 1869
Height and Complexion- Black 62
Father or Mother? Married?- Father Jacob Castleman- mother Gracie Ann- husband Wilson
Name of Children- Louisa wife of John Hill in Jefferson
Place of Birth- Hardy Co. Va
Residence- Gretna Jefferson Parish
Occupation- Washing & Ironing
Remarks- Been out here 29 yrs.- father died in Va year Lucy was sold away- mother died about 3 months before father- husband died in Gen. Hospital was in 77th Regt. Co. B- when she left Va she left children; Louisa (afterwards sold out here first to Baton Rouche & then down here when Baton Rouge was taken), Jonathan (sold away before his mother was), Arena, Jacob (sold to Baton Rouge with Louisa), Fanny & Hannah Catherine- brothers; Jacob & Richard in Va, Charles (sold away before her said to have been drowned)- sisters Harriet & Nancy Green in Va, Marina & Harriet both dead.
Signature- x

Account Number- 1007
Name- William McKinney
Date of Application- Mar. 8, 1869
Height and Complexion- Black 44
Father or Mother? Married?- Father John- mother Christy- wife Louisa (dead)
Place of Birth- Georgetown DC
Residence- 140 White St.
Occupation- Cistern Maker works for Mr. Hendricks on Rattsan 8th corner Clio
Remarks- Raised in Washington DC- been out here 22 yrs.- children Mothiel & Arreel dead- father was sold away before Wm. can remember- mother in Washington- brother can't remember name in Washington- sister Mary Ellen sold out here 7 yrs. before Wm.
Signature- x

Account Number- 1008
Name- Matt Turner
Date of Application- Mar. 9, 1869
Height and Complexion- Black 22
Father or Mother? Married?- single
Name of Children- Louisa Turner 7 months old- her mother is Mary Turner
Regiment and Company- Co. I 80th U.S.C.T.
Place of Birth- Baton Rouge La
Residence- No. 105 Perdido St.
Occupation- Porter at Gen. Bussery
Remarks- Been out here 3 years- father Robert Turner resides at the mouth of Red River La- mother Louisa died about 3 yrs. before the war on Red River- one sister Emily wife of William Allen lives in Donaldsonville La- Matt had another wife

Mary who left him about 2 yrs. ago and went to Baton Rouge.
Signature- x

Account Number- 1009
Name- Henderson L. Smoot
Remarks- see record 420

Account Number- 1010
Name- Elodis Toussant
Date of Application- Mar. 9, 1869
Height and Complexion- Dark Brown 38
Father or Mother? Married?- Father Etienne Carrere- mother Justine Mederic- step mother Charlotte Dial- husband Augustus
Name of Children- Mary 18, Elodie 8 & Paul 10
Place of Birth- New Orleans
Residence- 120 Union St.
Occupation- Seamstress
Remarks- Husband was killed at Port Hudson- Father with daughter- mother died here in 1834- brother Barthelmy in city- half sisters Delphine Carrere & Linotte in city- brothers Amede & Albert dead.
Signature- x

Account Number- 1011
Name- Edmund Yarrell
Date of Application- Mar. 9, 1869
Height and Complexion- Dark Brown 31
Father or Mother? Married?- Father George- mother Susan
Regiment and Company- Co. I 51st U.S.C.T.
Place of Birth- Martin Co. NC
Residence- Freret between Gravier & Perdido
Occupation- Foreman at McCluskey & Mason Coal Yard
Remarks- Came out here about 25 years ago to Louderdale Co. Miss- in the city 3 yrs. next July- former wife Eliza separated from her- left parents in NC- hasn't heard from them in 12 yrs.- brothers; Eli in NC and others but he can't remember them- sisters; Charity, Penny, & Edny were sold away before Edmund- Oct. 31, 1870 wife's name Louisa Jones- born Natchez Miss- 27 yrs. old-light mulatto- father John Jones- mother Sophy- in case of sickness Louisa Yarrell is empowered to draw on presentation of Bank Book.
Signature- x

Account Number- 1012
Name- Nathaniel Taylor
Date of Application- Mar. 10, 1869
Height and Complexion- Black 27
Father or Mother? Married?- Father Henry- mother Rose- wife Mary Thomas
Regiment and Company- Co. A 86th U.S.C.T.
Place of Birth- Red River
Residence- on Antonio Marrerro place St. Bernard Parish
Occupation- Farmer
Remarks- Raised in St. Bernard Parish- came here when 4 yrs. old- father died in St. Bernard Parish 2 yrs. ago last Feb.- mother died there last Sept.- brother John in city, William Henry in St. Bernard Parish- sister older than him dead- his brother John says there were one brother & three sisters who are dead- Taylor left Mary Thomas and got married in April 1869 to Caroline Johnson.
Signature- x

Account Number- 1013
Name- Pauline Dozier
Date of Application- Mar. 10, 1869
Height and Complexion- Black about 35
Father or Mother? Married?- Father Souneau Jougot- mother Charlotte- husband John
Name of Children- Mary 20, Joseph 14, Nelda 9, Louisa 6 & George Hamolet 6
Place of Birth- Plaquemines Parish
Residence- Bagatelle St. between Girod & Urquhart Sts.
Occupation- cook for Antoinette Regean
Remarks- Father died in Plaquemines Parish when she was small- mother died same place before father- husband died here about 5 yrs. ago- brother Jules on Adolph Regean's place down coast- brothers Manuel & August both dead- sister Nelda in St. Bernard Parish.

138

Signature- x

Account Number- 1014
Name- Frederick George Smith
Date of Application- Mar. 10, 1869
Height and Complexion- White 33
Father or Mother? Married?- Father Francis- mother Sophia- wife Ann Ellenor
Name of Children- George 4
Place of Birth- Hastings Surrey Co. England
Residence- Washington St. at Oliver Pearce's factory
Occupation- Under Warehouse man in Thompson's Sugar Refinery Common St.
Remarks- Came here Dec. 14, 1868- mother dead- father in England- sister Anna Charlotte & Augusta Josephine both in England.
Signature- yes

Account Number- 1015
Name- John Jenkins
Date of Application- Mar. 10, 1869
Height and Complexion- Black born Feb. 6, 1835
Father or Mother? Married?- Father John - mother Lizzie
Regiment and Company- Co. B 39th U.S.C.T.
Place of Birth- Gooseland Co. Va
Residence- Ellick Hill Gotesland Co. Va
Occupation- Soldier
Remarks- Came out here as a soldier in 1867- parents in Va- brother George & Henry at home- sisters; Norah wife of James Miles in Richmond Va & Betty at home- Wm. R. Banks came with him is in Co. F same Regt.- May 1, 1869 John Jenkins is now in Co. G 25th US Infantry and detached in the Commissary Dept. in the city.
Signature- x

Account Number- 1016
Name- William Robinson Banks
Date of Application- Mar. 10, 1869
Height and Complexion- Brown 22 Aug. 31, 1869
Father or Mother? Married?- Father Hanover- mother Matilda

Regiment and Company- Co. F 39th U.S.C.T.
Place of Birth- Richmond Va
Residence-Richmond Va
Occupation- Soldier
Remarks- Came out in the Army in 1867- parents in Richmond- brothers; Thomas in N O, Hanover & Joseph in Richmond- sisters Charlotte & Sarah both at home- by consolidation of the regiment he is now a private in Co. B 25th US Infantry and detached in the Commissary Dept. in this city.
Signature- yes

Account Number- 1017
Name- Peter Victor
Date of Application- Mar. 11, 1869
Height and Complexion- Light 29
Father or Mother? Married?- Father Charles Perry- mother Emmy- wife Caroline
Name of Children- Emma 4 & Nema 1 yr.. 6 mos.
Regiment and Company- Co. G 1st La (73) U.S.C.T.
Place of Birth- New Orleans
Residence- 100 Ursulines St.
Occupation- Steam boating
Remarks- Father died in St. Charles Parish when Peter was about 10- mother & sister Mary in city
Signature- x

Account Number- 1018
Name- Joseph Gillem
Date of Application- Mar. 11, 1869
Height and Complexion- Black 52 next Oct.
Father or Mother? Married?- Father Jacob- mother Isabella- wife Zabella
Regiment and Company- 10th Heavy Artillery Co. B
Place of Birth- Williamsburg Va
Residence- 197 Dauphin St.
Occupation- Drayman
Remarks- Came out when 25 yrs. old- has been here 26 yrs.- wife's four children Mary, Frances, Mary Lewis & Joseph- father sold away before Joseph- mother died in Va 8 yrs. before Joseph

139

was sold- sister Winny wife of Olmstead Young in Va- half brother John Sanders sold about time father was- other brothers dead don't know names.
Signature- x

Account Number- 837
Name- Agnes Miles
Date of Application- Mar. 11, 1869
Height and Complexion- Black 50 Feb. 19, 1869
Father or Mother? Married?- Father Daniel Lee- mother Nancy- husband Daniel
Place of Birth- Fayette Co. Ky
Residence- 61 Derbigny St.
Occupation- Washing
Remarks- Came here when about 6 yrs. of age- children 2 dead not named- father was sold away from N O 30 yrs. ago- mother died here in 1857- sisters; Lucy wife of Luzene McCarthy in city, Mary Jane, Eliza, Nelly (dead), Emily, Mazilla- brothers; John, Harlan, Jordan (dead), & Henry.
Signature- x

Account Number- 837
Name- Mary A. Fox
Date of Application- Mar.11 , 1869
Height and Complexion- Light 30
Father or Mother? Married?- Father Moris Russell- mother Priscalla- husband Thomas
Name of Children- Sarah 13
Place of Birth- New Orleans
Residence- 277 St. Louis St.
Remarks- Father died here 8 yrs. ago- mother in city- child Moris dead- sister Eliza wife of Ben Brazil in city.
Signature- yes

Account Number- 837
Name- Sally Pullam
Date of Application- Mar. 11, 1869
Height and Complexion- Black 85 Mrs. Pullam is quite fleshy
Father or Mother? Married?- Father Ransom Easten- mother Molly- husband John
Name of Children- adopted son John 23
Place of Birth- Louisville Ky
Residence- Basin St. between Mellophone & Thalia
Occupation- Washing
Remarks- Been here 47 yrs.- husband died here 1 yr.. 4 mos. ago- father sold away when Sally was small- mother died here 23 yrs. ago- brothers; George Wilson, Moses Wilson, James Wilson all dead- sister Hannah dead.
Signature- x

Account Number- 67
Name- Ellen Gray wife of Anthony Gray
Height and Complexion- Black about 42
Father or Mother? Married?- Anthony Gray
Name of Children- William Green & Rosaline from another husband both dead
Place of Birth- Kentucky
Residence- Washington between Clara & Magnolia
Occupation- Washer & Ironer
Remarks- Father's name can't say- mother died when she was 3 weeks old- has no brother or sisters- no relatives.

Name Index

A

Abbott, Francis	85
Abbott, George	46
Abbott, Isaac A.	84, 109
Abbott, Melinda	85
Abbott, Victorine	46
Aber, Sophie	37
Aber, William	36, 37
Abrahamsen, Julius	98
Abram, Charlotte	104
Adams, Alexander	83
Adams, Elizabeth	83
Adams, Henry	83
Adams, Maria	30
Adams, Mrs. Clark	18
Adams, Nelson	50
Aldron, Charles	136
Aldron, Malise	136
Aldron, Sidney	136
Alexander, John	68
Alexander, Joseph Thomas	47
Alexander, Mary Constance	47
Alexander, Renette	56
Alexander, Rosalie	68
Alexander, Sarah	47
Alexander, Sandy	47
Alexander, Severin	68
Alexander, Spencer	79
Alexander, William	24
Alexis, John B.	76
Alexis, Rosalie	42, 76
Allen, Aleck	24
Allen, Alfred	18
Allen, Annie	126
Allen, Celestine	126
Allen, Charles	12
Allen, Emily	137
Allen, George	12
Allen, Henry	126
Allen, Revd. James	112
Allen, Jane	18
Allen, Jerry	18
Allen, Joe	12
Allen, Monerva	12
Allen, William	24, 137
Alexander, Dicy	129
Allis, Corinne	66
Allis, Newton	66
Alphonse, Gustave	55
Alphonse, James	55
Alphonse, Mary	55
Alphonse, Theresa	55
Alvord, J. C.	2
Ambry, Peter	41
Amson, M.A.	7
Anderson, Alfred	83
Anderson, Ausy	130
Anderson, David	106
Anderson, Edward	26, 102
Anderson, Elijah	130
Anderson, Ellen	106
Anderson, Elyza	60
Anderson, Emily	60
Anderson, Frank	130
Anderson, Giles	60
Anderson, Jack	130
Anderson, John	106
Anderson, Joseph E.	2
Anderson, Lewis	130
Anderson, Marie T.	2
Anderson, Mary	130
Anderson, Nancy	130
Anderson, Richard	70
Anderson, Rosetta	60
Anderson, Sicily	130
Anderson, Tom	130
Anderson, William	2
Andres, Lizzie Stewart	10
Andres, William	10
Andrew, William	118
Andrews, Ellen L.	31
Andrews, Gustavus A.	31
Ann, Charles	46
Ann, Lucinda	46
Ann, Maria	46
Ann, Willie	46
Anthony, Capt.	113
Antoine, C.C.	4
Antoine, Elizabeth	136
Antoine, Elizabeth H.	4
Antoine, F.C.	136

Name Index

Antoine, Felix C.	4	Babbin, Edward	68
Antoine, Lewis C.	4	Babbin, Sarah	68
Antoine, Joseph	4	Babbin, Simon	69
Archy, John	96	Bacchus, Mary	49
Armistead, Alexander	137	Bacchus, Rosette	107
Armor, Estelle	20	Badrop, Davy	86
Armor, John	20	Badrop, Lucy	86
Armstead, Ellen	77	Bailey, Adeline	12
Armstrong, Alexander	6	Bailey, Albert	27
Armstrong, Mary	17	Bailey, Alexander	12
Arnaud, Ramar	2	Bailey, Edward	27
Asher, Felice	55	Bailey, Emma	31
Asher, James F.	55	Bailey, Jane	27, 112
Asher, Wm.	55	Bailey, Joseph	22
Askin, Caroline	56	Bailey, Sylvester	27
Askin, Daniel	56	Baker, Ben Jackson	13
Askin, Jerry	56	Baker, Hannah	73
Askin, Susan	56	Baker, John	73
Atkins, Harriet	9	Baker, Mary Susan	13
Atkins, Thomas	9	Bakum, Nancy	25
Attakapy, Rose	70	Baldwin, Lucy	33
Auguste, Francois	80	Ballard, Margaret	14
Auguste, Hermina	80	Ballard, William	14
Auguste, Laurent	80	Banks, Charlotte	139
Auguste, Made.	104	Banks, Hanover	139
Auguste, Mirtile	80	Banks, Joseph	139
Augustin, Charlotte	25, 53	Banks, Matilda	139
Augustin, Eve	53	Banks, Sarah	139
Augustin, Mary	53	Banks, Thomas	139
Augustin, Simon	25, 53	Banks, William Robinson	139
Augustus, Emma	20	Banks, Wm. R.	139
Augustus, Margaret	24	Banwoode, Nancy Melinda	108
Augustus, Nathan	20	Banwoode, Walker	108
Augustus, Perry	24	Baptiste, Andrew J.	5
Augustus, William	20	Baptiste, Auguste	43, 130
Austin, Abraham	67	Baptiste, Augustine	130
Austin, Abram	67	Baptiste, Edmonia	121
Austin, Beverly	67	Baptiste, John	48
Austin, Irany	67	Baptiste, Mary	67
Austin, Louisa	67	Baptiste, Oguch	121
Austin, Milly	67	Baptiste, Oscar Charles	130
Austin, Minny	67	Baptiste, Victorine	43, 130
Austin, Priscilla	67	Barnes, Edward	46, 47
		Barnes, Mathilda	46
B		Barnett, Daniel	136, 137
		Barnett, Daniel Jefferson	137

Name Index

Barnett, David	50	Beard, Mary	30, 46
Barnett, Durby	137	Beard, William	15
Barnett, Eliza	137	Beasley, Mary	120
Barnett, Fanny	51, 137	Beasley, Maxwell	120
Barnett, George Washington	137	Beaumont, Ida	38
Barnett, Jenny	51	Beaumont, Maria Louisa	38
Barnett, Joe	51	Beaumont, Peter	38
Barnett, Jep	137	Beauregard, Tilman	48
Barnett, Joe	51, 137	Becker, John P.	116
Barnett, Lucy	137	Becker, Margaret	116
Barnett, Lysa	50	Becknell, Peter	76
Barnett, Nancy	51, 137	Becson, Marsha	35
Baron, Peter	122, 125	Beer, Henry	95
Baron, Prudence	122, 125	Beer, Max	94
Baron, Robert	77	Beer, Moses	95
Baron, William Alexander	122, 125	Beer, Mrs.	95
Barr, D.E.	75	Begger, Adele	99
Barr, Rev. D.E.	95	Bell, Alice	70
Barrie, Carris	78	Bell, Allen	5
Barrie, Charles	78	Bell, Annie	78, 79, 108
Barrie, Julia	78	Bell, Anthony	101
Barrie, Melly	78	Bell, Benjamin	101
Barrow, Milly	92	Bell, Bui	5
Barrow, Sarah	92	Bell, Eliza	101
Barrow, William	92	Bell, Georgiana Christina	101
Barry, Ebenezer	9	Bell, Graham	5, 32
Barry, Eliza	9	Bell, Gus	101
Barry, Hannah	9	Bell, Henry	41, 100, 101
Barry, Randolph	9	Bell, Ida Victoria	5
Basil, Otto	5	Bell, Jane	41
Bass, Adelada	131	Bell, Lewis	5
Bass, Arthur	132	Bell, Madison	70
Bass, John M.	131	Bell, Martha	101
Bass, Louis	131	Bell, Mary	101
Batchess, Mr.	92	Bell, Mary E.	5
Batron, Jean	104	Bell, Nathan	5
Battice, Adele	91	Bell, Polly	101
Battice, Augustin	91	Bell, John	5
Battice, Isabella	67	Bell, Rachel	101
Battice, John	67, 91	Bell, Sam	5
Battice, Marie Agnes	91	Bencar, Adolph	34
Battice, Rafael	91	Bender, Chs.	40
Bawley, Mary	78	Bender, Harriet	40
Beal, Surgeon	23, 24	Bender, John	40
Beard, Jane	15	Bender, Oathanna	40
Beard, John	30	Berdon, Amanda	17

143

Name Index

Benedict, Mr.	53	Bertrand, Marie	104
Benford, Clark	83	Bienaime, Dede	118
Benford, Curtis	83	Biggs, Adeline	15
Benford, Jemima	83	Biggs, Louis	15
Benford, Phed	83	Bingman, Anthony	115
Bennett, Ben	88	Bingman, Cynthia	115
Bennett, Charley	88	Bingman, John	115
Bennett, Ellen	88	Bingman, Mary	115
Bennett, James	88	Birge, John	46
Bennett, Lively	88	Blackson, Andrew	94
Bentson, Arthur	87	Blackwell, F.	97
Bentson, Charlotte	87	Blan, Edward	40
Bentson, John	87	Blan, Elizabeth	40
Bentson, Milly	87	Blan, Emily	40
Berard, Prosper	58	Blan, Maria	40
Berard, Celina	113	Blan, Schack	40
Berard, Charlotte	113	Blan, Susan	40
Berard, Edward	113	Bland, Elizabeth	122
Berard, Emile	113	Bland, Sam	122
Berard, Ernestine	113	Blue, Fanny	13
Berard, Henri	113	Blunt, Milly	98
Berard, Hortense	113	Blye, Louisa	85
Berard, Louise	113	Blye, Louisa	21
Berard, Prosper	58, 113	Bockee, Capt.	60
Berard, Rose	113	Bodreau, C.C.	51, 52
Berard, Zelphire	113	Bodreau, Mrs.C.C.	51, 70
Berg, Marie Louise Jean	61	Body, Silvy	129
Berkins, Christiana	40	Body, Wm.	129
Berkins, William	40	Bogan, Ann Eliza	120
Berkley, Abraham	47	Bogan, Caroline	120
Berkley, Alfred	47	Bogan, Henry	120
Berkley, Lavinia	47	Bogan, James	120
Berkley, Mary	47	Bogan, John	120
Berry, Elijah	32	Bogan, Judy	120
Berry, Elizabeth	120	Bogan, Minervy	120
Berry, Ellen	106	Bogan, Oliver	120
Berry, Emilia	120	Bogan, Peter	120
Berry, James	106	Bogan, Rosa	120
Berry, James B.	120	Bogan, Sally	120
Berry, Martha Ann	120	Bogan, Simon	120
Berry, Polly	32	Bonaparte, Nathaniel	88
Berry, Thomas	106	Bond, Ann Maria Francis	120
Bertrand, Bertrand	104	Bonseigneur, Paul	24
Bertrand, Denis	104	Booker, John	65
Bertrand, Eugenie	104	Boree, Anatole L.	38, 112
Bertrand, Jean	104	Boree, Auguste Louis	38

Name Index

Boree, Aurore Adelaide	38	Bradley, William	52, 100
Boree, Josephine	38	Brady, Ellen	38
Boree, Marie Louise	38	Brady, M.B.	20
Borel, Alonzo	66	Branch, Edey	103
Borel, Ambrose	66	Branch, Eliza Antoinette	103
Boreland, Lavina	95	Branch, George	103
Boreland, Margaret	95	Branch, Green	103
Boreland, Peter	95	Branch, Harriet	103
Boreland, Robert	95	Branch, Jack	103
Boreland, William	95	Branch, Malvina	103
Bossiere, Xavier	128	Branch, Meajor	103
Bostram, Wilhelm	109	Brant, Anderson	85
Bowie, Nancy	24	Braxton, Anderson	31
Bowie, Robert Washington	24	Braxton, Annikus	31
Bowland, Arthur	58	Braxton, Charles	8
Bowland, Epham	58	Braxton, Claremtime	30
Bowland, Madison	58	Braxton, Diana	85
Boyd, James	116	Braxton, David	31
Boyd, Jenny	116	Braxton, Frederick	8
Boyd, John	116	Braxton, Harriet	31
Boyd, Kiah	116	Braxton, John	31
Boyd, Margaret	116	Braxton, Keser	8
Boyd, Mary	116	Braxton, Lucy	30
Boyd, Nancy	116	Braxton, Mary Diana	21
Boyd, Susan	116	Braxton, Reuben	30
Boyd, William	116	Braxton, Rose	31
Boyer, Caroline	16	Braxton, Tom	30
Bracy, Sarah	75	Brazier, Aaron	118
Brackstone, Dinah	11	Brazier, Amos	118
Bradford, Isaac	74	Brazil, Ben	140
Bradford, Mary	74	Brazil, Eliza	140
Bradley, Aaron	11	Breaux, Marcelin	16
Bradley, Caroline	100	Brige, John	30
Bradley, Charity	100	Briggs, Caroline	59
Bradley, Dorsey	102	Briggs, Malinda	61
Bradley, Dud	100	Briggs, Marthe	61
Bradley, Foster	99	Briggs, Moses	61, 81
Bradley, George	100	Briggs, Patsy	61
Bradley, Isaac	102	Briggs, Rebecca	61
Bradley, Isiah	102	Bright, Alice	29
Bradley, Jim	52	Bright, Cornelius	29, 78
Bradley, Joe	100	Brill, Nathen	133
Bradley, John	100	Briller, Charles	131
Bradley, Lizzie	99	Briller, James	130, 131
Bradley, Nancy	52, 102	Briller, Judy	131
Bradley, Rachel	52, 54, 91	Briller, Silvy	131

Name Index

Brinkley, Sarah	80
Briscoe, Holday	78
Brooks, Aleck	77
Brooks, Bill	61
Brooks, David	119
Brooks, Delph	61
Brooks, Dennis	119
Brooks, Frank	119
Brooks, Hannah	119
Brooks, Harriet	77
Brooks, Henrietta	119
Brooks, Jane	88
Brooks, Jerry	119
Brooks, John	77, 98
Brooks, Mary Ann	119
Brooks, Patsy Ann	61
Brooks, Kitty	98
Brooks, Rosina	82
Brooks, Samuel	61
Brooks, Sarah	98
Brooks, William	119
Brothers, William	24
Broussard, Etienne	110
Brown, A.J.	92
Brown, Abraham	30
Brown, Abram	53
Brown, Alfred	72
Brown, Alexander	89
Brown, America	92
Brown, Ann	16, 34
Brown, Ann Eliza	22
Brown, Annie	16
Brown, Barby	115
Brown, Ben	53, 60
Brown, Benjamin	86, 115
Brown, Cezar	60
Brown, Chapman	53
Brown, Charles	98
Brown, Collin	53
Brown, Capt. Daniel	30
Brown, Daniel	130
Brown, Davy	53
Brown, Delphind	45
Brown, Edward	45, 86
Brown, Edwin	53
Brown, Emma	34
Brown, Ester	58
Brown, Eveline	98
Brown, Fannie	56
Brown, Fred	53
Brown, George	72
Brown, Gus	45
Brown, Harris	53
Brown, Isaac	30
Brown, Isaac Washington	32
Brown, Jacob	30
Brown, Joseph	86
Brown, Joshua	53
Brown, Julia Ann	88
Brown, Lew	127
Brown, Lewis	58
Brown, Lucinda	72
Brown, Lucy	57
Brown, Lydy	53
Brown, Malvina	72
Brown, Manda	66
Brown, Maria	56
Brown, Margaret	30
Brown, Margaret Jane	8
Brown, Martha	123
Brown, Mary	30, 32
Brown, Mary Ann	34
Brown, Melia	98
Brown, Nancy	8
Brown, Poiner	86
Brown, Reuben	56
Brown, Robert	34, 51, 57, 123
Brown, Sarah	56
Brown, Steven	32
Brown, W.A.	34
Brown, William	34, 60
Bruce, August	64
Bruce, Dave	64
Bruce, Elmond	64
Bruce, Fine	64
Bruce, Jane	64
Bruce, Joseph	110
Bruce, Lewis	64
Bruce, Malinda	64
Bruce, Pheobe	64
Bruno, Mary Louise	37
Bryan, Anderson	60

Name Index

Name	Page	Name	Page
Buck, Billy	129	Burns, Selvine	111
Buford, Aime	104	Burns, Thomas	87
Buford, Ellen	104	Burridge, Alexander	22
Buford, Henry	104	Burridge, Delia	22
Buford, Raswall	104	Burrill, Martha	23
Bullard, Peter	49	Burrill, Robinson	23
Bumbray, Enoch	7	Burrow, Ralph	43, 118
Bumbray, Mary	6	Burton, Eliza	55
Bumbray, James	6	Burton, Joe	55
Bumbray, James Jr.	6	Burton, Sergt. William	55
Bunton, Ancel	7	Bush, Alice	36
Bunton, Annie	7	Bush, Dick	36
Bunton, Catharine	7	Bush, Dinah	36
Bunton, Frederic	7	Bush, George	36
Bunton, Martha	7	Bush, Giles	36
Bunton, William	7	Bush, Jenny	36
Burbank, Alfred	70	Bush, Mary	36
Burbank, James	70	Bush, Noah	36
Burchard, J.M.	107	Bush, Rose	36
Burchard, Jenny	107	Bush, Sam	36
Burchard, Loulou	107	Bush, Sandy	36
Burchard, M.	107	Bush, William	36
Burchard, Willy	107	Butchern, Mary	34
Burg, Mrs.	94	Butchern, Norbin	34
Burke, Daphne	28	Butler, Albert	69
Burke, Edward	19	Butler, Col.	96
Burke, Emily Robertson	28	Butler, Delphine	69
Burke, Emma	19	Butler, Hannah	99
Burke, John	28	Butler, Henry	78
Burke, Phelis	28	Butler, John	55, 69
Burke, Rebecca	28	Butler, Joseph	70
Burl, Elizabeth	20	Butler, Mary	69
Burnett, Charlotte	35	Butler, Nancy	99
Burnett, Edom	35	Butler, Robert	128
Burney, J.A.	24	Butler, Sarah	55
Burney, John Albert	24	Butler, Thomas	99
Burns, Emile	111	Butler, William	99, 135
Burns, Isaac	87	Butler, William Jr.	99
Burns, James	111	Butler, Zeb	69
Burns, Jane	87	Button, Edmund,	86
Burns, Joseph Washington	110	Byass, Barbain	83
Burns, Julia Ann	87	Byass, Jim	83
Burns, Martha	87	Byrd, Elizabeth	89
Burns, Mary Ann	111	Byrd, John	89
Burns, Robert	87	Byrd, Lucy	89
Burns, Sara	87	Byrd, Sydney	89

Name Index

Byrd, Victoria	89

C

Cairnes, Henry	17
Caldwell, Cray	34
Calhoun, Jane	74
Caliste, Cecilia	121
Caliste, Iule	121
Camille, Henry	71
Campbell, Henry	115
Campbell, Jacob	42
Campbell, Martha	34
Campbell, Mary Ann	42
Campbell, Prescilla	115
Campbell, Yorick H.	115
Campbell, William	115
Cambridge, Leonard	135
Cannon, Claiborn	87
Cannon, Emilia	87
Cannon, Mary Jane	87
Cannon, Steven	87
Cantrelle, Mary Vassern	61
Capla, Alfred	46
Capla, Felicie Fleury	46
Capla, L.J.P.	46
Capla, Lucien	46
Carey, John	65
Carey, Michael D.	65
Carpenter, Isabella	26
Carpenter, John	26
Carnes, Esther	93
Carr, Charlotte	91
Carr, Emily	91
Carr, Lafayette	91
Carr, Lewis	91
Carrere, Albert	138
Carrere, Amede	138
Carrere, Barthelmy	138
Carrere, Delphine	138
Carrere, Etienne	138
Carrere, Linotte	138
Carter, Addison	82
Carter, Anthony	92
Carter, Caroline	92
Carter, Cecilia	66
Carter, Charlotte	82
Carter, Daniel	68
Carter, Delphine	82
Carter, Ellen	92
Carter, Ellsey	92
Carter, Elyza	68
Carter, Emma Maria	66
Carter, Esther	82
Carter, Harrison	75
Carter, Henderson	34
Carter, Henry	3, 92
Carter, Hiram	1, 2, 51
Carter, James	59
Carter, John	3, 86
Carter, Joseph	19
Carter, Josephine Seymour	59
Carter, Juddy	82
Carter, Louisa	59, 101
Carter, Lucy	137
Carter, Malchior	82
Carter, Manda	82
Carter, Mary Jane	34
Carter, Mathilda	19, 86
Carter, Mellie	86
Carter, Peter	86
Carter, Puss	68
Carter, Robert	66
Carter, Rose	92
Carter, Simon	3
Carter, Timothy	59
Carter, Titine	92
Carter, William	19, 137
Caruthers, Ben	11
Casmer, Jemima	76
Casmer, Lewis	76
Casmer, Merritt	76
Casmer, Susan	76
Castleman, Arena	137
Castleman, Catherine	137
Castleman, Charles	137
Castleman, Fanny	137
Castleman, Gracie Ann	137
Castleman, Hannah	137
Castleman, Harriet	137
Castleman, Jacob	137
Castleman, Jonathan	137

Name Index

Castleman, Marina	137	Chillis, Sally	102
Castleman, Richard	137	Chinn, Charles	135
Cass, Louis	66	Chinn, Fletcher T.	135
Cass, Louisa	66	Chinn, Isaac	135
Cass, Soloman	66	Chinn, Martha	135
Cavanaugh, Harriet	12	Chinn, Roxanne	135
Cazenau, Fanny	23	Chinn, Sarah	135
Celestin, Angele	87	Chinn, Scott	135
Chace, William	45	Chinn, Walter	135
Chambers, Maria	92	Chinn, Writhe	135
Chambers, Nancy	92	Choppin, W. Valerien	91
Chamburger, John	15	Chretien, Hypolite	2
Chamburger, Josephine	15	Christian, Henry	19
Champ, Harriet	79	Christian, Julia	19
Chandler, Philip	4	Cilicise, John	48
Chapman, Alfred	34	Citizen, James	129
Chapman, Ann	70	Citizen, Nancy	129
Chapman, Chadwick	34	Clark, Arthur	66
Chapman, Julia	34	Clark, Becky	66
Chapman, Mahala	34	Clark, Betty	66
Chapman, Nelly	34	Clark, Charles	99
Charle, Mrs. Francis	58	Clark, Dr.	84, 118, 119
Cheek, Clara	13	Clark, Eliza	99
Cheek, Jacob	13, 117	Clark, Elizabeth	100
Cheek, James	13	Clark, Ellsworth	99
Cheek, Noah	13	Clark, Emma	75, 100
Cheek, Rachel	13	Clark, Fanny	66
Cheek, Susan	13	Clark, Felice	100
Cheeks, Jacob	42, 135	Clark, Jim	73
Cheneau, Anatole	104	Clark, Joe	66, 75
Cheneau, Cecile	104	Clark, Joseph	100
Cheneau, Henry	104	Clark, Lewis	100
Cheneau, Lewis	104	Clark, Mitchell	66
Cheneau, Louis	104	Clark, Steven	73
Cheneau, Marie	104	Clark, Tinman	66
Cheneau, Mary Jennie	104	Clark, Viney	66
Cheney, Miss	38	Clark, William	100
Chesse, A.L.	111	Clark, Wilson	72
Childrars, Minervy	123	Claude, Rosa	104
Chillis, Amy	102	Clay, Aggy	129
Chillis, Dinah	102	Clay, Benjamin	129
Chillis, Jim	102	Clay, Ellen	129
Chillis, Katy	102	Clay, George Washington	129
Chillis, Keziah	102	Clay, Georgiana	129
Chillis, Matt	102	Clay, Harrison	129
Chillis, Nelson	102	Clay, Harry	129

Name Index

Clay, Henry	69, 129	Cooper, Flora G.	64
Clay, Herod	122	Cooper, Forestine	64
Clay, Kasiah	70	Cooper, Humphrey	10
Clay, Lucinda	129	Cooper, Kay	64
Clay, Margaret	122	Cooper, Maria	10
Clay, Maria	129	Cooper, William	1, 128
Clay, William	70	Cooper, Wm.	129
Clayton, Celestine	15	Cook, Francis	3
Clinton, Comelia	33	Cook, Frederic	95
Cloth, Susan	76	Cook, Jane	63
Coates, Angeline	80	Corbin, Cora	105
Coates, Stephen	80	Cornish, Mrs.	106
Cobb, Daniel	81	Cosby, Amy	104
Cobb, Harriet	4	Cosby, David	103, 135
Cobb, Henry	81	Cosby, Frank	103
Cobb, Mary	81	Cosby, Madison	104
Cobb, Robert	4	Cosby, Mary Jane	103
Cobb, William	81	Cosby, Matilda	104
Coca, Philip	42	Cosby, Sarah	103
Cogfield, Abe	5	Cosby, Washington	104
Colbird, Hannah	71	Cosey, Peter	31
Colbird, Maria	72	Council, Adam	41
Colbird, Peter	72	Council, Amanda	41
Colbird, Sandy	72	Council, Edmond	41
Colbird, William	71	Council, Julia Ann	41
Cole, Julia B.	113	Council, Kitty	41
Cole, M.C.	113	Council, Lucy	41
Coleman, Ledy	67	Council, Mary	41
Collins, Ellen	32	Council, Stephen	41
Collins, Nelson	25	Coundry, Rose	24
Collins, Joseph	17	County, Betsy	84, 118, 119
Collins, Theresa	25	County, Celina	84
Collis, Amos S.	71	County, Celine	111
Colquitt, Mowning	25	County, Emma	84, 111
Colquitt, Washington	25	County, Frederic	84
Conway, Angelina	64	County, Frederick	118
Cook, Baylor	47	County, George	84, 111
Cook, Emelia	47	County, Harry	84, 118
Cook, Frank	47	County, Jacob	119
Cook, George	47	County, Julia	119
Cook, Nancy	47	County, Lucy	84, 111
Cook, Richard	47	County, Maria	118
Cook, Richmond	47	County, Melvina	114
Cook, Virginia	47	County, Ned	119
Cooke, John Wesley	42	County, Netty	118
Cooper, Charles L.	64	County, Sam	114

150

Name Index

County, Thomas	84, 111, 119	Crump, Edward	20, 111
County, Warren	114, 119	Crump, Ellen	20
Coursay, Adam	69	Crump, Fanny	20, 111
Coursay, Annie	69	Crump, Jack	20, 111
Coursay, Basil	69	Crump, John	20, 111
Coursay, Daniel	69	Crump, Mary	20, 111
Coursay, Ellen	69	Crump, William	20, 111
Coursay, Elvira	69	Curan, Rosine	96
Coursay, Jenny	69	Custis, Berry	78
Coursay, Jesse	69	Custis, Emma	78
Coursay, Lorilla	69	Custis, Joseph	78
Coursay, Maria	69	Custis, Malvina	78
Courtney, Janey	68	Cyrus, Candess	17
Courtney, Joe	68		
Courtney, Rachel	68	**D**	
Courtney, Soloman	68	Dalbz, Philomene	104
Courtney, Wiley	68	Daly, Briget	112
Courtney, Willis	68	Dancer, Charles	102
Couvertie, Angele	109	Dancer, Edmund	102
Couvestie, Mary Coralie	79	Dancer, Mary	102
Cox, Charles	19, 113	Daniel, Annie	54
Craig, Emma Jane	112	Daniel, Ben	54
Craig, Henry	112	Daniel, Delia	65
Craig, James	112	Daniel, James Washington	54
Craig, Joseph	112	Daniel, Laura	54
Craig, Mary Elizabeth	112	Daniel, Leana	54
Craig, Mary Jane	112	Daniel, Washington	54
Crawford, Allen	91	Daniels, Antoinette	42
Crawford, Jenny	91	Daniels, Emile	42
Crawford, Capt. John James	42	Daniels, Jacques Joseph	42
Crawford, Milly	91	Daniels, Lucile	42
Crawford, Nancy	65	Daniels, Victoria	42
Cray, Alphus W.	16	Daret, Dr.	17
Cray, Cely	128	Daunoy, Robert	30
Cray, Charles	127, 128	Davenport, Maria	16
Cray, Daniel	128	Davenport, Wm	16
Cray, Eliza	128	Davidson, Annie	73
Cray, Fanny	128	Davidson, James	16
Cray, Henderson	128	Davidson, John	13
Cray, Isaac	128	Daville, Eugene	41
Cray, Lucy	128	Davis, A.J.	4, 114
Cray, Maria	128	Davis, A.J. Jr.	4
Cray, Rachel	128	Davis, Alexander	75
Cripps, Charles	105	Davis, Amelia	60
Cripps, Hermes	105	Davis, Andrew	81
Cripps, Hortense	105		

Name Index

Davis, Benjamin	81
Davis, Castillo	77
Davis, Celestin	97
Davis, Charles	77
Davis, Elizabeth	24
Davis, Emilia	10
Davis, Evariste	97
Davis, Francis A.	60
Davis, Henrietta	64
Davis, Henry	33
Davis, James	19
Davis, Joe	89
Davis, John	24, 89
Davis, Lucian	77
Davis, Martha	89
Davis, Martha Stewart	75
Davis, Melia	99
Davis, Milly	81, 89
Davis, Mr.	20
Davis, Moses	89
Davis, Nelly	89
Davis, Patience	77
Davis, Peggy	77
Davis, Prescilla	43
Davis, Priscilla	130
Davis, Rachel	97
Davis, Rhyna	77
Davis, Thomas	97
Day, James	68
Day, Lucy	68
Day, Mary H.	9
Day, Sam	76
Day, Sarah Ann	68
Day, William H.	9
Dean, Dr. W.	23
De Gar, Antoine	126
De Gar, Bob	126
De Gar, Eglantine	126
De Gar, Francois	126
De Gar, Frank	126
De Gar, Hester	126
De Gar, John	126
De Gar, Narcisse	126
de Graffenreid, Chanorde	12
Delaney, Isabella	128
Delaney, John	128
Denny, Phene	129
Denny, Sam	129
Dent, Alfred	132
Dent, Arre	132
Dent, Josephine	132
Dent, Louis	132
Derbigny, Charles	38
Deshields, Mr.	14
Dever, Jennie	86
Dever, Joseph	86
Dever, Nathaniel	86
Dial, Charlotte	138
Diamond, William	7
Dicey, Cecilia	117
Dicey, Mary	76
Diggs, Maria	38
Diossy, Eva	80
Diossy, Rev. R.K.	41, 80, 94
Diossy, Sarah E.	80
Dirden, Darkess	120
Dirden, Lucy	120
Dirden, Martha	120
Dirden, Mr.	120
Dirden, Primus	120
Donato, Emile	35
Donato, Helen Roberts	35
Donato, Joseph	35
Dore, Chs.	3
Dore, Elizabeth	3
Dorse, Emily	107
Dorsey, Adelaide	61
Dorsey, Ann	2
Dorsey, Georgiana	61
Dorsey, John	2, 61
Dorsey, John Henry	2
Dorsey, Joseph	61
Dorsey, Louisa	61
Dorsey, Marie	61
Dorsey, Nelda	61
Dossey, Celia	62
Doughty, Charles C.	98
Doughty, Revd.	98
Douglas, Allen	133
Douglas, Dempsey	133
Douglas, Dinah	133
Douglas, Ermin	133

Name Index

Douglas, Huldy	133	Dunford, Maricria	124
Douglas, James	133	Dunford, Mr.	42
Douglas, Lucy	133	Dunford, Therese	124
Dow, Lorenzo	77	Dunlap, Mary	1
Doyle, Henry	6, 60	Dunlop, Mary Ann	125
Dozier, George Hamolet	138	Dunlop, Nathaniel	125
Dozier, John	138	Dunn, Delia	103
Dozier, Joseph	138	Dunn, Francis Sophronia	125
Dozier, Louisa	138	Dunn, Joseph	125
Dozier, Mary	138	Dunn, Richard	103
Dozier, Nelda	138	Dunn, William	103
Dozier, Pauline	61, 138	Dupare, Jules	125
Drake, Warren	2	Duplantier, Alfred	32
Drake, Warren Jr.	2	Duplantier, Bienville	32
Dubois, Etienne Jr.	110	Duplantier, Louisa	32
Dubois, Etienne Sr.	110	Dupre, John	97
Dubois, Henriette	110	Dupre, Laure	97
Dubois, Rose Caroline	110	Dupuy, Eugenie	48
Dudon, Benj.	73	Durfee, Katish	74
Duest, Catharnia	98	Durfee, Capt. Luke	74
Duest, Henry	98	Durant, Thomas J.	53
Dull, Mary J.	50	Durnford, Andrew	1
Dull, Peter	49	Durnford, Benit	1
Dumas, Aimee	57	Dutch, Rev. Joseph	33
Dumas, Alexander	6, 57	Dutton, James	23
Dumas, Charlotte	6, 57	Dyer, Abraham	80
Dumas, Harriet	6, 57	Dyer, Benjamin	90
Dumas, Maria Simms	6, 57	Dyer, Ellen	90
Duncan, Caroline	94	Dyson, John Baptiste	126
Duncan, Dr. 1	23		
Duncan, Fanny	94	**E**	
Duncan, Henderson	118	Easten, Molly	140
Duncan, Jane	123	Easten, Hannah	140
Duncan, John	18	Easten, Ransom	140
Duncan, Lizzie	94	Ebar, Louise	46
Duncan, Maria	94	Ebar, Modeste	46
Duncan, Mary	66	Ebar, Sella	46
Duncan, William	94	Edington, Harriet	56
Dunford, Amelie	1	Edington, James	56
Dunford, Bennett	124	Edmond, Jean	128
Dunford, Breno	124	Edmond, John	1, 79
Dunford, Cedelze	124	Edmond, Julia	1, 79
Dunford, Clara	124	Edmond, Laurence	79
Dunford, Emily	124	Edmond, Mary Lorenza	1, 79
Dunford, Joseph	124	Edwards, Charles	50
Dunford, Manassas	124		

153

Name Index

Edwards, Claiborne	16	Fields, Howard	17
Edwards, Frances	50	Fields, Martha	12
Edwards, Joseph	96	Fields, Martha Ann	17
Edwards, Margaret	96	Finney, Armstead	88
Edwards, William	57,84	Finney, Camille	88
Edwards, Zelphie	57	Finney, Hortense	88
Edwards, Zelphire	84	Finney, Louisa	88
Elder, Caroline	135	Finney, William	87
Elder, Jack	135	Fische, Hautess	120
Ellis, Cyrus	5	Fische, Louisa	120
Ennis, Alford	134	Fische, Peter	120
Ennis, Charles	134	Fisher, Andrew	133
Ennis, Edmund	134	Fisher, Nancy	133
Ennis, Isaac	134	Fisher, Nicissy	133
Ennis, Jones	134	Fisher, Ony	133
Ennis, Permelia	134	Fisher, Peggy	133
Epps, Dave	115	Fisher, Soloman	133
Epps, Frederic	115	Fisher, Thomas	133
Epps, John	115	Fisher, William	132
Epps, Phil	115	Fishon, Margaret	74
Epps, Philis	115	Fishon, Phillis	74
Epps, Robert	115	Fitzgerald, George	103
Epps, William Henry	115	Fitzgerald, Jim	103
Esnard, John Benjamin	90	Fitzgerald, John	103
Esnard, Rosa	111	Fitzgerald, Josephine	103
Esnard, T.	90	Fitzgerald, Julia	103
Etrenne, Marie Louise	4	Fitzgerald, Matilda	103
		Fitzgerald, Violet Amelia	103
F		Flagg, Mary	27
Fairview, Mr.	68	Flagg, O.J.	27
Farrar, Eliza	18	Flash, A.	1
Fax, Mary	32	Fletcher, Alfred	10
Fax, Sarah	32	Florey, H. T.	95, 107
Fax, Thomas	32	Flory, Andrew	13
Ferguson, Hatcher	89	Flory, Denson	13
Ferguson, Jane	83	Flory, Mary Ann	13
Ferguson, Melinda	89	Fobb, Harriet	70
Ferguson, Victorine	117	Fobb, Tony	70
Ferrand, Marie	107	Foley, John	85
Ferrier, Alexis	83	Foley, Julia	85
Ficius, Henry	17	Foley, William	67
Field, Martha	65	Fontenett, Alice	78
Fields, Aime	11	Forbush, Aleck	105
Fields, Edward	10, 75, 111	Ford, Martin	29
Fields, Fanny	10	Ford, Mary Letitia	49
		Foreman, Bristor	3

Name Index

Fornientin, Alexander	48	Gadson, Maria	12
Fornientin, Numa	48	Gale, Charity Ann Maguerite	48
Forrest, Joseph	51	Gale, John	48
Forrest, Mary Ann	51	Gale, Marguerite	48
Forrest, Michael	53	Galley, Adeline	79
Forrest, Panilus	53	Galley, Charles	79
Forrest, Priscilla King	53	Galley, Emmeline Washington	79
Fortier, John	51	Galley, Emilia	79
Foster, Charles	130	Galley, William	79
Foster, Lewis	124	Gannon, Noble	25
Foster, Lucinda	130	Gardner, Daniel	65
Foster, Widow	30	Gardner, Eliza	114
Fox, Mary A.	106, 140	Gardner, Henriette	108
Fox, Moris	140	Gardner, James	65
Fox, Sarah	140	Gardner, John	65
Fox, Thomas	140	Gardner, Kate	110
Francis, Caroline	37	Gardner, Louisa	108
Francis, John	64, 67	Gardner, Lucy	65
Francis, Lucinda	64	Gardner, Maria	65
Francis, Sarah	64	Gardner, Nancy	108
Franklin, Ben	136	Gardner, Peggy	68
Franklin, Eliza	117	Garrison, Aleck	74, 77
Franklin, Flaggy	136	Garrison, Harris	74, 77
Franklin, George	83	Garrison, Melly	77
Franklin, Lucy	136	Gauche, John	131
Franklin, Mary	136	Gaule, Mary	100
Franklin, Milly	135	Gaule, Michael	100
Franklin, Rachel	136	Gayle, Margaret	50
Franklin, Rosa	116	Geal, Mary	115
Frazier, Mary Jane	60	Georgia, Adam	121
Frazier, Moses	60	Gibbs, Mary Ann	90
Fredberg, Major	75	Gilbert, Lewis	9
Frederick, Dick	96	Gilbert, Sarah	9
Frederick, Susan	96	Giles, Aby	105
Frelow, James	64	Giles, George	105
Frizzell, David	14	Giles, Jane	105
Frizzell, Franklin	14	Giles, John	105
Frizzell, Harriet	14	Giles, Joseph	105
Frizzell, Johnson	14	Giles, Louisa	105
Frizzell, Louisa	14	Giles, Phil	53
Frost, Margaret	11	Giles, Simon	105
Fuller, Joseph	15	Giles, Susan	53
Fuller, Millis	18	Gill, Agnes	4
		Gill, Hannah	4
G		Gill, Michael	4
		Gill, Pleasant	4

Name Index

Gillem, Frances	139	Green, Anderson	42
Gillem, Isabella	139	Green, Barbry	105
Gillem, Jacob	139	Green, Benjamin	49
Gillem, Joseph	139	Green, Caroline	125
Gillem, Mary	139	Green, Celestin	79
Gillem, Zabella	139	Green, Celestine	79
Givens, D.A.	34	Green, Christina	123
Givins, William	45	Green, Clarissa	49
Glasco, Caroline	12	Green, Dan	134
Glasco, Rebecca	12	Green, Daniel	79
Glasco, Rosa	12	Green, David	42
Gleason, Honora	110	Green, Dinah	42
Glenn, Thomas J.	43	Green, Denis	33
Glover, Rhody	78	Green, Dolly	117
Goland, J. B.	107	Green, Dorthulia	123
Goodman, Nathan	80	Green, Elizabeth	36, 42
Gooe, Anderson	47	Green, Elizabeth Louisa	41
Gooe, Dicey	47	Green, Frank	9
Gooe, Isaac	47	Green, Frederick	79
Gordon, Lysa	102	Green, Gardner	56
Gordon, Rachel	102	Green, George	11, 21, 85
Gordy, Margaret	77	Green, George Henry	134
Gordy, Michael	77	Green, Geo W.	15
Gore, Charles	123, 124	Green, Hannah	41
Gore, Charlotte	124	Green, Henry	19, 56, 79, 134
Gore, Elizabeth	123	Green, Rev. Henry	41, 74, 111
Gore, Geuin	123	Green, Isam	123
Gore, Guillamen	123	Green, Jacob	134
Gore, Joseph	123	Green, James	49
Gore, Phillis	123, 124	Green, John	117
Gossum, W.	10	Green, Joseph	9, 79, 123, 125
Goulon, Colin	96	Green, Lange	79
Goulon, Estelle	96	Green, Lewis	42
Gownes, Byron	28	Green, Lid	40
Graham, Gen.	55	Green, Lizzie	79
Graham, Sam	93	Green, Lorena	123
Graham, Susan	93	Green, Loretta	134
Grandpre, Henry T.	77	Green, Luda	56
Grandpre, Theophite	77	Green, Margaret	11
Graves, Mary Jane	115	Green, Maria	134
Gray, Anthony	5, 140	Green, Mary	79
Gray, Dicy	5	Green, Mary Jane	36, 134
Gray, Ellen	5, 140	Green, Mellie	41
Gray, Felice	55	Green, Milton	96
Green, Aaron	134	Green, Nancy	137
Green, Alexander	79	Green, Parish	41

Name Index

Green, Penny	123
Green, Richard A.	56
Green, Riddy	123
Green, Rosaline	140
Green, Sally	123
Green, Susan	134
Green, Susan A.	56
Green, Thomas	79
Green, Walton	36
Green, Wellington	123
Green, Wesley	42
Green, William	117, 140
Gregory, Andrew	50, 55, 93
Gregory, Ann	9
Gregory, George	93
Gregory, Issac	9
Gregory, James	93
Gregory, Mackey	93
Gregory, Maria	50, 93
Gregory, Mary	93
Griffin, Allen	30
Griffin, Emma	31
Griffin, John	30
Griffin, Mary H.	59
Griffin, Nancy Gale	30
Griffin, Washington	31
Griggs, Alice	28
Griggs, Ann	28
Griggs, John	28
Griggs, Mary	28
Gross, Charles	54
Gross, Clara	54
Gross, Daniel	21
Gross, Ida	54
Gross, Susan	54
Gross, Walker	54
Grouex, Evarico	124
Groves, Rachel	97
Grundy, Laura	47
Grundy, Maria	46
Gulick, John W.	33
Gulick, Joseph A.	33
Gustaff, Joseph	89

H

Hagan, J.P.	111
Hagwood, Agar	102
Hailey, Charles	83
Hailey, Charles H.	83
Hailey, Charles Henry	97
Hailey, Eulalie	83, 97
Hailey, Henry	83
Hailey, Sylvy	83
Hailey, Thos.	83
Hale, Albert	25
Hale, Alfred	25
Hale, Ambrose	57
Hale, Eliza	56, 62
Hale, Maria	25
Hale, Viney	25
Hale, Violet	25
Hales, Ida	63
Haley, Eliza	61
Hall, Adam	126
Hall, Ananias	126
Hall, Ben	126
Hall, Bridget	131
Hall, Charity	131
Hall, Effie Ann	126
Hall, Eliza	1
Hall, Hanover	126
Hall, Irena	126
Hall, Jennie	37
Hall, John	131
Hall, Margaret	131
Hall, Mimy	126
Hall, Narcissa	37
Hall, Philip	126
Hall, Robert	131
Hall, Sarah	37, 126
Hall, Thomas	126
Hall, Tony	37
Hall, William	1
Hall, Wm.	130, 131
Halloway, Harriet E.	88
Haman, Mr.	120
Hammus, Monroe	31
Hampton, Lizzie	18
Hampton, Wade	18
Hancock, Alfred Daniel	90
Hancock, George W.	90

Name Index

Hancock, Lewis	90	Harris, Martha	97
Handy, Becky	107	Harris, Mary	97
Hanson, Henry	74	Harris, Milton	13
Hanson, Philis	74	Harris, Mr.	15
Hanson, Wilson	74	Harris, Peter	35
Hantney, Louisa	70	Harris, Rachel	97
Harbuck, Greenberry	63	Harris, Richard	35
Harkins, Charles	108	Harris, Rudolph	65
Harkins, Delia	107	Harris, Sam L.	122
Harkins, Francis	108	Harris, Sarah	65, 90
Harkins, Jack	108	Harris, Sarina	65
Harkins, Jim	107	Harris, Walter	13
Harkins, Tom	108	Harris, Washington	44
Harper, Katharine	51	Harris, William	35, 55
Harris, Abbinter	90	Harris, William R.	99
Harris, Adam	60, 85	Harris, Wm R.	8
Harris, Aga	31	Harrison, Benjamin	12
Harris, Allen	90	Harrison, David	12
Harris, Allison	44	Harrison, Edmond	16
Harris, Andrew James	97	Harrison, Fanny Sels	12
Harris, Ann Rebecca	97	Harrison, J.W.	23
Harris, Arena	97	Harrison, Madison	16
Harris, Ben	65	Harrison, Malvina	16
Harris, Cicero	105	Harrison, Martha	12
Harris, Daphne	35	Harrison, Rudolph	12
Harris, Dekeeser	97	Harrison, Sarah	12
Harris, Eliza	44	Harrison, William	23
Harris, Elizabeth	97	Harrison, Wilson	16
Harris, Emanuel	97	Hatchet, Margaret	86
Harris, Fanny	65	Hawkins, Joseph	15
Harris, Geo. W.	18	Hayden, Catherine	14
Harris, George	97	Hayden, Charlotte	14
Harris, George Washington	97	Hayden, Frederick	14
Harris, Henry James	18	Hayden, John	14
Harris, Irena	97	Hayden, Josephine	14
Harris, Joe	31	Hayes, Jordan	134
Harris, John	18, 97	Hayes, Ann	135
Harris, John Henry	18, 97	Hayes, Heiram	135
Harris, Julia	44	Hayes, Isaac	135
Harris, Lizzie	44	Hayes, Jordan	134, 135
Harris, Louisa	90	Hayes, Louisa	135
Harris, Madison	13	Hayes, Mahala	135
Harris, Manuel	97	Hayes, Rufus	135
Harris, Margaret	15, 90	Hays, Anna	81
Harris, Maria	8, 35	Hays, Charles W.	81
Harris, Mark	44	Hays, Emily Letche	22

Name Index

Hays, Getchie	81
Hays, Margaret	81
Hays, Rebecca	81
Hays, Sarah Ann	75
Hays, Wm.	4
Hazelup, Becky	107
Hebert, Larty	46
Hecand, Foedora	52
Henderson, Albert	121
Henderson, Andre	46
Henderson, Andrew	30
Henderson, Archy	121
Henderson, Augustus	121
Henderson, Cooley	124
Henderson, Jane	121
Henderson, John	121
Henderson, Mary	124, 127
Henderson, Nancy	127
Henderson, Robert Thomas	127
Henderson, Sophy	124
Henderson, Tilda	121
Henderson, William	127
Henderson, Wm.	61
Hendricks, Mr.	137
Hennison, Wilson	77
Henry, Augustus	129
Henry, Catherine	129
Henry, Charles	62
Henry, Dicy	129
Henry, Emma	62
Henry, Harriet	61
Henry, James	9
Henry, Jessy	43
Henry, John	129
Henry, Mary	62
Henry, Mary Agnes	62
Henry, Nancy	9
Henry, Patsy	129
Henry, Peggy	129
Henry, Richard	62
Henry, Sally	44
Henry, William	129
Henry, William M.	68
Henry, Wm.	61
Herrim, Jane	26
Hill, Aaron	60
Hill, Abner	60, 85
Hill, Arron	85
Hill, Emily	60
Hill, Gloster	60
Hill, Joe	85
Hill, John	137
Hill, Joseph	45
Hill, Louisa	129, 137
Hill, Mary	45
Hill, Thomas	45
Hill, Thomas J.	74
Hill, Yosty	85
Hillborn, Judith	7
Hinkling, James	93
Hinkling, Sam	93
Hinkling, Samuel	93
Hinkling, Smith	93
Hinkling, W.C.	93
Hinson, Bob	127
Hinson, Eliza Ann	127
Hitman, Peter	23
Hodge, Bill	16
Hodge, Billy	16
Hodge, Caroline	16
Hodge, Elisa	43
Hodge, George	16
Hodge, Henry	43
Hodge, Jam	16
Hodge, Jane	16
Hodge, John Henry	43
Hodge, Mary	16
Hodge, Robert	16
Hodge, Sally	16
Hodges, A.C.	49
Hodges, John	49, 59
Hodgins, Frank	64
Hodgins, Sarah Ann	64
Holland, Coleman	93
Holland, Joseph E.	22, 51
Holland, Minter	93
Holland, Sarah Ann	22, 51
Holliday, Celina	98
Holliday, Emma	98
Holliday, Lucy	98
Holliday, Mary	98
Holliday, Sarah Brooks	98

Name Index

Holliday, Spenser	98
Holliday, William	98
Hollman, William	92
Holt, Geo. Arnold	19
Hooker, Sarah	78
Hopes, Alexander	127
Hopes, Baoler	127
Hopes, Charles	127
Hopes, Hannah	127
Hopes, James	127
Hopes, Mitchell	127
Hopes, Mony	127
Hopes, Rueben	127
Hopes, Silvy	127
Hopes, Simon	127
Hopes, Tabby	127
Hopkins, Annison	131
Hopkins, Ed	20
Hopkins, Elisha	131
Hopkins, James	131
Hopkins, Louisa	131
Hopkins, P.	106
Hopkins, Wesley	131
Horton, Henry	39
Horton, Leonore	39
Horton, Lucy	39
Hossler, Charles	49
Hossler, Milly	49
Howell, Clara	134
Howell, Ellen	134
Howell, Judge	134
Howell, Judge R.K.	66
Howell, May	134
Howell, Minnie	134
Howell, Rufus King	133
Hubbard, Jenny	99
Hubbard, Milah	99
Hubbard, Peter	99
Hubbard, Sallie	99
Hubbard, Wallow	99
Hubeau, Ernest A.	49
Hubeau, Ernestine	49
Humphrey, Daphne	84
Humphrey, Era	84
Humphrey, Harriet	37
Humphrey, Mary	84
Humphrey, Stephen	84
Humphrey, Susan	84
Hunt, Edward	54
Hunt, Elisa	54
Hunt, Mary	54
Hunt, Sarah	54
Hunter, Alfred	23
Hunter, Andrew	23, 136
Hunter, Doctor	136
Hunter, Eliza	18
Hunter, Ellen	23, 136
Hunter, Flora	106
Hunter, Frank	106
Hunter, Frederick	23
Hunter, James	18, 136
Hunter, John	23, 136
Hunter, L.	97
Hunter, Leah	136
Hunter, Margaret	136
Hunter, Mary	23, 136
Hunter, Mary	23
Hunter, Patsy	23, 136
Hunter, Phillip	23, 123
Hunter, Robert	136
Hunter, Thomas	87
Hunter, Will	23
Hunter, William	23, 136
Hurlburt, Joseph	66
Hutchinson, Arthur	136
Hutchinson, Charley	136
Hutchinson, Cornelia	136
Hutchinson, George	136
Hutchinson, Harriet	136
Hutchinson, Henrietta	136
Hutchinson, John Wallace	136
Hutchinson, Mary Jane	136
Hutchinson, Thomas	43
Hutchinson, William	136
Hyatt, Dick	78
Hyatt, Isaac	78
Hyland, Ann	40
Hyland, Julia	40
Hyland, William	39

I

Name Index

Ingraham, Henrietta	136	Jackson, Thomas	18
Ingraham, Jas. H.	136	James, Alfred	88
Iron, Anna	62	James, Augustin	96, 97
Iron, Mary	62	James, Burrell	88
Iron, Paldo	62	James, Eliza	88
Iron, Sally	62	James, Elizabeth	97
Iron, Sambo	62	James, Frank	88
Iron, Sye	62	James, Jacob	88
Isabelle, Andrew	69	James, Joseph	97
Isabelle, James	69	James, Joseph Augustin	97
Isabelle, Jamesetta E.	57	James, Marie Antoinette	97
Isabelle, Patrick J.	69	James, Mary Antoinette Jean	96
Isabelle, Robert	69	James, Nathan	88
Isabelle, Robert H.	57, 92	James, Samuel	97
Isabelle, Thomas	69	Jarvis, James	109
Isabelle, William	69	Jarvis, Maky	109
Ivius, Ermine	14	Jarvis, William	109
Ivius, Henry	14	Jason, Mr.	130
		Jasper, Anachersis	48
		Jasper, Fanny	48
J		Jefferson, Eliz	91, 92
Jackson, Aaron	38	Jefferson, Hannah	27
Jackson, Andrew	35, 55	Jefferson, John	91
Jackson, Catherine	18, 83	Jefferson, Nicholas	98
Jackson, Celia	55	Jefferson, Thomas	27, 98
Jackson, Celina	13	Jena, Nancy	58
Jackson, Celine J.	3	Jena, Napoleon	58
Jackson, Ellen	72	Jenkins, Addison	6
Jackson, Elmira	35	Jenkins, Betty	139
Jackson, Frances	35	Jenkins, George	139
Jackson, Gustave	55	Jenkins, Gilbert	21
Jackson, Henry	86	Jenkins, Henry	139
Jackson, Ida	38	Jenkins, James	20
Jackson, Jenny	73	Jenkins, Jane	21
Jackson, John	73	Jenkins, John	139
Jackson, Julia Ann	18	Jenkins, Lizzie	139
Jackson, Lewis	52	Jenkins, Mary	21
Jackson, Louisa	63	Jenkins, Medard	21
Jackson, Lucy	18, 82	Jenkins, Scipio	7
Jackson, Manuel	52	Jenkins, Susan	6
Jackson, Margaret	73	Jennings, Frank	59
Jackson, Nat	72	Jennings, Gus	39
Jackson, Prescilla	18	Jennings, Henry	59
Jackson, Sarah	38	Jennings, N.R.	2
Jackson, Simms	55	Jennings, Sarah	59
Jackson, Spenser	5	Jennings, Winnie	59

Name Index

Jerridan, Louisa	14
Jetter, Ned Williams	57
John, Moon Charles	49
Johnson, Abraham	22, 72
Johnson, Aimee	52
Johnson, Albert	113
Johnson, Alfred	44
Johnson, Amy	71
Johnson, Ann Dossy	29
Johnson, Ben	50
Johnson, Betsy	4, 101
Johnson, Caroline	138
Johnson, Charles	62
Johnson, Clara	10
Johnson, Crelia Ann	124
Johnson, Constance	43
Johnson, C.W.	33
Johnson, Daniel	101
Johnson, Dicy	71
Johnson, Edward	96, 112, 132
Johnson, Eli	96
Johnson, Eliza	101
Johnson, Ellen	61, 72
Johnson, Emily	96, 117
Johnson, Emma	24
Johnson, Fanny	13, 43
Johnson, Francis	96, 131
Johnson, George	101
Johnson, Henry	72
Johnson, Jacob	43
Johnson, James	101, 124
Johnson, James H.	88, 108
Johnson, Jasper	72
Johnson, Jeanette	44
Johnson, Jeremiah	8
Johnson, Jerry	71
Johnson, Joe S.	4
Johnson, John	21, 124
Johnson, Johnny	6
Johnson, Joseph	50
Johnson, Josephine	43
Johnson, Judith	15
Johnson, Judy	71
Johnson, Laura	8, 73
Johnson, Levi	7, 72
Johnson, Louisa	124
Johnson, Lucy	50
Johnson, Margaret	22
Johnson, Maria	62
Johnson, Mary	6, 8, 71, 73
Johnson, Mary Jane	96
Johnson, Mason	22
Johnson, Milly	96
Johnson, Nancy	124
Johnson, Patsy	71
Johnson, Philip	117
Johnson, Rachel Ann	44
Johnson, Rebecca	2
Johnson, S.	112
Johnson, Silas	44
Johnson, Sophia	52
Johnson, Sophie	71
Johnson, Thomas	15
Johnson, Turner W.	22
Johnson, William	6, 71, 96, 101
Johnson, William C.	2, 74
Johnson, William Henry	52
Johnson, Winters	52
Johnson, Wither	71
Jones, Amanda	122
Jones, Amy	122
Jones, Anna	121
Jones, Anthony	121
Jones, Archy	122
Jones, Becky	91
Jones, Benjamin	92
Jones, Bervick	121
Jones, Caleb	91
Jones, Clementine	89
Jones, Courtney	121
Jones, Dalphe	3
Jones, Daniel	34, 96
Jones, Delsy	53
Jones, Duncan	133
Jones, Easter	3
Jones, Edmund	117, 118
Jones, Edward	91
Jones, Eli	18, 96
Jones, Elizabeth	122
Jones, Ellen	115
Jones, Ephraim	121
Jones, F.W.	70

Name Index

Jones, Frank	122	Jougot, Charlotte	138
Jones, Frederic	3	Jougot, Jules	138
Jones, Frederick	3	Jougot, Manuel	138
Jones, Hembry	53	Jougot, Nelda	138
Jones, Joe	3	Jougot, Souneau	138
Jones, John	138	Julian, Barbara	37
Jones, Lisa	117	Justice, Jennie	127
Jones, Lorena	121	Justice, Kitty	127
Jones, Louisa	121, 138	Justice, Louisa	127
Jones, Lucy	91	Justice, Simon	127
Jones, Malvina	121	Justice, Sophy	127
Jones, Manson	3		
Jones, Margaret	122	**K**	
Jones, Meriky	118	Kaulle, Major	42
Jones, Minerva	121	Kelper, Andre	3
Jones, Nadey	121	Kennedy, John	63
Jones, Rachel	3	Kenner, Nancy	71
Jones, Robert	121	Kenner, Spencer	71
Jones, Rueben	118	Kettle, Anna	73
Jones, Seward	99	Kilgore, Clara	91
Jones, Silvy	121	Kilman, Mr.	121
Jones, Spotman	3	Kimball, Jane	109
Jones, Sophia	3	King, Abraham	15
Jones, Sophy	138	King, Bridget	15
Jones, Stevens	3	King, Elisha	15
Jones, Susan	18, 96	King, Eliza	133
Jones, Susanne	82	King, Elizabeth	15
Jones, Warren	118	King, Esther	15, 19
Jones, Woodson	3	King, Henry	15, 19
Jones, William	82	King, Hester	15
Jordan, Amanda	63	King, Homer	15
Joseph, Adele	110	King, Leah	15
Joseph, Cora	11	King, Leven	15
Joseph, Delphine	110	King, Margaret	15, 128
Joseph, Frank	117	King, Milly	15
Joseph, Gabriel	61	King, James	15
Joseph, Hannah	110	King, John	133
Joseph, Joe	110	King, Rufus	133
Joseph, John	110	King, Sharper	15
Joseph, Joseph	110	King, Sally	15, 19
Joseph, Mary	110	Kinsley, Isabella	114
Joseph, Paul	110	Kirby, Abram	129
Joseph, Pauline	110	Knole, Angeline	31
Joseph, Peter	11	Knole, Annie Mae	31
Joseph, Victor	110	Knole, George	31
Jougot, August	138		

Name Index

Kock, Charles	78	Lee, Harlan	140
Krause, Mary K.	63	Lee, Henry	140
Krause, U. O.	62	Lee, John	28, 140
Kyder, Evelina	115	Lee, Jordan	140
		Lee, Joseph	28
L		Lee, Major	28
Lackey, Jane	82	Lee, Margaret	28
Lackey, William	82	Lee, Maria	28
Lacorbiere, Marie	108	Lee, Mary Jane	140
Lacorbiere, Rosa	108	Lee, Mazilla	140
Lacorbiere, Uranie	108	Lee, Nancy	140
Lacorbiere, V.	108	Lee, Nelly	140
Lacorbiere, Victor	108	Lee, Sarah	28
Lacoste, Alfred	10	Lecount, A.C.	2
Lacour, Pierre	108	Lester, Fanchonette	65
Lameston, William	132	Lester, John B.	65
Landry, Phebe	73	Lester, Joseph	65
Lange, Alexander	70	Levi, Major	65
Lange, Annette	70	Leviste, E.	1, 2, 3
Lange, Antoine	70	Lewis, A.W.	89
Lange, Eliza	70	Lewis, Dr. A.W.	5, 14, 68
Lange, John Baptiste	70	Lewis, Adam	27, 105
Lange, Lizzie	70	Lewis, Alexander	27
Lange, Manette	70	Lewis, Alonzo	27
Lange, Paulin	70	Lewis, Amanda	63
Lange, Raphael	70	Lewis, Anderson	61
Lange, Victoria	70	Lewis, Benjamin	89
Langston, Henrietta	53	Lewis, Carolina	89
Langston, Rosa	53	Lewis, Clarice	82
Latapie, Mr.	23	Lewis, Daniel	89
Lathrop, C.C.	3	Lewis, Edmond	89
Latting, R. J.	7	Lewis, Edward	7
Laud, Joseph	89	Lewis, Edwin W.	89
Leary, Priest	107	Lewis, Edwin Walker	5
Leason, Thomas	72	Lewis, Ellen	61
Leaton, Thomas	54	Lewis, Emma	105
Leblanc, Coralie	68	Lewis, Esther	27, 105
Leduc, Joseph	31	Lewis, Francis	132
Leduc, Sarah Mellon	31	Lewis, George	105
Lee, Anna	12	Lewis, Henrietta	27
Lee, Benj. A.	128	Lewis, James	61, 105
Lee, Daniel	140	Lewis, John	7, 82
Lee, Eliza	140	Lewis, Josephine	82
Lee, Emily	140	Lewis, Judy	89
Lee, George	12	Lewis, Julia	7
		Lewis, Kitty	105

Name Index

Lewis, Lewis		105	Lovely, Rosy	31
Lewis, Louisa		61	Lovely, Wm	31
Lewis, Mary	89, 105, 106,	139	Lowry, Arrena	95
Lewis, Peter		105	Lowry, Beverly	95
Lewis, Phoebe		105	Lowry, Daniel	95
Lewis, Phroline		82	Lowry, John	95
Lewis, Pryor		105	Lowry, Mathilda	95
Lewis, Rebecca		61	Lowry, Mary	95
Lewis, Reuben		105	Lowry, Patience	98
Lewis, Richard		52	Lowry, Peter	95
Lewis, Rosetta		89	Lowry, Phillis	95
Lewis, Sarah	7, 26, 52,	105	Lowry, Rebecca	95
Lewis, Sarah Adeline		89	Lowry, Tom	95
Lewis, Uassala		105	Lubin, Ellen Baptiste	1
Lewis, William	8,	105	Lubin, Marguerite	1
Lindor, Eliza Maurice		24	Lubin, Mary	1
Lindor, Felix		24	Luke, Corinne	29
Lindor, Marie Adele		24	Luke, Francois	29
Linton, James		10	Luke, Johnson	29
Little, Catherine		65	Luke, Lewis	29
Little, George		65	Luke, Rasberry	29
Livingston, Augustus		119	Luke, Samuel	29
Livingston, Frederick		119	Lyall, John	53
Livingston, Patience		119	Lynch, Wm. F.	72
Livingston, William		119		
Llorens, F.G.		99	**M**	
Lockman, David		21	Macgibbon, Duncan	123
Lockwood, Mary		117	Macgibbon, James	123
Lockwood, Mary Ann		46	Macgibbon, John	123
Lockwood, William J.	46,	117	Macgibbon, Katy	123
Londe, Jos. L.		87	Macknami, Susan	19
Long, Mitchell		57	Macon, Capt. T.L.	16
Long, Mrs.		70	Maddox, Dr.	119
Long, Sarah Ann		57	Maddox, Thomas	2
Lopez, Alice Morgan		56	Madoss, Jordan	37
Lopez, Emma		56	Madoss, Lucy	37
Lopez, Frederick		56	Maherty, Ben	84
Lord, Francis		86	Maherty, Carolina	84
Lord, Frank		86	Maherty, Elina	84
Lord, Jenny		86	Maherty, Ephraim	84
Lord, John		86	Maherty, Mathilda	84
Lord, Milly		86	Maherty, Melly	84
Lord, Rosalie		86	Maherty, Minerva	84
Lord, Rose		86	Maherty, Parelly	84
Lord, Sarah		86	Major, Edward	14, 109
Lougus, Samuel		3		

Name Index

Major, Maria	14	Martinez, Marie	15
Malard, Albert	79	Mason, Adaline	134
Malard, Alice	79	Mason, Granville	134
Malard, Angelina	79	Mason, Henry	134
Malard, Arthur	79	Mason, Jane	134
Malard, Ernest	79	Mason, Joseph	134
Malard, Ernestine	79	Mason, Partheana	134
Malard, Fracois	79	Mason, Rose Ann	134
Malard, Laura	79	Mason, Roy	134
Malbourn, Betsy	17	Massana, J.	25
Mallen, Adolph	123	Mather, Melie	3
Mallen, Edward	123	Mathews, Jane Ann	17
Mallony, George	78	Mathews, Peter	17
Mallony, Mary	78	Mathews, William Henry	17
Malone, Montelius	25	Maurey, Charlotte	79
Malone, Salomon Robert	26	Maxey, William Henry	8
Malone, Truelive	25	Maxwell, Frank	66
Mandeville, St. Calair	28	Maxwell, Mr.	66
Mangel, Fanny	129	May, Frances	26
Mangel, Lewis	129	May, Harriet	26, 102
Mann, Caroline	120	May, William	26, 102
Mann, Clementine	69	Maybray, Green	36
Mann, Martha	69	Maybray, Harriet	36
Mann, Mary	69	McBride, Alzere	74
Mann, Sandy	69	McBride, Elmire	74
Mann, Silas	120	McBride, Madison	74
Maritche, Nelson	1	McBride, Marcus	74
Marmillion, Mr.	118	McBride, Madison	74
Marrerro, Antonio	138	McBride, Patsy	74
Marshall, Harriet	67; 112	McBride, Sally	74
Marshall, James	67	McBride, Stephen	74
Marshall, John	107, 108	McBride, Susan	74
Marshall, Mr.	73	McCabe, Aleck	119
Marshall, Robert Jr.	42	McCabe, Britt	119
Marshall, Susan	107	McCabe, Caroline	119
Martin, Corey Ann	125	McCabe, Claiborne	119
Martin, Jance	125	McCabe, George	119
Martin, Jane	125	McCabe, Jim	119
Martin, Lazeine	125	McCabe, Lucy	119
Martin, Martin	125	McCabe, Lusanna	119
Martin, Mary	125	McCabe, Maria	119
Martin, Phillis	125	McCabe, Mary	119
Martin, Salis	125	McCabe, Milton	119
Martin, Theodore	48	McCabe, Ned	119
Martin, Viny	125	McCabe, Sam	119
Martin, William	125	McCabe, Sally	119

Name Index

McCabe, Seymour	119	McLain, Sandey	53
McCall, Richard	77	McLain, Susan	53
McCarthy, Lucy	140	McMurren, Cyrus	38
McCarthy, Luzene	140	McMurren, John	38
McCary, Wm	47	McMyler, J.J.	94
McConnell, David	60, 93	McMyler, James J.	37
McCray, Alpheus	63, 66	McNalley, Margaret	58
McCray, Henry	63	McNalley, Patrick	58
McCray, Marceline	63, 66	McNease, John	44, 45
McDaniel, James F.	73	McNease, Sarah	45
McDaniel, Muriel	73	McRae, Chas.	35
McDonald, A.C.	41	McTire, Ligibeth	126
McFerlane, Laura	102	McTire, Sally	126
McGee, Meyer	20	McTire, Sam	126
McGuire, George	64	McWarren, Cyrus	38
McIntire, Robert	70	McWilliams, Peter	107
McKay, Aaron	123	Mederic, Justine	138
McKay, Margaret	123	Meekins, Major	10
McKay, Martha	123	Menard, E. M.	101
McKay, Nancy	123	Menard, J.W.	101
McKensy, Daniel	29	Menard, Willis Tirrell	101
McKensy, Maria	29	Mercer, Dr. W.N.	117
McKensy, Martin	29	Merritt, Ariann	64
McKinney, Agnes	126	Merritt, Charley	64
McKinney, Angeline	126	Merritt, Fanny	64
McKinney, Ann	126	Merritt, George	64
McKinney, Arreel	137	Merritt, Robert	14
McKinney, Christy	137	Merritt, Sally	64
McKinney, Frank	126	Messiah, Anna	121
McKinney, Henry Franklin	126	Messiah, George	121
McKinney, Horatio	126	Messiah, John	121
McKinney, John	137	Messiah, Leonore	121
McKinney, Julia Ann	126	Messiah, John	121
McKinney, Louisa	137	Messiah, Virginia	121
McKinney, Mary Ellen	137	Michel, Coralie	24
McKinney, Mothiel	137	Middleton, Elizabeth	53
McKinney, Tom	126	Middleton, Gilbert	133
McKinney, William	137	Middleton, Margaret	133
McLain, Charlotte	53	Miles, Agnes	140
McLain, Fanny	53	Miles, Barney	100
McLain, Griffin	53	Miles, Becky	100
McLain, Jesse	53	Miles, Benjamin	100
McLain, Julius	53	Miles, Daniel	140
McLain, Lydy	53	Miles, Henry	100
McLain, Sally	53	Miles, James	139
McLain, Sanders	52	Miles, John	100

Name Index

Miles, Norah	139	Moore, Elie	13
Miles, Sarah	100	Moore, Esther	113
Miles, William	100	Moore, George	13, 85
Miller, Ben	8	Moore, Graham	13
Miller, Benjamin	8	Moore, Hubbard	37
Miller, Henrietta	8	Moore, James	8
Miller, Jacob	31	Moore, Maria	8
Miller, James	58	Moore, Mathilda	37
Miller, Love	8	Moore, Melden	13
Miner, Anna Jane	55	Moore, Morgan	67
Miner, Rev. Samuel S.	55	Moore, Oliver	8
Mitchell, Alfred	93	Moore, Peter	120
Mitchell, Aspasie	81	Moore, Roddy	86
Mitchell, Celeste	81	Moore, Susan	8, 37
Mitchell, Charles	93	Moore, Thomas Overton	120
Mitchell, Doria	93	More, Edward	126
Mitchell, Ellen	93	Morell, John	67
Mitchell, Emma	33	Morell, Mary	67
Mitchell, George	76	Morell, Wesley G.	75
Mitchell, Henry	33, 81, 101	Morell, William	67
Mitchell, Isabella	93	Morse, Laura	14
Mitchell, James Henry	93	Morgan, Josephine	69
Mitchell, Jane	77	Morgan, Louisa	11
Mitchell, Kitty	93	Morgan, William	11
Mitchell, Leontine	33	Morris, Annette	21
Mitchell, Louisa	77	Morris, Alerenia	21
Mitchell, Mary	33	Morris, Alexine	21
Mitchell, Paul	77	Morris, Arthelia	31
Mitchell, Pauline	81	Morris, Augusta	21
Mitchell, Pelagie Marie	81	Morris, Charlotte	1
Mitchell, Plummus	33	Morris, Dow	71
Mitchell, Rosanna	33	Morris, Elsie	21
Mitchell, Syvanie	81	Morris, Harriet	31
Molemasse, Frank	128	Morris, Henry	31
Moman, William	45	Morris, Juddy	71
Monroe, Sallie	36	Morris, Justina	21
Montegut, Alphonsine	107	Morris, Littleton	21
Montegut, Felicie	107	Morris, Louisa	21
Montegut, Felix	107	Morris, Lydia	21
Montegut, Marie	107	Morris, Maria	21
Montegut, Michel	107	Morris, Mary	27
Moore, Alick	13	Morris, Milton	85
Moore, Anna	8	Morris, Salomon	31
Moore, Cesar	8	Morris, Sam	21
Moore, Cynthia	8	Morris, Surenna	21
Moore, Daniel	120	Morris, Susan	31

Name Index

Morris, William	21, 71
Morris, William Henry	21
Morse, Alexander	9
Morse, George	9
Morse, Georgiana	9
Morse, Henrietta	9
Morse, Henry	9
Morse, Isabella	9
Morse, Nicey Henrietta	9
Morton, Elsie	131
Morton, George	131
Morton, Matilda	131
Morton, Wyatt	131
Moses, Charlotte Ann	26
Moses, Levi	26
Moses, Solomon R.	89
Mott, John N.	26
Murphy, Samuel	21
Murrell, Ann	27
Murrell, Diana	6
Murrell, John	27
Murrell, Joseph	27
Murrell, Mars	6
Murrell, Martha Ann	6
Murrell, Mary Jane	27
Murrey, John A.	17

N

Nair, Issac	7
Nalciers, Auguste	39
Nalciers, Jules	39
Nalciers, Marie	39
Nance, Berry	128
Nance, Dave	128
Nance, Henry	128
Nance, Isabella	128
Nance, Jackson	128
Nance, Jane	128
Nance, Lazarus	128
Nance, Maria	128
Nance, Sarah	128
Nance, Stephen	128
Nancy, Charly	121
Narice, John	73
Narcissa, Clara J.	66
Narcisse, Aline	14
Nash, David	76
Nash, Elizabeth	114
Neal, Bill	119
Neal, Louisa	119
Neck, April	7
Neck, Hester	7
Neck, Lucy	7
Neck, Mary	7
Nelson, Clemenci	100
Nelson, Emile	100
Nelson, Jackson	63
Nelson, John A.	100
Nelson, Lysa	102
Nelson, Numa	100
Nelson, Samuel	50
Nelson, William	102
Newman, Rev. J.P.	25, 66, 87
Nicholas, Marie	58
Nicolls, Milty	124
Noble, Jordan B.	25
Norman, Oliver	71
Norwood, Eliza	11
Norwood, Isiah	11
Norwood, Mary	11

O

Obar, DeMatile	127
Obar, Gus	127
Obar, Eliza	127
Obar, Frances Elizabeth	127
Obar, Joe	127
Obar, Joseph William	127
Obar, Katrine	127
Obar, Odelia	127
Obar, Thomas William	127
Obar, William	126
Ogilvie, Jules	135
O'Hare, Patrick	74
O'Hare, Susan	74
Oliver, George Calvin	116
Oliver, Harriet A.	116
Oliver, Harry A.	116
Olmstead, Caroline	29
Olmstead, Hurlde	29

Name Index

Olmstead, John	29	Parker, Harry	128
Orbin, Henry	119	Parker, Henry	132
Osborne, Mons	137	Parker, Henry Lang	6
Owen, Agar	30	Parker, James	13
Owen, Susan	30	Parker, James Henry	132
Owen, William	30	Parker, Jefferson	128
Owens, Alfred	121	Parker, Julia	13, 132
Owens, Albert	121	Parker, Lorenzo	132
Owens, Amanda	121	Parker, Lucy	128
Owens, Archy	120	Parker, Mary	128
Owens, Charles	121	Parker, Pheobe	128
Owens, Edmund	72	Parker, Richard	13, 132
Owens, Elias	120, 121	Parker, Robert	132
Owens, Eliza Ann	121	Parker, Roddy	78
Owens, George	121	Parker, Troy	128
Owens, John	121	Parrent, Adeline	19
Owens, Lucy	120	Parrent, Ambrose	19
Owens, Martha	121	Parrent, Ann	19
Owens, Peggy	72	Parrent, Mary Ann	19
Owens, Sarah	121	Parris, Milberry	15
Owens, Scylla	120	Parris, Jacob	14
		Parker, Albert	123
		Parker, Alfred	123
P		Parker, Charity	123
Packer, George Henry	103	Parker, Charles	130
Packer, Mary	103	Parker, Clementine	123
Packer, Mildred Ann	103	Parker, Elijah	123
Packer, Patsy Jane	103	Parker, Eliza	130
Packer, Philip	24, 103	Parker, Glasgow	123
Packer, Thomas	103	Parker, Harry	71
Packwood, Marie Louise	70	Parker, Henry	123
Page, David	28	Parker, James	71, 123
Page, Diana	28	Parker, Jane	58
Page, Emily	28	Parker, John	58
Page, James	28	Parker, Josephine	123
Page, Joseph	130	Parker, Jules	71
Page, Mary Ann	130	Parker, Julia	123
Page, William Raymond	130	Parker, Lorenzo	123
Paillerse, Alfred	81	Parker, Lucy	123
Pailles, A.	128	Parker, Martha	71
Parker, Albert	4, 13, 48, 132	Parker, Mary	123
Parker, Charles	16	Parker, Richard	123
Parker, Delia	128	Parker, Robert	123
Parker, Delphy	128	Parker, Rosalie	71
Parker, Elijah	11	Pascal, Mrs.	25
Parker, Eliza	16	Patterson, Adelaide	65

Name Index

Patterson, John	65	Pierce, Maggie E.	101
Patton, Isaac	14	Piermont, Margaret	23
Pawny, John	123	Piermont, Mary Jane	23
Pawny, Miney	123	Piermont, John	23
Pearce, Oliver	139	Piermont, Julia Ann	23
Pease, Lumas Hoyt	127	Piermont, Rebecca	23
Peek, Fanny	119	Piermont, William	23
Peek, Sam	119	Pierre, Anna	36
Perniell, Charles	41	Pierre, Mr.	36
Perniell, Dicia	40	Pilman, Bill	125
Perniell, Jane	41	Pilman, Charles	125
Perniell, William	40	Pilman, Elizabeth	125
Pero, Jessy	72	Pilman, Joanna	125
Pero, Magaritte	72	Pilman, Joseph	125
Pero, Matildie	72	Pilman, Mary	125
Pero, Paul	72	Pilman, Zinette	125
Perret, Malvina	114	Piquery, Emma	121
Perret, Mariann	114	Piquery, Francis Adele	121
Perry, Charles	139	Piquery, Josephine	121
Perry, Emmy	139	Piquery, Nancy	121
Perry, Lucy	126	Piquery, Theodore	121
Perry, Mary	139	Piquery, Theodule	121
Perry, Peter	126	Pitchen, Mary	89
Perry, S.	29	Pitman, Albert	117
Petaway, Douglas	122	Pitman, Corinne	117
Petaway, Franklin	122, 129	Pitman, Eliza	117
Petaway, Harriet	122	Pitman, Zelie	117
Petaway, Mary Ann	122	Place, Emilia	21
Peter, Anthony	92	Pleasant, Frd (Fred)	3
Peter, Hannah	91	Pleasant, John	131
Peter, John	91	Plumley, Col.	11
Peter, Jno.	129	Poindexter, Mathilda	109
Peter, Philip	118	Poindexter, Robert	109
Pettis, W.	10	Polk, Ceclis	33
Philip, Miami	57	Populus, Annica	131
Philips, Irma	24	Populus, Armand	131
Philips, Lorenza	24	Populus, Artoulou	131
Philips, Miami	51	Populus, Florentia	131
Philips, Modeste	24	Populus, Henri	131
Phine, Barbara	58	Populus, Henry	131
Phine, Gracey	58	Populus, Jorquena	131
Phine, Philip	58	Populus, Maria	131
Pierce, Capt. H.H.	97, 98	Populus, Theodora	131
Pierce, H.H.	101	Porter, Adeline	33
Pierce, John	41	Porter, Becky	88
Pierce, Lawyer	6	Porter, Cecile	39

Name Index

Porter, Esther	113	Quilland, James Hervey	66
Porter, Friday	33	Quilland, Lewis	66
Porter, Friday Jr.	32	Quilland, Newton	107
Porter, John	25	Quilland, Newtown	66
Porter, Lucinda	33	Quilland, Susan	66
Porter, Nat	39		
Porter, Savilla	33	**R**	
Porter, William	88		
Potter, John C.	29	Rafael, Hermogene	35
Powell, Duke	113	Randall, Anderson	25, 96
Pralon, Jean	1	Randall, Emilia	11
Prerie, Mary Jane	3	Randall, Peyton	11
Presas, Jos	99	Randall, Rosine	25
Preston, Isabella	114	Randall, Walker	11
Preston, William	114	Randolph, Nancy	72
Price, Alice	136	Randolph, Robert	72
Price, George W.	136	Ransom, Betsy	135
Price, George Washington	136	Ransom, Charlotte	135
Price, George W.	136	Ransom, Hannah	135
Price, Jimmy	136	Ransom, James	135
Price, Joseph	136	Ransom, Polly	135
Price, Lavinia	136	Ransom, Richard	135
Price, Mary	136	Ransom, Sarah	135
Price, Oranys	136	Rawley, Joe	22
Price, Thaddeus	136	Ray, David	45
Priestley, Charlotte	6	Ray, Ennis	15
Priestley, Stephen	6	Ray, Jenny	137
Proctor, Bill	41	Ray, Robinson	137
Prudhomme, Lestor	18	Raymond, Alphonsine	132
Pryor, Lucy	133	Raymond, Arthur	21
Pullam, John	140	Raymond, Clothilde	21, 132
Pullam, Sally	140	Raymond, Coralene	132
Purcell, John Jr.	33	Raymond, Ermina	132
		Raymond, Fred	132
Q		Raymond, Frederick Robert	21
		Raymond, Harriet	132
Questy, Annette	132	Raymond, Mrs. Joseph	9
Questy, Jacob	132	Raymond, Peter	132
Questy, Jacques	132	Raymond, Phillisene	132
Questy, John	132	Raymond, Pierre	21
Questy, Joseph	132	Raymond, Reta	132
Quickly, George	121	Raymond, Robert	132
Quilland, Anna Walker	66	Reed, Ann	133
Quilland, April	66	Reed, Caroline	132
Quilland, Hannah	107	Reed, Celestine	132
Quilland, Hervey	66	Reed, Charles	26

Name Index

Reed, Delia	26
Reed, Edward	133
Reed, Elyzabeth	85
Reed, Emmeline	70
Reed, George	106
Reed, Howard	133
Reed, Jane	132
Reed, John McCoy	71
Reed, Johnson	85, 95
Reed, Laura	26
Reed, Lizzie	133
Reed, Maria	85
Reed, Martha Ann	133
Reed, Mary	132
Reed, Page	133
Reed, Ransom	107
Reed, Richard	133
Reed, Silvy	133
Reed, Thomas	26
Reed, William	71, 133
Reedy, A.J.	51
Reedy, Cassana	51
Reedy, Harriet Louisa	51
Reedy, Harriet Wilhelmina	51
Reedy, Houston	51
Regand, Frederic	95
Regean, Adolph	138
Regean, Antoinette	138
Reynolds, Delia	94
Reynolds, Jason Joseph	94
Reynolds, John P.	94
Reynolds, Samuel J.	94
Rice, Dr.	23
Rice, Lily	23
Rice, Rosella	7
Richard, William	128
Richardson, George	28
Richardson, John	113
Richardson, Lucy Ann	85
Richardson, Nancy	113
Richardson, Rachel	17
Riche, Charley	17
Riche, Jane	17
Riche, Lewis	17
Riche, Louis	17
Riche, Margaret Jane	17
Riche, Mary	17
Riche, Sally	17
Riche, William	17
Ricks, Elizabeth	30
Ricks, Hermogene	30
Ricks, Isabella	29
Ricks, Mary	49
Ricks, Peter	29, 30, 135
Ricks, Theodore	30
Ridley, Ann	92
Ridley, Augustus	92
Ridley, Charles	92
Ridley, Eliza	92
Ridley, Isabella	92
Ridley, Jane	92
Riefel, Mrs. Octave	58
Riley, Darkey	3
Riley, Gabriel	124
Riley, Georgia	105, 116
Riley, John	105
Riley, Margaret	124
Riley, Sarah Jane	88
Rivers, Mathilda	18
Rixon, Patrick	126
Robbins, Thomas	15
Roberts, Berthea	122
Roberts, Dick	122
Roberts, Edwin	30
Roberts, Emily	122
Roberts, Frank	122
Roberts, John	73, 122
Roberts, Julia	30
Roberts, Margaret	59
Roberts, Mary Jane	30
Roberts, Romeo	73
Roberts, Samuel	59
Roberts, Virginia	122
Roberts, Walter S.	59
Roberts, Winnie	122
Robertson, Alfred	13
Robertson, Ann	27
Robertson, Dudley	1, 76
Robertson, Elijah	27
Robertson, Ella	43
Robertson, Henry	1
Robertson, Jack	27

Name Index

Robertson, Jacob	134	Ross, Maria	4, 94
Robertson, Johanna	32	Ross, Orlena Celestine	49
Robertson, John	17	Rovira, Adolphus	114
Robertson, Lou	115	Rovira, Alexis	114
Robertson, Lizzie	134	Rovira, John	114
Robertson, Mahala	43	Royal, Celestin	2
Robertson, Manuel	76	Royal, Celestine	2
Robertson, Margaret	85	Royal, E.P.	12
Robertson, Maria	76	Royal, Rev. E.P.	135
Robertson, Phil	134	Royal, Rev. Eugene P.	118
Robertson, Polly	134	Royal, James	12
Robertson, Richard	32	Royal, Louisa	12
Robertson, Robert	74, 134	Royal, Martin	12
Robertson, Roxana	13	Royal, Philip	12
Robertson, Sally	76	Royal, Polly	12
Robertson, Sarah	1	Royal, Sarah	12
Robertson, Sisily	134	Royal, Sophia	2
Robertson, Susan V.	13, 99	Royal, Syllis	12
Robertson, Tom	134	Royal, Victorine	12
Robertson, William	1, 76	Royal, W.E.P.	37
Robin, Courtney	55	Rubere, Ferdinand	105
Robin, Mr.	3	Rubere, Roxanne	105
Robinson, Alexander	79	Rucker, Ann	126
Robinson, Burril	136	Rucker, Richard	126
Robinson, Dorcas	135	Russell, Louisa	38, 109
Robinson, Emily	20	Russell, Moris	140
Robinson, Frank	66	Russell, Oliver	38, 109
Robinson, James	63	Russell, Priscalla	140
Robinson, Martha	136	Russell, William	59
Robinson, Mary	66	Russell, William B.	107
Robinson, Nelly Ann	79	Rutherford, Mathilda	34
Robinson, Rosetta	5	Ryan, Ann	39
Robinson, William	135	Ryan, Frank	38, 39
Rodriguez, Henriette	62	Ryan, Julia	39
Rodriguez, Lazare	62	Ryan, Melinda	38, 39
Rodriguez, Mathilde	62	Ryan, Silas	38
Roe, Charles T.	107	Ryder, Charles F.	128
Roe, Jane	107	Ryder, Elnora D.	128
Rondanez, Dr. L.C.	116	Ryder, Elnora M.	128
Rondanez, Louis Charles Jr.	116	Ryder, Isabella	128
Rook, Bolin	80		
Rook, Emmy	80	**S**	
Rook, James	80	Sabatier, Mr.	109
Rook, Quentan	80	Sanders, Celie	3
Ross, Rev. Anthony	5, 35, 111	Sanders, Daniel	10
Ross, Emeline	5		

Name Index

Name	Page
Sanders, Emilia	3
Sanders, Georgiana	10
Sanders, Ive	3
Sanders, John	3, 140
Sanders, Jve(?)	3
Sanders, Louisa	23
Sanders, Marinda	10
Sanders, Nancy	81
Sanders, Virginia	81
Sandford, David	102
Sauvenet, J.B.	110
Sauvinet, Charles Silas Jr.	48
Sauvinet, C.S.	48, 68, 127
Saville, Mr.	25
Saxton, Louisa	2
Scantling, Abraham	73
Scantling, Peggy	73
Scott, Barry	44
Scott, Elizabeth	4
Scruggs, Alfred	112
Scruggs, Harriet	112
Scruggs, Lishy	112
Scruggs, Ned	112
Scruggs, William	112
Seig, R.	108
Seldon, Caroline	60
Seldon, Cesar	60
Seldon, Henry	93
Seldon, John G.	15
Shaw, Christiana	40
Shaw, Daniel	40
Shaw, Harriet	40
Shaw, Mary Ann	40
Shearer, J. W.	34
Sheehan, Annie	112
Sheehan, James	112
Sheehan, John	112
Sheehan, Kate	112
Sheehan, Margaret	112
Sheehan, Michael	112
Sheehan, Patrick	112
Shelburn, Charlotte	77
Sheppard, Jackson	75
Sheppard, Julien	75
Sheppard, Rossette	75
Sheppard, Rubin	75
Sheppard, Thomas	75
Sheridan, Maria	66
Sheridan, Samuel	66
Sherman, Josephine	131
Shields, Elizabeth	117
Shield, Margaret	23
Shields, Martha	117
Shields, Sally	113
Shields, Wilmer	117
Shoenocker, John	50
Short, William	117
Shorter, Anny	118
Shorter, Ausey	118, 119
Shorter, Charles	118
Shorter, Emiline	118
Shorter, Eureline	118
Shorter, George	118
Shorter, Kizzy	118
Shorter, Maria	118
Shorter, Ned	118
Shorter, Rachel	118
Shorter, Sawny	118
Shorter, Thomas	118
Shortridge, James	14
Shortridge, J.P.	17
Shurbare, Selina	132
Silas, Margaret	69
Simmons, Dennis	2
Simon, Caroline	56
Simon, Honore	56
Simon, Mathieu	56
Simon, Morris	56
Simon, Pauline	56
Simpson, Annie	2
Simpson, Francois	2
Simpson, Mary	2
Simpson, Nelly	2
Simpson, William	2
Simson, Ann	132
Simson, Crawford	132
Simson, Henry	132
Simson, Julius	132
Simson, Seny	132
Singleton, Alexander	16
Skelley, Ellen	100
Skelley, Timothy	100

Name Index

Skinner, Ander	56	Smith, Louisa	13, 105, 113
Skinner, Clara	52	Smith, Luconda	104
Slater, Mr.	108	Smith, Mary	39, 52, 84
Slaughter, Daniel	83	Smith, Melinda	84
Slaughter, Green	83	Smith, Molly	80
Slaughter, Lucy	83	Smith, Moses	84
Slaughter, Mary	83	Smith, Mrs.	73
Slocomb, Mr.	12	Smith, Nellie,	39
Smith, Adam	84	Smith, Olive	72
Smith, Agnes	76	Smith, Patience	84
Smith, Alexine	21	Smith, Paul	39
Smith, Amos	130	Smith, Rachel	26
Smith, Ann	117	Smith, Robert	19, 72
Smith, Ann Ellenor	139	Smith, Robert C.	93
Smith, Anna Charlotte	139	Smith, Robert P.	92, 93, 100
Smith, Anthony	84	Smith, Rosalie	69
Smith, Augusta Josephine	139	Smith, Samuel	42, 130
Smith, Betty	40	Smith, Sarah	39, 42
Smith, Carolina	130	Smith, Silvy	110
Smith, Charles	54	Smith, Simon	21, 72
Smith, Charlotte	31	Smith, Sophia	69, 139
Smith, Clara	105	Smith, Thomas	84
Smith, Daley	96	Smith, Tom	31
Smith, David	69	Smith, Tony	84
Smith, Elizabeth	39	Smith, William	21, 39
Smith, Ellen	130	Smith, Wright	72
Smith, Ely	130	Smoot, Eliah	40
Smith, Emanuel	105	Smoot, Henderson L.	40, 138
Smith, Emberly	84	Smoot, Nancy	40
Smith, Esther	39	Smooth, Aga	1
Smith, Frances	113	Solanes, Emma Ryder	128
Smith, Francis	139	Spencelbuy, M r.	73
Smith, Frank	52	Sperry, W.	14
Smith, Frederick George	139	Spicer, Frank	122
Smith, George	39, 139	Spruel, Bannister	120
Smith, Gracy	105	Spruel, Charles	33
Smith, Green	104	Spruel, Daphny	120
Smith, Harriet	39, 70	Spruel, David	120
Smith, Henrietta	39	Spruel, Eliza	33, 120
Smith, Jacob	104, 118	Spruel, Ephraim	120
Smith, James H.	113	Spruel, George	33, 120
Smith, John Duncan	26	Spruel, Louisa	120
Smith, Joseph	110	Spruel, Mary Jane	120
Smith, Laura	39	Spry, Ben	127
Smith, Lee	105	Stallwood, George A.	103
Smith, Lincoln	84	Stallwood, Henry	103

Name Index

Stanford, Delia	22	Summer, Orton	90
Stanford, Spencer	22	Summer, Peter	90
Stansbury, Charles	94	Summer, Pleasant	90
Stansbury, Elyza	94	Summer, Ralph	90
Stansbury, Henrietta	94	Summer, Tom	90
Stansbury, Henry	94	Sutton, Betsy	113
Stark, Peter	62	Sweeney, Polly Ann	62
Stark, Wire	62	Sweeney, Primus	62
Starkes, D.C.	98	Sylvester, Fanny	36
Starkes, Douglas	99	Sylvester, Mahala	36
Stevenson, Christina	81	Sylvester, Margaret	36
Stevenson, Daphne	6, 81	Sylvester, William	36
Stevenson, Joseph	6, 81		
Stevenson, Wilby	81	**T**	
Steverson, Charles	135	Talbot, Andrew	20
Steverson, Victoria	135	Taliaferro, Randall	86
Steward, Cornelia	134	Tatum, Joseph	42
Steward, Levins	78	Taylor, Angeline	37
Steward, Margaret	10, 78	Taylor, Canilla	116
Steward, William	134	Taylor, Caroline	47
Stewart, Emanuel	35	Taylor, Cecilia	62
Stewart, Henry	5	Taylor, Charles	62, 125
Stewart, John H.	35	Taylor, Cornelia	26
Stewart, Maria	5	Taylor, Ed	26
Stewart, Nancy	35	Taylor, Esau	7
Stewart, Nelly	36	Taylor, Esther	26, 116
Stewart, Page	36	Taylor, Evaline	83
Stickman, Margaret	121	Taylor, Frank	24
Stickman, William	121	Taylor, Hannah	117
Stone, Dr.	127	Taylor, Henrietta	26, 116
Stoney, Joe	134	Taylor, Henry	26,29,83,116,138
Stoney, Silvy	134	Taylor, Humphrey	90
Strange, Cornelia	25	Taylor, Hy	47
Strange, John	25	Taylor, Jenny	116
Strange, Stevens	25	Taylor, Jim	62
Strong, Miller C.	33	Taylor, Joe	62
Stubbs, Thos.	54	Taylor, John	138
Stump, Christopher	122, 123	Taylor, Jordan	26, 116
Stump, David	123	Taylor, Josephine	125
Stump, Emeline	123	Taylor, Julia	47
Stump, Jane	123	Taylor, Kitty	29
Stump, Sam	123	Taylor, Lavinia	47, 125
Sullivan, Dr.	67	Taylor, Levy	62
Summer, Elzie	90	Taylor, Lewis	125
Summer, Ephraim	90	Taylor, Lucinda	7, 62
Summer, Jordan	90		

Name Index

Name	Page
Taylor, Lucy	116
Taylor, Lucy Ann	26
Taylor, Lydy Ann	125
Taylor, Maria	29
Taylor, May Eliza	62
Taylor, Milly	125
Taylor, Nathaniel	138
Taylor, Newman	26, 116
Taylor, Phil	62
Taylor, Polly	90
Taylor, Reuben	29
Taylor, Richard H.	90
Taylor, Rose	138
Taylor, Rosetta	24, 47
Taylor, Sam	62
Taylor, Sophy	62
Taylor, Therison	62
Taylor, Vincent	26, 116
Taylor, William	125
Taylor, William Henry	138
Teelers, Annie	11
Teelers, David	11
Teelers, Melly	11
Teelers, Nancy	11
Teelers, Simon	11
Tennant, William	12
Theodore, John B.	76
Theodore, Rosalie	76
Thomas, Amanda	63
Thomas, Ann Maria	126
Thomas, Cavallier J.	131
Thomas, Charles	63
Thomas, Charlotte	58
Thomas, Clementine	126
Thomas, Doet	7
Thomas, Dolly	63
Thomas, Dorthea	32
Thomas, Esther	94
Thomas, George	94
Thomas, Gustavus A.	15
Thomas, Horace	126
Thomas, Isaac	126
Thomas, James	126
Thomas, John	94
Thomas, Joseph	113
Thomas, Mary	118, 138
Thomas, Mary Jane	16
Thomas, Nelly	79
Thomas, Prince Albert	16
Thomas, Robert	8
Thomas, Sydned	118
Thomas, William	63
Thomas, Willis	5
Thompson, Alpha	92
Thompson, Ann	42, 67
Thompson, Beverly	126
Thompson, Cornelius	17
Thompson, Dennis	33
Thompson, Edward	42
Thompson, Eugene Joseph	48
Thompson, James Henry	7
Thompson, Joseph Alexander	7
Thompson, Lazarus	29
Thompson, Louisa	51
Thompson, Maria	126
Thompson, Moses	29
Thompson, Rose	27
Thompson, Sarah	67
Thompson, Susan	17
Thompson, Willis	92
Thoroughgood, Alfred	128
Thoroughgood, Harriet	128
Tillman, Adeline	19
Tillman, Henry	19
Tillman, Samuel	10
Tillman, Jane	10
Tiro, Ben	113
Todd, Elyzabeth	88
Todd, Prescilla	88
Todd, Thomas	88
Todd, Walter	88
Tolliver, Betsy	74
Tolliver, William	74
Tompkins, Benjamin	122
Tompkins, Hannah	122
Tompkins, Harriet	122
Tompkins, Kit	122
Tompkins, Sally	122
Tompkins, Soloman	122
Tompkins, Virginia	122
Topp, Louisa	89
Toussaint, Mary	95

Name Index

Name	Page
Toussant, Augustus	138
Toussant, Elodie	138
Toussant, Elodis	138
Toussant, Mary	138
Toussant, Paul	138
Towns, Elijah	130
Townsend, Moses	23
Townsend, Roxeann	23
Trevigne, Charles Nerestan	108
Trevigne, Hortensia	108, 110
Trevigne, Paul	108, 110
Trevigne, Paul Sr.	110
Trevigne, Simeon Nerestan	110
Trotter, Caroline	58
Trotter, Eliza	8
Trotter, Joe	8
Trotter, Letitia	8
Trotter, Mary	8
Trotter, Sam	8
Trotter, Samuel	8
Trotter, Sarah	8
Tucker, Crecy Ann	77
Tucker, Dr. George	17
Tureand, Adolphe	3
Turner, Darly	37
Turner, James	117
Turner, John	13
Turner, Revd. John	99
Turner, Jonas	37
Turner, Louisa	137
Turner, Mary	117, 137, 138
Turner, Mary E.	13, 99
Turner, Matt	137
Turner, Melinda	37
Turner, Nancy	48
Turner, Nancy "Bright"	5
Turner, Paul	117
Turner, Phil	37
Turner, Robert	137
Turner, Sumpter	7
Turner, Theopile	117
Turner, Thomas	37
Turner, W.W.D.	117
Turner, Wm.	5
Turpin, Edward	31
Tyler, Capt. Henry	49

U

V

Vance, Charles W.	111
Vance, Revd. James M.	111
Vance, Mathilda	111
Vedder, Col. N.	59
Veel, Ella	126
Veel, Sam	126
Verret, Eulalie	61
Vichy, Henry	134
Vichy, Versy	134
Victor, Caroline	139
Victor, Emma	139
Victor, Henriette	104
Victor, Jean	104
Victor, Nema	139
Victor, Peter	139
Vors, Charles	125
Vors, John	125
Vors, Nicholas	125
Vors, Priscilla	126
Vors, William	125

W

Wagner, William	133
Waldon, Archy	11
Waldon, Charles	11
Waldon, Manuel	11
Waldon, Elizabeth	11
Waldon, Goliath	11
Waldon, Guy	11
Waldon, John	11
Waldon, Robert	11
Waldon, Sam	11
Waldon, Slatia Ann	11
Waldon, William	11
Wale, Alexandre	109
Walk, Ann Eliza	27
Walk, Kitty	27
Walk, Robert F.	27
Walker, Bromwell	54
Walker, Elizabeth	112
Walker, George	98

Name Index

Walker, Hannah	78, 107, 108	Washington, Lucy Ann	117
Walker, Henderson	59	Washington, Ludrick	14
Walker, Jane	31	Washington, Margaretta	1
Walker, John	126	Washington, Maria	117
Walker, Joshua	54	Washington, Martha	137
Walker, Lewis	78, 108	Washington, Mathilda	18, 96
Walker, Maria	54	Washington, Matilda	137
Walker, Mollie	51	Washington, Isaac	73, 108
Walker, Nicholas	59	Washington, Isabella	73
Walker, Patsy	51, 54	Washington, John	1
Walker, Sarah Jane	60	Washington, Riley	73
Walker, Sophy	126	Washington, Sandy	53
Walker, Stephen	14	Washington, Sarah	14
Walker, William	54	Washington, Sarah Ann	7
Walker, Zachariah	54	Washington, Silvy	14
Wallace, Phebe	12	Washington, Twissie	27
Wallace, Virginia	69	Washington, William	53, 137
Walsch, Michael	50	Washington, Willis	137
Warburg, Daniel	108	Waterman, Alexander	50
Warburg, Josephine	108	Waterman, George	50
Warburg, Uranie	108	Waterman, Grant	50
Ware, Sergt. Silas	58, 59	Waterman, Mary	50
Ware, Wennsota	58	Watkins, Nathaniel	10
Ware, William	58	Watson, Betsy	119
Warren, Harry	9	Watson, Charlotte	5
Warren, Margaret	9	Watson, Emily Anna	5, 119
Warren, Nancy	9	Watson, Richard	119
Warren, Silas	9	Webster, Alfred	124
Washington, Ann	41	Webster, Dan	124
Washington, Aaron	26	Webster, Demps	124
Washington, Becky	53	Webster, Green	124
Washington, Candiss	53	Webster, Jesse	124
Washington, Caroline	18, 96	Webster, Louisa	124
Washington, Ch.	52	Webster, Lucy	124
Washington, Charles	137	Webster, Sarah	124
Washington, Coleman	14	Webster, William	124
Washington, E.	27	Weeks, Annie Eliza	44
Washington, Edmond	53	Weeks, Blacksmith	44
Washington, Eliza	73	Weeks, Hamilton	44
Washington, Elizabeth	26	Weeks, Katy	44
Washington, Ermine	14	Weeks, Rebecca	44
Washington, George	59, 76, 137	Wells, Katherine	65
Washington, George A.	135	Wells, Minerva	65
Washington, Hannah	73	Wells, Robert	65
Washington, Josephine	137	Wells, William	65
Washington, Lizzie	52	West, Henry	49

Name Index

West, Priscilla	51	Whitley, Jessie		36
Weston, Albert	19	Whitley, Phrosine		69
Weston, Charles	19	Wickham, Charles		114
Weston, Richard	19	Wickham, Thomas Warrenton		114
Whalan, Harriet	12	Wickham, William C.		114
Whalan, Isaac	12	Wilde, Alice		122
Whalan, Martha	12	Wilkinson, Kesar		36
Whally, Anna	105	Wilkinson, Major		36
Whally, Catherine	105	Wilkinson, Peter		36
Whally, Clementine	105	Wilkinson, Samuel		36
Whally, Horace	105	William, Alphonse		133
Whally, Leontine	105	William, Alice		133
Whally, Martha	105	William, Clara		133
Whally, Monique	105	William, Joshua		133
Wheeler, Elijah	31	William, Mary		133
Wheeler, Lavissa	31	Williams, Abram		80
Whidby, Eliza	120	Williams, Alfred		21
Whidby, Jas	120	Williams, Anna Eliza		112
White, Adeline	116	Williams, Cecile		135
White, Andrew	31	Williams, Celeste		80
White, Beverly	43	Williams, Celestine		135
White, Carter	17	Williams, Celie		80
White, Cherry	31	Williams, Charity		106
White, Chloe	17	Williams, Charles		38, 80
White, Delila	7	Williams, Charley		52, 54
White, Eliza	31	Williams, Charlotte		80
White, Fanny	31	Williams, Clintin		52
White, Francis	17	Williams, Diana		111
White, Hanna	32	Williams, Edith		20
White, Harry	7	Williams, Edward		2
White, John	116	Williams, Rev. Emperor		111
White, Joseph	7	Williams, Field		79, 80
White, Leymour	43	Williams, Francis William		111
White, Louisa	51	Williams, George		42, 135
White, Mathilda	41	Williams, Hannah		22
White, Phonetta	116	Williams, Henry		18, 22, 106
White, Richard B.	7	Williams, Homer		116
White, Robert	17	Williams, James		38
White, Samuel	43	Williams, Jane		57
White, Samuel P.	7	Williams, John		87
White, Sarah	116	Williams, Joseph		21
White, Sophia	43	Williams, Leah		135
White, William	17	Williams, Maria		26
Whiten, Billy	49	Williams, Martha		2, 80
Whiten, Charles	49	Williams, Martine		21
Whiten, Judy	49	Williams, Mary	38, 67, 111, 134	

Name Index

Williams, Mathilda	18, 112	Wilson, John	77
Williams, Maudier	52	Wilson, John P.	75
Williams, Mellie	87	Wilson, John Shield	109
Williams, Moore A.	112	Wilson, Jule	114
Williams, Mr.	115	Wilson, Lettis	109
Williams, Nancy	116	Wilson, Margaret	44
Williams, Ned	57	Wilson, Maria	115
Williams, Noel	135	Wilson, Martha A.	75
Williams, Pauline	21	Wilson, Mary	77
Williams, Phileus	80	Wilson, Mary Ann	31
Williams, Rosa	131	Wilson, Milly	109
Williams, Rose Lee	5	Wilson, Minerva	115
Williams, Sandy	134	Wilson, Moses	140
Williams, Sallie	80	Wilson, Mr.	52
Williams, Save	21, 22	Wilson, Nancy	109
Williams, Sophia	57	Wilson, Nelson	129
Williams, Vina	80	Wilson, Patrick	109
Williams, Washington	80	Wilson, Peggy	75
Williams, Wellington	22	Wilson, Perry	77
Williams, Winston	22	Wilson, Richard	75
Williamson, Anna	9	Wilson, Roberson	129
Williamson, Binah	12	Wilson, William	44
Williamson, Harriet	9	Wilson, Winny	129
Williamson, Mary Adele	9	Wilton, D.	126
Williamson, James C.	9	Windsor, George	82
Wilson, Albert	114, 115	Winehill, N.	105
Wilson, Anderson	129	Winley, Flora A.	106
Wilson, Andrew	115	Winley, Louisa	106
Wilson, Aneke	129	Winley, Primus	106
Wilson, Amy	109	Winley, Zeke	106
Wilson, Arthur	87	Winston, Caroline	34
Wilson, Bill	124	Winston, Clara	35
Wilson, Charley	77	Winston, Elias	35
Wilson, Charlotte	129	Winston, John F.	34
Wilson, Edward Lee	75	Winston, Mary	35
Wilson, Elyza	77	Winston, Patrick	35
Wilson, George	114, 129, 140	Winston, Tom	35
Wilson, Georgiana	24	Wolfe, Anna	106
Wilson, Harriet	44, 129	Wolfe, Elizabeth	106
Wilson, Henry	31, 113	Wolfe, Francis	106
Wilson, Isaac	77, 109	Wolfe, Jane	106
Wilson, Jack	109	Wolfe, Julia	106
Wilson, Jackson	77	Wolfe, Mary	106
Wilson, James	44, 59, 140	Wolfe, Terence	106
Wilson, Jim	109	Wolfe, Terence Sr.	106
Wilson, Joseph	44	Woodney, Wideny	5

Name Index

Wood, Ann	33
Wood, Mrs.	11
Wood, Violet	33
Wooden, Arice	76
Wooden, Willis	76
Woodruff, G.W.	121
Woods, Ann	130
Woods, Benjamin	130
Woods, Charlotte	76
Woods, Edward	76
Woods, Ellen	129
Woods, Frank	129
Woods, Henry	76
Woods, Jerome	4
Woods, Joseph	130
Woods, Mary	4
Woods, Mary E.	4
Woods, Mr.	130
Woods, Philip Jason Fred.	129, 130
Woods, Rachel	129, 130
Woods, Samuel	4
Woods, William	4
Worthen, Henry	23, 50
Wright, Emily	63
Wright, Henderson	95
Wright, Henry	63
Wright, John	26, 69
Wright, Julia Ann	95
Wright, Louisa	26
Wright, Susan	26
Wright, Thomas	95
Wright, Virginia	95
Wyche, Floyd	34

X
Y

Yarrell, Charity	138
Yarrell, Edmund	138
Yarrell, Edny	138
Yarrell, Eli	138
Yarrell, Eliza	138
Yarrell, George	138
Yarrell, Louisa	138
Yarrell, Penny	138
Yarrell, Susan	138
Yarrington, Col.	115
Yarrington, Elizabeth	115
Yarrington, Julia	115
York, Esther	54
York, Jacob	54
York, James	53
York, Mark	54
York, Rhody	54
Young, A.L.	36
Young, Bennett	30
Young, Edward	118
Young, Fanny	28, 30
Young, Isaac	118
Young, Maria	100
Young, Olmstead	140
Young, Robert	74
Young, Rosa	74
Young, Selvy	118
Young, William	118
Young, Winny	140

Z

Zemar, Adolph	99
Zemar, Lavinia	99
Zenon, Emile	58
Zenon, Hillare	58
Zenon, Modeste	58
Zenon, Victorine	58
Ziegler, George H.	85
Ziegler, George K.	85

www.ingramcontent.com/pod-product-compliance
Lightning Source LLC
Chambersburg PA
CBHW071424160426
43195CB00013B/1802